Len Deighton was born in London in 1929. At the age of seventeen he became a photographer attached to the RAF Special Investigation Branch. Following his discharge in 1949 he did a variety of jobs, including working in a railway marshalling yard, and in 1952 won a scholarship to the Royal College of Art. After graduating in 1955, with characteristic unpredictability, he joined BOAC as a steward. He resigned in the summer of 1956 (anticipating by one week his almost certain dismissal for an innocent involvement with a gold-smuggling organization based in Hong Kong) and embarked on yet another circumnavigation of the world, this time financed by his earnings as a designer and illustrator. In 1969 he became art director of an advertising agency.

Deighton's first novel, *The Ipcress File*, was published in 1962 and was an immediate and spectacular success. Since then he has gone from strength to strength, varying his literary output from espionage novels to war and general fiction, cookery and other non-fiction. Acclaim for his work has been universal and unparalleled.

I have been impressed by Len Deighton ever since he was greeted as the mere successor to Ian Fleming. Apart from his virtues as a story-teller, his passion for researching his backgrounds gives his work a remarkable factual authority.

I don't know the world of espionage, but I do know that of show business, and his 'Close-up', a study of a film actor in decline, seemed to me quite faultless in its delineation of every aspect of the cinema, from camera technique to tax evasion. With 'Bomber' and 'Fighter' he established himself as an expert on a period with which, since he was born in 1929, he could not be expected to be directly familiar, at least not as an adult. Yet the authority of these books seems absolute.

Anthony Burgess, *The Observer*

Also by Len Deighton

The Ipcress File
Horse Under Water
Funeral in Berlin
Billion-Dollar Brain
An Expensive Place to Die
Only When I Larf
Declarations of War
Close-Up
Spy Story
Yesterday's Spy
Twinkle, Twinkle, Little Spy
Bomber
SS-GB

Action Cookbook
Où Est le Garlic

Len Deighton

Fighter

The True Story of the Battle of Britain

With an Introduction by
A.J.P. Taylor

TRIAD PANTHER

Published in 1979 by Triad/Panther Books Ltd
Frogmore, St Albans, Herts AL2 2NF

ISBN 0 586 04611 9

Triad Paperbacks Ltd is an imprint of
Chatto, Bodley Head & Jonathan Cape Ltd and
Granada Publishing Ltd

First published in Great Britain by
Jonathan Cape Ltd 1977

Made and printed in Great Britain by
Richard Clay (The Chaucer Press) Ltd
Bungay, Suffolk
Filmset in Times

Contents

Issued by the Ministry of Information  *in co-operation with the War Office and the Ministry of Home Security.*

If the INVADER comes

WHAT TO DO — AND HOW TO DO IT

THE Germans threaten to invade Great Britain. If they do so they will be driven out by our Navy, our Army and our Air Force. Yet the ordinary men and women of the civilian population will also have their part to play. Hitler's invasions of Poland, Holland and Belgium were greatly helped by the fact that the civilian population was taken by surprise. They did not know what to do when the moment came. *You must not be taken by surprise.* This leaflet tells you what general line you should take. More detailed instructions will be given you when the danger comes nearer. Meanwhile, read these instructions carefully and be prepared to carry them out.

I

When Holland and Belgium were invaded, the civilian population fled from their homes. They crowded on the roads, in cars, in carts, on bicycles and on foot, and so helped the enemy by preventing their own armies from advancing against the invaders. You must not allow that to happen here. Your first rule, therefore, is :—

(1) IF THE GERMANS COME, BY PARACHUTE, AEROPLANE OR SHIP, YOU MUST REMAIN WHERE YOU ARE. THE ORDER IS "STAY PUT".

If the Commander in Chief decides that the place where you live must be evacuated, he will tell you when and how to leave. Until you receive such orders you must remain where you are. If you run away, you will be exposed to far greater danger because you will be machine-gunned from the air as were civilians in Holland and Belgium, and you will also block the roads by which our own armies will advance to turn the Germans out.

II

There is another method which the Germans adopt in their invasion. They make use of the civilian population in order to create confusion and panic. They spread false rumours and issue false instructions. In order to prevent this, you should obey the second rule, which is as follows :—

(2) DO NOT BELIEVE RUMOURS AND DO NOT SPREAD THEM. WHEN YOU RECEIVE AN ORDER, MAKE QUITE SURE THAT IT IS A TRUE ORDER AND NOT A FAKED ORDER. MOST OF YOU KNOW YOUR POLICEMEN AND YOUR A.R.P. WARDENS BY SIGHT, YOU CAN TRUST THEM. IF YOU KEEP YOUR HEADS, YOU CAN ALSO TELL WHETHER A MILITARY OFFICER IS REALLY BRITISH OR ONLY PRETENDING TO BE SO. IF IN DOUBT ASK THE POLICEMAN OR THE A.R.P. WARDEN. USE YOUR COMMON SENSE.

Re… they… where… where… them… you to… are, and… fore, is…

(4) …

…OUT OF ACTION WHEN NOT IN USE. IT IS NOT ENOUGH TO REMOVE THE IGNITION KEY; YOU MUST MAKE IT USELESS TO ANYONE EXCEPT YOURSELF.

IF YOU ARE A GARAGE PROPRIETOR, YOU MUST WORK OUT A PLAN TO PROTECT YOUR STOCK OF PETROL AND YOUR CUSTOMERS' CARS. REMEMBER THAT TRANSPORT AND PETROL WILL BE THE INVADER'S MAIN DIFFICULTIES. MAKE SURE THAT NO INVADER WILL BE ABLE TO GET HOLD OF YOUR CARS, PETROL, MAPS OR BICYCLES.

VII

The six rules which you have now read give you a general idea of what to do in the event of invasion. More detailed instructions may, when the time comes, be given you by the Military and Police Authorities and by the Local Defence Volunteers; they will NOT be given over the wireless as that might convey information to the enemy. These instructions must be obeyed at once.

Remember always that the best defence of Great Britain is the courage of her men and women. Here is your seventh rule :—

(7) THINK BEFORE YOU ACT. BUT THINK ALWAYS OF YOUR COUNTRY BEFORE YOU THINK OF YOURSELF.

Illustrations

Plates

Figures

Maps by Jean Paul Tremblay

Introduction

by A. J. P. Taylor

Bismarck once asked Count Helmuth von Moltke whether he could guarantee victory in the coming war against Austria. Moltke replied, 'Nothing is certain in war.' War is indeed full of surprises and the Second World War had many, from the German breakthrough at Sedan in May 1940 to the dropping of the two American bombs on Japanese towns in August 1945. No action, however, was as surprising and unexpected as the aerial combats between the Royal Air Force and the Luftwaffe in the summer of 1940. Imaginative novelists, and particularly H. G. Wells, had described future engagements between vast armadas of the air. Few of those who determined air strategy in practice believed that such forecasts had any reality.

The key to the story is that the air commanders before the Second World War had very little previous experience to draw on. The materials and methods of war are of course constantly changing. Generals acquire rifles, machine guns, and tanks. Admirals acquire bigger battleships and submarines. But they have some idea from earlier wars of the problems that are likely to face them. The air commanders had no such resource. The war in the air of the First World War had been largely a matter of dogfights between individual aircraft. The few bombing raids had caused terror and little effective damage. Those who determined air strategy after the war had to proceed by dogma alone, a dogma that was little more than guesswork.

The dogma was simple: 'The bomber will always get through.' General Giulio Douhet said this in Italy; Billy Mitchell said it in the United States. Both were detached theorists. It was more important that Lord Trenchard said it in England, for Trenchard was Chief of Air Staff for ten years, from 1919 to 1929. Trenchard was determined to have an independent air force, and the only way for it to be more than an auxiliary of the army and navy was to have a strategy of its own. This strategy was independent bombing. The air commanders practised this strategy successfully. The British bombed defenceless villages in Iraq; the Italians bombed defenceless villages in Abyssinia; the Germans bombed defenceless villages in Spain; the Japanese bombed defenceless cities in China.

But was there no defence? The air chiefs answered unanimously: none. The only answer was to possess an even stronger bomber force than the enemy with which to destroy his bases and his industrial resources. The British, thanks to Trenchard, accepted this doctrine wholeheartedly. They calculated the strength of the largest air force in Europe and made this their yardstick, just as British Admirals had made the German navy their yardstick before the First World War. In the early days the French air force provided the yardstick, though it is difficult to believe that there was ever a serious chance of a war between France and Great Britain. In the 1930s the German Luftwaffe became the obvious rival. The British Air Staff clamoured for more bombers and, when the RAF slipped behind, declared that Great Britain was in imminent danger. Everything, it seemed, turned on the bomber race.

In December 1937 there was a revolution in British air policy. It was sensational though little regarded. The year before, Sir Thomas Inskip had been made Minister for the Co-ordination of Defence. He was an unimpressive figure whose appointment had been dismissed as the most surprising since Caligula made his horse a consul. But Inskip had a clear lawyer's mind. He recognized that the British were losing the bomber race with Germany. Then he proceeded to the striking conclusion that it was not necessary for them to win it. For while the Germans aimed at a short war and therefore wanted a knock-out blow, the British merely needed to survive until blockade and perhaps the aid of allies brought victory in a long war. In his own words, 'The *role* of our Air Force is not an early knock-out blow . . . but to prevent the Germans from knocking us out.'

Inskip had also a practical argument. Previously it had been plausible and perhaps even reasonable to claim that there was no defence against bombers and that they would always get through. Now there were new assets on the British side. Their new fighters, especially the Spitfire, were faster and more formidable than any that had gone before and could challenge the German bombers. Radar was being developed by British scientists and with it the British fighters would know when the bombers were coming. Defence was possible after all. Of course this, too, was a dogma, not based on experience. In Inskip's view it was worth trying.

He had a still more practical argument. Fighters cost less than bombers to build. Therefore more could be produced for the same money and the great British public, who understood nothing of the difference between fighters and bombers, would be the more impressed. This argument was decisive with the Cabinet, which accepted Inskip's recommendation on 22 December 1937. The Air Marshals raged and Trenchard declared in the House of Lords that the decision 'might well lose us the war.' But the revolution in British air policy had begun. Some of Inskip's arguments, such as his reliance on blockade, were mistaken. But he deserves some credit as the man who made British victory in the Battle of Britain possible.

The second man who exercised decisive influence also arrived at his position in an almost accidental way. Sir Hugh Dowding was the senior member of the Air Council. He had every claim to become Chief of Air Staff in 1937. But he was a quiet, reserved man, obstinate in pressing his views and not a good mixer. He was pushed off to become head of Fighter Command, then regarded by the other Air Marshals as a second-rate post. Dowding considered the problem of fighter strategy in his cool, rational way. Far from him was any romantic idea of vast armadas contending in the skies or of dog-fights such as there had been in the First World War. The sole task of Fighter Command, as Dowding saw it, was the defence of Great Britain and this could be accomplished by defeating the German bombers. Without them the German fighters would be harmless. Dowding planned an economical campaign to husband his fighter force at all costs.

Dowding's single-minded concentration on the defence of Great Britain often brought trouble for him after the war started. When the Germans broke through in Flanders the French pleaded for more British fighter squadrons. Churchill acquiesced. Dowding resisted this emotional decision and got his way after the Chief of Air Staff appealed to the Cabinet on his behalf. In July, when the Germans began to attack British shipping in the Channel, Dowding again refused to involve his fighters in this to him irrelevant conflict. Dowding also had trouble within his own force. Some of the area commanders resented Dowding's cautious policy and clamoured for the tactic of the 'big wing.' All along Dowding suffered from disloyalty as well as from lack of understanding.

There was a third decisive figure in the Battle of Britain. In May 1940 Churchill made Lord Beaverbrook Minister of Aircraft Production. Beaverbrook's task was to produce aircraft as quickly as possible without regard to established procedure. He discharged this task successfully and to the great annoyance of the Air Marshals. Beaverbrook was an isolationist who had little interest in the continental war. He came alive only when the defence of Great Britain was in question. He formed a close alliance with Dowding, who shared his outlook. Beaverbrook turned out fighters where the Air Marshals called for bombers. He sent new fighters direct to the squadrons. He trampled over all bureaucratic obstacles. Dowding paid him this tribute: 'The country owes as much to Lord Beaverbrook for the Battle of Britain as it does to me. Without his drive behind me I could not have carried on during the battle.' Thanks to Beaverbrook,

Fighter Command possessed more aircraft at the end of the Battle than it had possessed at the beginning. But as Len Deighton shows, not even Beaverbrook could remedy the wastage of pilots.

The decisive difference between the British and the Germans is that the British, directed by Dowding, knew what they were doing and the Germans did not. Though the Germans constantly boasted of their overwhelming might in the air, they had never contemplated the problems involved. Like the British Air Marshals they simply clung to the dogma that the bomber would always get through. A full-scale attack on Great Britain had never entered into their plans. Indeed they had never considered a direct attack on Great Britain. All of them from Hitler downwards assumed that Great Britain would make peace once France was defeated, and even the defeat of France came much sooner than they had expected.

The armistice between Germany and France was signed on 22 June. Hitler said to General Alfred Jodl, 'The British have lost the war, but they don't know it; one must give them time, and they will come round.' Hitler gave the British a month. Then on 19 July he addressed the Reichstag. After appealing to 'reason and common sense,' he threatened the British with 'unending suffering and misery' unless they made peace. Lord Halifax, though himself inclining towards a compromise peace, was given the task of brushing Hitler's peace offer aside on the radio. Hitler's bluff had been called. He had now to make good his threats. On 21 July 'Sea-lion,' the invasion of Great Britain, was decided on in principle. Ten days later the date for invasion was provisionally fixed for 15 September. Hitler was sceptical from the start and doubted whether the invasion was 'technically feasible.' In other campaigns, such as in France and later in Russia, he had gone to the front himself and taken command. With the preparations for Sea-lion, he retired to the Berghof and watched the proceedings with detached curiosity.

Sea-lion has attracted a great deal of attention. As a

practical operation it never existed. The army chiefs accumulated a considerable force with which they would overrun England once others had arranged the landings for them. They themselves made no contribution to the problem. Erich Raeder, the Grand Admiral who commanded an almost non-existent German fleet, regarded navy invasion as impossible unless the British had already surrendered. He went through the motions of assembling river barges and coastal steamers in order to please the Generals and to avoid annoying Hitler. But he never took the talk of invasion seriously.

The Luftwaffe was therefore on its own. Göring was delighted to undertake the task. Like other air chiefs he believed that the bomber would always get through. 'Eagle Attack,' the Luftwaffe offensive, and Sea-lion had no connection. Hitler's instruction was 'to establish conditions favourable to the conquest of Britain.' But the Luftwaffe simply assumed that fleets of bombers, escorted by fighters, would sail over England and pulverize the British into surrender – Guernica on a larger scale. The Luftwaffe did not co-ordinate its acts with the needs of the other services. It made few attacks on British warships and often bombed harbours and airfields that the army would need if it ever landed. Luftwaffe strategy was in fact a supreme assertion of the theory favoured by the Air Marshals that bombing unsupported by land and sea forces could win a war.

The Luftwaffe's attempt to reduce Great Britain by bombing failed, perhaps by a narrow margin. It also suffered from the German failure to consider its problems in advance. The attempt was a rushed affair where no German had time to stop and think, and in any case Göring rarely thought. Raeder was hypnotized by the prospect of the Royal Navy. No German remarked how British ships had been driven back by air attack during the Norwegian campaign. Again no one in Germany seems to have considered independent landings by paratroopers. Many people in England expected them to do so. At all events during my service in the Home Guard in the summer of

1940 I spent my time patrolling the Oxford gas works (with an unloaded rifle) in the firm belief that the entire weight of the German paratroop force would be directed against them.

The Battle of Britain was a fairly small affair. Hitler called off Sea-lion on 17 September and there was never any attempt to repeat it. Hitler was not seriously troubled by this set-back. Sea-lion was a botched plan, rushed up in a hurry and without importance in German strategy. Hitler's mind was already set on the invasion of Russia and he did not fear that Great Britain, though unsubdued, could do him any real harm. The British on the other hand were invigorated. They believed that they had won a great victory or rather that the pilots of Fighter Command had won a great victory for them. And so they had. The British were a maritime people. They had learned from previous wars that their task was to survive, and victory in the Battle of Britain enabled them to do so. To some extent their confidence was misplaced. Great Britain came nearer to defeat in the prolonged Battle of the Atlantic against the U-boats than she did in the Battle of Britain. But psychologically the Battle of Britain was the more decisive.

The Battle of Britain had an unforeseen consequence, unpleasant to all concerned. Almost unintentionally the Germans turned from daylight to night bombing while the Battle was still on. They continued this campaign throughout the winter, as many British cities bore witness. The British attempted to counter this campaign by night bombing of their own. It seemed that the bomber would always get through after all. This expectation again proved wrong. No decisive results were achieved. The Germans virtually broke off their campaign in May 1941, perhaps because the Luftwaffe was needed in Russia and the Mediterranean. The British continued their campaign throughout the war, again indecisively. Bombing was not effective until long-range fighters could accompany the bombers, and this had to wait until 1944. Yet this had already been demonstrated in the summer of 1940.

The Battle of Britain had a more profound result. It put Great Britain back in the war. After the fall of France it seemed that Great Britain could make no stroke against Germany except such marginal acts as the attack on the French fleet at Oran. Hitler himself, to adopt MacArthur's phrase, was content when he left Great Britain 'to wither on the vine.' Suddenly the British showed that they were still in the war and still fighting. The Battle of Britain, though a defensive battle, was at any rate a battle. Thanks to it, Great Britain was still taken seriously as a combatant Great Power, particularly in the United States. As an uncovenanted blessing, Italy gave the British further opportunities for victory in the winter of 1940. These victories may have been irrelevant to the defeat of Germany but they showed that the British were in action all the same.

It would be agreeable to record that the victors were duly honoured as Nelson had been posthumously after the Battle of Trafalgar. Some of them were. Churchill honoured the fighter pilots with the immortal phrase, 'Never in the field of human conflict was so much owed by so many to so few.' One man was passed over. The Air Marshals were angry that their dogmatic faith in independent bombing had been disproved. The advocates of the 'big wing' received official approval after the Battle was over, as Len Deighton describes. On 25 November Dowding was relieved of his command and passed into oblivion. Yet 'he was the only man who ever won a major fighter battle or ever will win one.'

Such were the strategical ideas and lack of them that lay behind the Battle of Britain. There were more practical considerations. In the last resort battles are decided by the men and machines that take part in them. I am afraid that many of us who write about wars neglect this side of it and write in great sweeping terms. Len Deighton does not. After all, if the aeroplane had not been invented, the Battle of Britain could not have been fought, and quality of aircraft is the central feature of Len Deighton's book. His brilliant analysis makes clear the technical problems of aircraft design in the interwar years. The Germans talked big and almost gave the impression that with such ingenuity and drive they ought to have won. I suspect that Erhard Milch is by way of being Len Deighton's hero.

Yet, however ingenious the Germans were in design, and however forceful in production, they lost the Battle of Britain, or to be more precise did not win it, which comes to the same thing. Dowding's superior strategy counted for much but each individual combat in the skies counted also. Here, too, Len Deighton provides a detailed account, fuller than any previously written, of how the British and Polish pilots prevailed. Indeed, in one way or another, he explains everything that happened in those days, now distant, of August and September 1940.

Figure 1

The two German Air Fleets had a boundary line (heavy broken line) that extended over England. The German single-seat fighters (Bf 109s) were concentrated at Cherbourg and the Pas de Calais under the command of *Jagdfliegerführer – Jafü* – of Air Fleets 2 and 3 respectively. The line marked Bf 109 shows the extreme range of the Messerschmitts, but combat would make this much shorter, as the pilots used full throttle and more fuel.

The most important bomber units – *Kampfgeschwader 1* (KG 1), etc. – are shown as at the airfield of *Geschwader* staff. *Kampfgruppe 100* (KGr 100), shown as the most westerly Luftwaffe unit, was the German pathfinder force.

From *Marine Gruppe West* four-engined Focke-Wulf FW 200s were sent out into the Atlantic – sometimes flying all the way round to Stavanger, Norway – and provided the weather reports that the Air Fleets needed to plan their attacks.

The vitally important RAF sector airfields, where the Operations Rooms were situated, are ringed; other fighter airfields are shown as solid black dots. Bawdsey was the home of British radar development. The extent of the normal 10-metre Chain Home radar coverage, for aircraft up to 15,000 feet, is shown as a light broken line. It includes inland areas where the German aircraft formed up, but at this range it was little more than what the operators called 'mush.'

Göring's private train went back to Germany, and then to the Pas de Calais. It is shown at Beauvais, its original site, which was also the HQ of *Fliegerkorps I*. Other *Fliegerkorps* HQ are shown as F. These, like the Air Fleet HQs, had advanced HQs nearer the coast.

Lowestoft marks the place where Peter Townsend went after the Dornier Do 17, and Cromer is where Douglas Bader also found a Dornier. (See text for 11 July.)

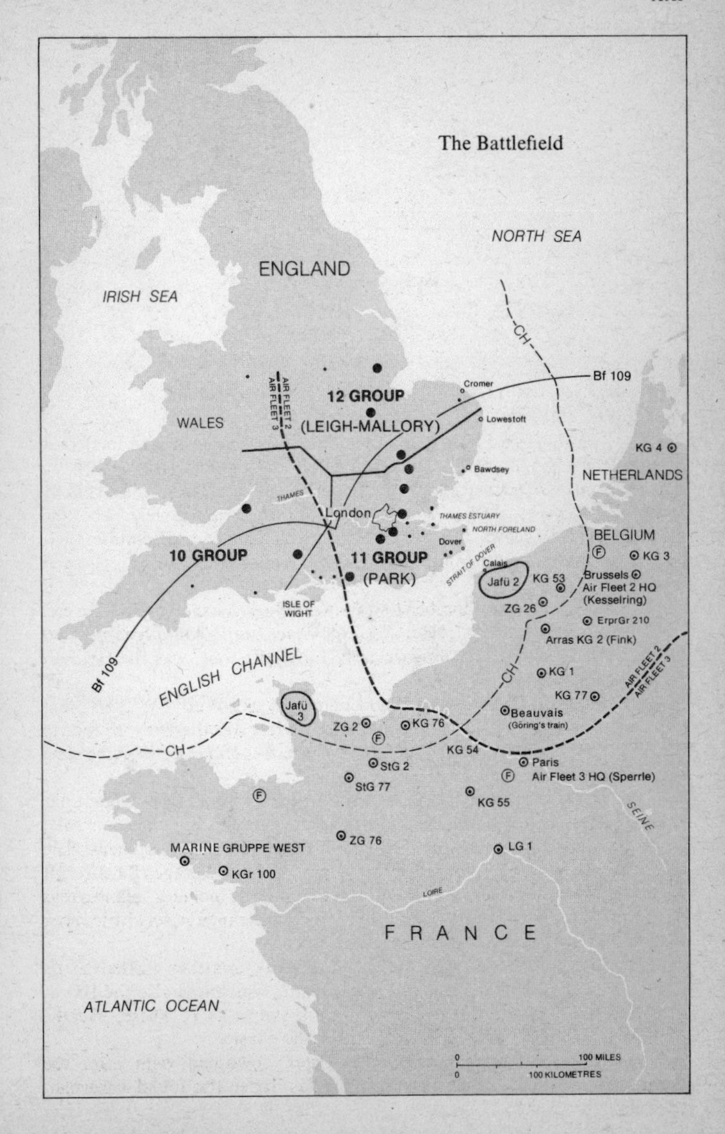
The Battlefield
NORTH SEA
ENGLAND
IRISH SEA
CH
Bf 109
Cromer
12 GROUP
(LEIGH-MALLORY)
AIR FLEET 2
AIR FLEET 3
WALES
Lowestoft
KG 4
Bawdsey
NETHERLANDS
THAMES
London
THAMES ESTUARY
NORTH FORELAND
BELGIUM
Dover
10 GROUP
11 GROUP
(PARK)
STRAIT OF DOVER
Calais
Jafü 2
KG 53
KG 3
Brussels
Air Fleet 2 HQ
(Kesselring)
ISLE OF WIGHT
ZG 26
ErprGr 210
Arras KG 2 (Fink)
Bf 109
ENGLISH CHANNEL
KG 1
KG 77
Jafü 3
Beauvais
(Göring's train)
ZG 2
KG 76
KG 54
StG 2
Paris
Air Fleet 3 HQ (Sperrle)
StG 77
KG 55
SEINE
ZG 76
LG 1
MARINE GRUPPE WEST
KGr 100
LOIRE
FRANCE
ATLANTIC OCEAN
0
100 MILES
0
100 KILOMETRES

PART ONE

Strategy

Taedet caeli convexa tueri

(It becomes dispiriting constantly to watch the arch of heaven)

VIRGIL, *Aeneid*, BOOK IV

Sea-Lion *(Otariidae). A carnivore modified for aquatic life.*

ENCYCLOPEDIA

History is swamped by patriotic myths about the summer of 1940. Many of these were generated by the shame of that portion of the British public who – after the fall of France – declared that it was time to negotiate terms with Hitler's Germany. It was a view shared by men of the Left and of the Right. The former believing that the Hitler–Stalin peace pact would last, and the latter hoping that it would not.

The Swedish ambassador in London reported back to his Ministry in Stockholm that he had spoken with people, including Members of Parliament, who wanted to seek terms with Hitler. He reported a senior member of the British government as saying common sense not bravado would govern British policy. From Washington, the British ambassador was prepared to seek out contacts for such a move. In Lisbon Sir Samuel Hoare and in Berne David Kelly made contact with possible intermediaries to get German viewpoints.

Lloyd George, the 'Churchill' of the First World War, wanted peace with Hitler, had wanted it for some time, and seemed not to mind who heard him say so. In Berlin his name had already been mentioned as a possible leader of a puppet regime. Even in the tiny, five-man War Cabinet that Churchill had formed, there was not unanimous determination to go on fighting. Lord Halifax, the Foreign Minister (who had only narrowly missed becoming Prime Minister instead of Churchill), suggested that they prepare a reply to Germany, to have ready if Hitler offered peace on reasonable terms. Chamberlain, now in Churchill's War Cabinet as Lord President, supported the idea of compromise.

Sardonic then was Churchill's choice of Halifax to go on the BBC and reject unequivocally Hitler's peace offer. For Churchill there would be no talk of peace terms. Already 65 years old, long derided as a warmonger, he declared his intention to fight, 'however long and hard the road may be.' Significantly perhaps, Churchill went to great trouble to get an important member of the Royal Family to the far side of the Atlantic where the Duke of Windsor became Governor of the Bahamas.

Churchill called himself Minister of Defence, artfully 'careful not to define my rights and duties.' Daily meetings with the Chiefs of Staff gave Churchill tight control of the progress of the war. The three service ministers were brushed aside and not even invited into the War Cabinet.

Churchill had his priorities right; Fighter Command's men and machines would decide whether or not Hitler came to London. Churchill, the first British Prime Minister to wear a uniform while in office (even Wellington did not do so), chose the uniform of the RAF. His only major change in the system, or the men who ran it, was to create a Ministry of Aircraft Production and give it to a newspaper tycoon to run.

But not until the Battle of Britain was won did Churchill gain the wholehearted support of the British public. No wonder then that he devoted so much of his time and energy, to say nothing of rhetoric, to convincing the British that they had won a mighty victory.

Broadcasting over the BBC on 11 September 1940, Churchill said, 'It ranks with the days when the Spanish Armada was approaching the Channel, and Drake was finishing his game of bowls; or when Nelson stood between us and Napoleon's Grand Army at Boulogne.' Later he was to point out that the great air battles of 15 September took place, like Waterloo, on a Sunday.

The Battle won, men forgot their ideas about a compromise peace with Hitler. Wartime propaganda, much of it primarily intended for American newspaper and radio correspondents, provided material from which a David and

Goliath myth was engineered. It suited all concerned, except the Germans, who still today insist that there was no such event as the Battle of Britain.

The Battle of Britain, although small in scale compared with the later fighting, was nevertheless one of the decisive battles of the Second World War. It converted American opinion to a belief that the British, given help, might win. This belief fed anti-German feeling. Until now dislike of Nazism had been repressed, because Americans felt that they couldn't do much about it. In 1940 they began to believe they could do something about it, and Britain provided a focal point for many disparate anti-Nazi elements, from émigrés to labour unions.

In military terms, the Battle proved that Britain was a secure base, from which the USA could fight Germany. More importantly, but less accurately, it convinced America that air-power was the decisive weapon with which to do it.

In June 1940 the French signed an armistice with the Germans. The British had been killed, captured, or had departed. The refugees turned round and began the walk home. Hitler took two old comrades on a tour of the 1914–18 battlefields, where he had served as a corporal.

Hitler now ruled a vast proportion of Europe: from the Arctic Ocean to the Bay of Biscay. Stalin, his new friend, was supplying oil, cattle, grain, and coal. Rumania, Hungary, and the Balkans were all anxious to do business with their rich and powerful neighbour, as teams of German technicians investigated the resources of the conquered lands.

The German victories had been a direct result of brilliant generalship and highly skilled, well-equipped armies with good morale. Yet by the spring of 1940 – in spite of months of war with Britain – the Wehrmacht had made no preparations whatsoever for any direct assault upon a hostile shoreline.

Unlike the Anglo-American armies later in the war, the Germans had no landing craft – for tanks, trucks, or men

Figure 2

By the summer of 1940 Hitler had created a centralized Europe ruled from Berlin. The USSR had invaded Poland and split it down the middle with Germany. That part of France not occupied by the German forces was little more than a satellite. The German mark was pegged artificially high in respect to other currencies so that wealth moved back into Germany without the victims realizing what was happening. Anxious to be in at the kill, Italy declared war in the final hours of France's agony and nibbled pieces of territory. The Balkan countries, given the choice of co-operating fully or being taken over, co-operated.

– no artificial breakwaters, no trained beach-masters, or any system of sea-route marking. In fact, the only army with any experience, or adequate equipment, was the Japanese army, which operated its own sea transport. It had made amphibious landings on the banks of the Yangtse river in 1938. At the time there had been a flutter of interest from military commentators but, apart from some experiments by the United States Marine Corps, no high commands envisaged a need for such techniques.

It was not until 12 July 1940 that the OKW – the High Command of the Wehrmacht – prepared a memorandum about invading England. Even then General Alfred Jodl, its author, described it as being 'in the form of a river crossing on a broad front.' He called it operation *Löwe* (Lion). Hitler took this memo and used it as a basis for his Directive No. 16, 'on preparations for a landing operation against England.' He changed the name to *Seelöwe* (Sea-lion).

Hitler's Directive No. 16, a top-secret document of which only seven copies were made, asked the army and navy chiefs for more proposals. But the Luftwaffe had a specific task: it must reduce the RAF morally and physically to a state where it could not deliver any significant attack upon the invasion units. To Göring that seemed possible.

In the heady days of that summer anything seemed possible. In Berlin representatives from the Welsh Nationalist movement were already talking of their coming role. So was a senior official of the IRA, which had been exploding bombs in England for several months before the war. The Welshmen made no progress with the Germans; the Irishman was sent home in a U-boat in August 1940, but died en route and was buried at sea, his body shrouded in a German naval ensign.

In France the German army was devoting some of its finest units to preparations for a great victory parade through Paris. *Generaloberst* Heinz Guderian, architect of the blitzkrieg, was in the capital, along with many other senior members of the army and air force. *Feldmarschall* Hugo Sperrle, commander of Air Fleet 3, had made it his headquarters.

Units rehearsed for the victory procession included massed motorcycles and tanks. German flags were prepared for all the façades in the Place de la Concorde, and blue hortensias for the Étoile. Press reports of the event were prepared but not yet dated. The only cloud on the horizon was a growing fear that the widespread publicity would invite a decidedly unfriendly flypast by the RAF. On 20 July caution prevailed; the whole scheme was abandoned and the men went back to their units.

By that time, Berlin had enjoyed a victory parade. It was a modest affair. Local conscripts of the 218th Infantry Division marched through the Brandenburg Gate. Joseph Goebbels, Minister for Public Enlightenment and Propaganda, took the salute. Hitler was not present. He was saving himself for the following evening, when the whole Reichstag and an astounding array of Generals had been summoned to hear his speech. Appropriately this glittering event took place in the Kroll Opera House. Hitler's speech was a long one and he used it to claim personal credit for the victories of 1940. 'I advised the German forces of the possibility of such a development and gave them the necessary detailed orders,' said the ex-Corporal to one of the most dazzling arrays of military brains ever gathered under one roof. 'I planned to aim for the Seine and Loire rivers, and also get a position on the Somme and the Aisne from which the third attack could be made.'

One eye-witness was William Shirer, who later described Hitler as an actor who this day mixed the confidence of the conqueror with a humility that always goes down well when a man is on top. Almost in passing, Hitler offered Churchill a chance to make peace. It was 'an appeal to reason,' said Hitler. Whether he hoped that his appeal would bring peace is still argued. Some say it was no more than a way of 'proving' to the German public that it was the British – and more specifically Churchill – who wanted the war. We shall never know. It was in Hitler's nature to seek opportunities and pursue those that seemed most promising. '*So oder so*,' he would repeatedly tell the men around him: achieve it either this way or that way.

When the applause of that multitude of Generals, politicians, and foreign dignitaries died away, Hitler began to distribute the honours. He created no less than twenty-seven new Generals. Mostly they were men who had commanded armies or panzer groups to win for him the great victories in Poland, Norway, and the west. But artfully Hitler arranged that yes-men such as Alfred Jodl and Wilhelm Keitel – who had told Hitler, 'my Führer, you are the greatest military commander of history' – got double promotions and seniority. While Gustav von Wietersheim – whose motorized infantry corps had consolidated the panzer thrust by which Guderian skewered France – was passed over because he had argued with the Führer in 1938. The lesson was learned by some.

So many new promotions were announced that there was not time for the Generals to receive Hitler's personal congratulations. As each name was called, a General stood up and gave the Nazi salute. There was then a brief pause while other officers leaned across to shake hands and, according again to Shirer, slap the back of the officer honoured.

By the time that Hitler had finished creating Generals, and no less than a dozen Field Marshals, there could have been few men in the opera house who did not understand that this was a cunning piece of megalomania that, while thoroughly debasing the coinage of high rank, defined Hitler as the man who owned the mint.

It was an unprecedented step. The Kaiser made only five Field Marshals in the whole of the First World War. Even General Erich Ludendorff had failed to find a baton in his knapsack. Now Hitler made twelve after less than a year of war, and the fighting had covered only a few weeks. But the new *Generalfeldmarschälle* were delighted. In Germany such exalted rank, from which the holder could neither be retired nor demoted (or even promoted), brought the provision of an office, a secretary, a staff officer, motor vehicles and horses, and full pay and privileges. And all this for life – or until defeat. A Field Marshal ranked above Reich Chancellor in the protocol lists but not above Führer, which was a new post invented by Hitler for himself.

In order to rescue Göring from the new squalor of Field Marshal rank, Hitler invented a post for him too. Göring received an extra-large baton. Hitler passed it to where

ILLUSTRATIONS

1 Winston Churchill takes charge On 10 May 1940 the German armour moved westward at dawn. By 8 a.m. the British Cabinet was in session and met for thirty minutes. Churchill was First Lord of the Admiralty and in this picture he is seen after leaving the garden door of 10 Downing Street to walk across Horse Guards Parade. Churchill told the man who took this picture, 'Plenty happened last night and something is happening today'. By six o'clock that evening Churchill had become Prime Minister.

The bowler-hatted man is Sir Kingsley Wood, the ineffectual Air Minister who had refused to let the RAF bomb German property. Until now he had been a yes-man for Prime Minister Chamberlain but this morning even Kingsley Wood had called for a change of leadership.

Churchill at this time was not the first choice of King or country and certainly not the first choice of the Conservative Party. Three days after this photo was taken, it was Chamberlain who was greeted by cheers and applause in the House of Commons, not Churchill. The third man in the photo is Anthony Eden.

2 German 'Sea-lion' exercises A barge crudely adapted to the needs of seaborne invasion is being tried out. At this time, and indeed throughout the war, virtually the whole German army was horse-drawn. Notice that the ramp has been fitted externally and does not compare with the fold-down bows of a proper landing craft. And any problems of getting this cart down the ramp would be nothing to the task of disembarking the horses needed to draw it.

And yet, had the RAF fighter force been eliminated, the other British coastal defences could have been neutralized by air attack and such German Sea-lion exercises would not have been so absurd, for the disembarkations could have been virtually without hazard and scenes like this might have been photographed anywhere along the English coast.

1

E.C. 27

3

4

5

Göring was sitting alone in the Speaker's Chair, and the *Reichsmarschall* could not resist opening the box to get a glimpse of it. And for Göring an old medal, the *Grosskreuz*, was revived. From this date onwards Göring can be seen in photographs wearing his special uniform with the huge cross dangling at his neck.

Three of Göring's Luftwaffe Generals became Field Marshals at the Kroll Opera House ceremony. One was the dapper little Erhard Milch, senior man at the Air Ministry, as well as Inspector General of the Luftwaffe. The other two were Albert Kesselring, commander of Air Fleet 2, and Hugo Sperrle of Air Fleet 3. Both men were double-jumped in promotion from *General der Flieger* to Field Marshal. Was this an idea of Göring's, to lessen Milch's power? Until this day he had been the Luftwaffe's only *Generaloberst*. If so, this divide-and-conquer policy

3 Air Vice-Marshal Keith Park The New Zealander who commanded Fighter Command's 11 Group was an ace fighter pilot of the First World War. By 1940 Park was regarded by many as the RAF's foremost expert on all aspects of fighter aircraft. For this reason Dowding sent Park – his right-hand man at Fighter Command HQ – to take over 11 Group, south-east England, which was sure to take the brunt of the German attacks.

During the pre-war years Park commanded a fighter unit at Tangmere and surprised his men by wearing a steel helmet on top of his flying helmet when he was in the air.

4 Air Vice-Marshal Trafford Leigh-Mallory He commanded RAF Fighter Command's 12 Group. Many people expected that Dowding would appoint him to command the more vital 11 Group area but Park got the job instead. From this bad beginning the relationship between the two men worsened. Leigh-Mallory did not stop at criticizing Keith Park but soon became Dowding's most bitter critic too. Eventually he got Dowding's job as C. in C. of Fighter Command.

5 Beaverbrook is appointed Minister of Aircraft Production Beaverbrook was a 'buoyant and vigorous' newspaper tycoon, in Churchill's words, and his appointment as head of the new Ministry of Aircraft Production was the only fundamental political change that Churchill made. This photograph was taken on 15 May 1940, one of the most important days in the history of 10 Downing Street, and shows the newly appointed Minister leaving after the meeting that Dowding attended.

was something Göring had learned from Hitler. To be an arbitrator between rival subordinates is a well-established device of the tyrant. It consolidates power. But in July, as the first skirmishes of the Battle of Britain were taking place, Göring and his three Field Marshals were about to learn that it was no way to win a battle.

Hermann Göring

Hermann Göring grew up in the gothic shadows of a castle at Veldenstein near Nuremberg. His father was a retired government official, once senior officer in German South-West Africa and Consul-General in Haiti. Göring's godfather – a wealthy bachelor named Epenstein – was a friend of his family. He owned the castle, lived in stylish quarters on the top floor, and shared his bed with Göring's mother. Her husband tolerated this arrangement.

While still a small child, Hermann went to boarding school. He grew up to be an ill-disciplined boy, so bold that he seemed incapable of recognizing physical danger. This seemed exactly the right qualification for military college, and so it proved. By the time war began, in the summer of 1914, Göring was a promising young infantry officer, although not promising enough to be accepted for flying training. So, without him, his closest friend, Bruno Loerzer, went off to get his wings.

As Loerzer finished pilot training, Hermann Göring was nearby, hospitalized by arthritis, after considerable front-line service. Göring could hardly walk, and there was no question of his returning to the trenches. Defying all military regulations, Loerzer put his friend into the back seat of his aeroplane, and they reported for duty, with Field Aviation Unit No. 25, as pilot and observer.

It says much for Göring's famous charm that the crippled young officer escaped a court-martial, and was allowed to become an aviator. For the Air Service it proved a wise decision. This lame subaltern became one of Germany's most famous fighter pilots. He won the coveted

Orden Pour le Mérite – the Blue Max – and succeeded von Richthofen to command *Jagdgeschwader 1*, the legendary 'flying circus.'

For Loerzer it was also a wise decision. Göring never forgot his friend's loyalty, and on 19 July 1940 at the Kroll Opera House he became a full Luftwaffe General.

In the final hours of the First World War, as communists fought to seize power throughout Germany, Göring came into conflict with a 'soldiers' soviet' in Darmstadt. Göring came off best, as he did later when faced with a mob intent on roughing up any officer in uniform, on the grounds that such men were responsible for the war which Germany had lost. But doubtless these events played a part in Göring's acceptance of the Nazi creed. And the Nazis' pathological hatred and fear of Jews went unchallenged by a man who had seen his father humiliated by his mother's Jewish lover.

In 1922 Hermann Göring joined the Nazi Party. The presence of this ex-officer war hero was very reassuring to the middle classes whose support the Nazis badly needed.

Göring was always the Nazi candidate for political office. He was used to show the voter how responsible the party could be when in power and how willing it was to conform to parliamentary democracy. And so it was Göring who became the President of the Reichstag and the Prime Minister of Prussia.

Hitler appreciated the importance of Göring. When the Nazis got power, Hitler gave him an authority second only to his own. Göring organized storm troopers, took over the Prussian Ministry of the Interior, formed the Gestapo, set up the first concentration camps, and took charge of the economy for the Nazi 'Four Year Plan.'

A fine horseman and a crack shot, Göring was able to combine his enthusiasm for hunting with a sincere concern for wildlife, and opposition to vivisection. In his youth he had been something of a womanizer but two contented marriages provided him with a stability that many of the other top Nazis did not have. He met his first wife, a countess, after flying through a snowstorm and landing on a frozen-over lake in Sweden. His passenger – a well-known explorer who'd engaged Göring to fly him home – offered him hospitality in his castle. It was there that Göring met his future wife.

For pleasure Göring read detective stories, his favourite authors being Agatha Christie and Dashiell Hammett, but he could talk with some authority on subjects as varied as mountaineering and the Italian Renaissance. And he could do so in Italian if need be.

Göring's rise to power gave him a life-style rarely equalled in the twentieth century. He had castles, several hunting estates with grand lodges, and town houses too. The most remarkable of all was Karinhall – named in memory of Göring's first wife – built between two lakes, with formal gardens, fountains, and bronze statues, as well as a large section of private countryside. His servants were dressed in comic-opera outfits: knee-length coats with rich facings, high white gaiters, and silver-buckled shoes. There was a swimming pool, a vast library, gymnasium, art gallery, and one of the world's most elaborate model-railway layouts. His study was larger than most houses, and in its ante-room there was a wall covered with photographs inscribed with varying degrees of enthusiasm: Boris, King of Bulgaria, 'to the great marshal,' Prince Paul, Regent of Yugoslavia, 'with thanks,' Hindenburg, 'to Göring.'

The pink, girlish complexion, overweight body, and many childish indulgences masked a personality capable of superhuman self-control. Göring, wounded during the 1923 putsch, became a morphine addict as a result of his treatment. He eventually cured himself of this addiction by willpower alone.

Five feet nine inches tall, Göring was dynamic – a fluent and persuasive enthusiast with a powerful handshake and clear blue eyes – and many of his antagonists fell prey to his charm.

Göring's civil power as Air Minister, his military rank as Commander in Chief of the Luftwaffe, and his political status made him incomparably more powerful than any other military leader in Germany. To retain his advantage, Göring was quick to point out to Hitler any failing of his rivals: the army Generals. The power and prestige of pre-war Germany had been largely due to the show of air-power that Göring's Luftwaffe had staged. Hitler responded by treating the Luftwaffe as a privileged 'Nazi' service, while describing his army and navy as 'Imperial' legacies of the old regime.

As a confidant of Hitler, and by 1940 named as Hitler's successor, Göring had personal access to the supreme command. As a 'General' who gave the army the closest possible co-operation, Göring was important to the men of the General Staff. As the air ace who inherited von Richthofen's command, Göring had an unassailable authority among his own flyers.

In 1940 the victories in the west gave the 47-year-old Göring new power, and new tastes of luxury. He went shopping for diamonds in Amsterdam, and took a suite at the Ritz Hotel in Paris. Göring liked Paris so much that he decided to move into a fine house on the Rue de Faubourg St Honoré. That this was the British Embassy – now unoccupied except for one caretaker – made it no less attractive.

Göring took the German ambassador with him to inspect the property but when they explained the purpose of their visit, the custodian said, 'Over my dead body, your Excellency,' and closed the door in their faces.

As far back as 1933, Hitler had authorized Göring to start a national art collection which would remain in Göring's hands for his lifetime but then become a public collection. The conquests of 1940, and the way in which the European currencies were all pegged artificially lower than the German Mark, gave new impetus to this collection. Many art treasures were simply seized: 'ownerless' Jewish collections and 'enemy possessions' were taken into new custody. To obtain paintings from unconquered countries, Göring simply swapped his surplus. A dealer in

Lucerne, Switzerland, received 25 French Impressionist paintings in exchange for 5 Cranachs and 2 German Primitives.

The regal splendour of Göring's life-style was completed by his train. Code-named 'Asia,' its vanguard was a pilot train which accommodated the staff – civilian and military – in comfort that extended to bathing facilities. There were also low-loaders for cars, and freight wagons for Göring's shopping.

The train in which Göring travelled, and sometimes lived, was specially weighted to provide a smooth ride. This luxury meant two of Germany's heaviest locomotives were needed to move it. One coach was designed as bedrooms for himself and his wife, and a study. Another coach was a modern cinema. A third was a command post with a map room. A fourth was a dining car. There were also carriages for his senior commanders and for guests, some of whom (Milch, for example) had a whole carriage to themselves. At front and back, there were special wagons with anti-aircraft guns and crews, although whenever possible the train was halted near tunnels as protection against air attack.

In the spring of 1940 Göring, who liked to be called 'the Iron Man,' ordered his train west to Beauvais in France, a suitable place to command his Luftwaffe for the attack upon England. Few doubted that *Der Eiserner* was about to lead his Luftwaffe to a unique military victory. To do it would be nothing less than a personal triumph.

The Rise of the New German Air Force

In November 1918, a defeated Germany was forbidden the use of military aviation. Since there was at that time virtually no other sort of aviation, about a hundred large companies were without work.

A.E.G. (manufacturer of the G.IV twin-engined bomber) had already planned for such a contingency. As early as 1917, they had formed Deutsche Luftreederei, an airline which would use the aircraft they built. So within three months of the war's end, the world's first civil aeroplane airline[1] connected Berlin with Leipzig, Weimar, and Hamburg.

Professor Hugo Junkers, another German aircraft manufacturer, was just as quick to adapt to the changing times. On the very morning that the Armistice was signed, he had held a senior staff conference to discuss the changeover to manufacturing civil aircraft. By 25 June 1919 – three days before the signing of the Versailles Treaty – the outstanding Junkers F-13 was test flown. And while the other transports in use were cumbersome old wood-and-fabric biplanes, Junkers's new machine was an all-metal cantilever monoplane, and such a breakthrough in design that sales were made in spite of the thousands of war surplus aircraft that were available at give-away prices. It was a period when many wartime flyers formed one-man airlines. But the manufacturers were in the most advantageous position to prosper, and Junkers had shares in several airlines.

Professor Hugo Junkers came from an old Rhineland family. He was a scientist, a democrat, and a pacifist. He was also a genius. While working on gas-stove design he became interested in the efficiency of layered metal plates for heat transfer. He built himself a wind tunnel to study the effect of heated gases on various shapes, and ended up as the most important pioneer of metal aircraft construction.

By 1918, as the First World War ended, Hugo Junkers was already 60 years old. He was a white-haired old man with a large forehead and clear blue eyes. He had a large family but was ready to 'adopt' brilliant newcomers.

The most successful of Junkers's protégés was a small, rather pop-eyed man named Erhard Milch. No account of

[1]The world's first passenger-carrying airline service was operated by Zeppelin airships before the First World War.

the Luftwaffe, its victories or its failures, would be complete without devoting some words to this strange personality.

Erhard Milch did not create the Luftwaffe (that was the role of General Hans von Seeckt and dated from his memo of 1923), but Milch wet-nursed the infant air force, and dominated it right up to the end.

Milch was born in March 1892 in Wilhelmshaven, where Milch senior was an apothecary of the Imperial German Navy. 'Loyalty to the Kaiser and loyalty to my country were the only political doctrines I received either as an officer or earlier in my parents' home,' he told the judge at Nuremberg at his war-crimes trial.

But the dominant influence upon Milch's life was a secret that troubled him throughout it. So much so that when, near the end of his life, a biographer discovered the truth, Milch suppressed it still. The facts are simple, but, even in this permissive age, bizarre.

Klara, who was to become Milch's mother, fell in love with her uncle. Such a marriage was forbidden not only by her parents but by Church law too. Eventually she did her parents' bidding and married another man – Anton Milch – but did so on the strict understanding that he would not father her children. It was a decision endorsed by the discovery that his mother was in an asylum, and incurably insane. And so she agreed to the arranged marriage on condition that her uncle – the man she truly loved – would be the father of her future children. Erhard Milch grew up to know the wealthy man who visited them as 'uncle,' not realizing that the visitor was his father.

So carefully did his parents guard their secret that it was not until 1933 that the by then middle-aged Milch discovered the truth behind the mysteries that had haunted his youth. And this was the result of an investigation started by an informer who said that Milch's father was Jewish. It was an accusation calculated to get him removed from the key job he had in the Nazi regime.

The rumours said that because Anton Milch was Jewish, his mother had invented a story about Erhard's illegitimate birth in order to get Erhard classified as 'Aryan.' The rumours continued throughout the war and after it. They were fomented by Milch's evasive replies at the post-war Nuremberg trials. Milch allowed these stories to circulate all his life, for the only way that he could refute them was by revealing a secret that he was determined to take to his grave.

'I'll decide who is Jewish and who is not Jewish,' Göring told several men who came to him with stories of Milch's birth. But such replies only convinced the accusers that Göring was a part of the cover-up.

But Göring knew all the facts of Milch's birth. He had in fact been behind the Gestapo's investigation of the mystery. It is difficult not to wonder what Göring himself made of the curious fact that his right-hand man had a secret about his mother that was even darker than Göring's own.

Milch was an observer with the German Army Air Service in the First World War. His organizational abilities gave him command of a fighter squadron in spite of the fact that he could not fly an aeroplane! So it was no surprise that Milch proved to be such an able employee in the Junkers organization. And yet his next change of job took him to the very top levels of commerce. When the German government bullied and cajoled thirty-eight separate airlines into becoming just one subsidized state monopoly, Milch was selected to be one of its bosses. This choice remained 'inexplicable' even to Milch: he still couldn't pilot a plane, had very little business experience and no technical knowledge of aviation or manufacturing.

But Milch learned very quickly. Soon he was paying Hermann Göring – by now an influential Nazi Reichstag deputy – a regular 'consultancy fee,' and his private papers later revealed the extent to which he was already compiling files of damaging material about his rivals and superiors.

By 1929 Milch was the chief executive of Lufthansa and a secret member of the Nazi Party. His enemies said that his membership was kept secret so that when he falsified

Lufthansa accounts (so that the Nazi Party never paid for the aircraft chartered from Lufthansa) no suspicion would attach to him. In 1932 alone, Hitler and other Nazi leaders flew 23,000 miles. Aircraft played a vital part in the Nazi political campaigning. If Milch provided this facility for nothing he certainly earned the rewards he subsequently collected.

Milch became a figure of growing political importance as Lufthansa built airport facilities, organized signal and meteorology networks, and radio beacons for air-corridors. Its personnel were trained in administration, supply, and engineering as well as all the mysteries of blind-flying and long-range navigation. Even in its first year, Lufthansa had a night passenger service Berlin–Königsberg to connect with Moscow, and was sending experimental flights far afield. Its G-24s went to Peking and its Dornier Wal flying boats to Brazil. As early as 1930, civil aviation in Germany (measured by passengers or by mileage) was as big as all the British and French civil aviation services combined! All gliding records were, at this time, held by Germany and Austria.

By 1932 (and this was a year before the Nazis came to power) Germany had a claim to be the leader of world aviation. The Graf Zeppelin airship – carrying about sixty people and freight – had circumnavigated the world, been on long cruises to Egypt, Iceland, and the Arctic, and in March 1932, begun a scheduled service between Friedrichshafen and Rio de Janeiro. This was to be the only transatlantic air service for another seven years! The experimental twelve-engined Dornier Do X had crossed both the South and North Atlantic and a German pilot in a German plane had made the first east–west crossing of the North Atlantic.

Professor Junkers's series of all-metal monoplanes had culminated in the classic Junkers Ju 52/3m. By 1932 it was in service on the Berlin–Rome and Berlin–London routes. Lufthansa now connected Berlin with Barcelona,

Moscow, and Athens, flying a daily average of 30,000 miles.

No country in the world had training facilities to compare with the *Deutsche Verkehrsflieger Schule* (German Air Transport School), where so many of the Luftwaffe's pilots learned to fly bombers. To supply candidates for Lufthansa's training, there were about 50,000 active members of gliding clubs of the *Deutsche Luftsportverband*. In 1932, the 20-year-old Adolf Galland, already a skilled glider pilot, applied for training as a Lufthansa pilot: of 4,000 applicants, only 18 were accepted. The examinations lasted ten days.

This intense interest in aviation was shared by the general public. The 14-year-old apprentices, working at any aircraft factory, would find glider construction a mandatory part of their apprenticeship, and would not become qualified tradesmen unless they possessed the glider pilot's licence.

When the Nazis gained power, Erhard Milch was the obvious choice to build in secrecy a new air force. Professor Hugo Junkers had by now become an outspoken critic of the Nazis. He was one of the most powerful individuals in German aviation, and by far the most brilliant. Milch decided that he could gain control of the aviation manufacturing industries by making an example of his one-time benefactor and employer.

Milch sent the police to arrest Junkers. He was accused of many offences, including even treason. Armed with the terrible power of the totalitarian state, Milch broke Junkers. The end of the interrogations came only when Junkers assigned 51 per cent of his various companies to the State. This was not good enough for Milch. He then demanded, and got, chairmanship of the companies for his own nominees. Still not satisfied, Milch put the ailing old man under house arrest, until he gave the State the remainder of his shares. Less than six months afterwards, Hugo Junkers died. Milch sent a delegation of mourners from the Air Ministry, with a suitably inscribed wreath.

This so angered Junkers's family that the men from the ministry returned to Berlin without attending the ceremony, rather than face their wrath.

Perhaps it is not too much to suggest that Milch found in the Nazis, with their despotic regality and regalia, elaborate rallies and displays, something to appeal to the ardent monarchist he had always been. Although his role as Göring's right-hand man brought him sometimes into arguments with his boss (who was marginally younger than Milch), his loyalty to Hitler and his Nazi kingdom was unquestioning.

And Hitler gave his two airmen a comprehensive slice of the kingdom. They had control of everything from Lufthansa ticket clerks to fighter pilots, and from the secret construction of military aircraft to the gliding clubs, which were now a part of the NSFK (Nazi Flying Corps). Such flexibility made these men the envy of other service chiefs, who had no such access to semi-trained personnel, and no access to Hitler via civil channels. Nor did other service chiefs have such control over the design and development of their weapons, and the supply of them, as the Air Ministry had over the aircraft industry.

But there is little to support the allegation that, even before the Nazis came to power, the German aircraft industry produced fleets of warplanes, thinly disguised as civil aircraft. Of seven major aircraft types used by the Luftwaffe for operations in the Battle of Britain, only two had prototypes flying before 1935. One of these – the Ju 52/3m – was undoubtedly designed as a transport aircraft, as its sale to the airlines of twenty-nine foreign countries, and its brief and unsuccessful career as a Spanish Civil War bomber, indicated. The other aircraft was the Dornier Do 17, which flew in prototype form in the autumn of 1934. But this 'Flying Pencil' was put into storage after flight testing, and was adapted for military use only after being discovered there.

Hitler gained power when the Reichstag passed his Enabling Act in March 1933. The Luftwaffe must be dated from the big aircraft-building programme that started in January 1934. But few of these machines were suitable for modern warfare, for air forces do not start with warplanes: the first need is training aircraft. And so, of the 4,021 aircraft the Luftwaffe ordered in January 1934, 1,760 were elementary trainers (Arado Ar 66 and Focke-Wulf FW 44). Only 251 were fighter types, and all of these were biplanes.

On 1 March 1935, the existence of the Luftwaffe was officially announced. It was accepted as a fact of life by the Allied powers that had forbidden it. In Berlin a huge and grandiose Air Ministry building provided a thousand offices, where ambitious men bickered. Göring had neither the technical knowledge nor the inclination to give the new air force a clear directive. Hitler asked only for the greatest possible number of combat aircraft in the shortest possible time. It was in this atmosphere that all thoughts of a long-range strategic bombing force languished.

There was no strong opposition to the four-engined long-range bomber (possession of which would have totally changed the Battle of Britain), it was simply a matter of priorities. The complex problems of manufacturing such aircraft would delay all the other programmes.

The priorities of the new air force preoccupied the men in the German Air Ministry. Petty jealousies and vicious vendettas flourished as empires were built. Milch was tough enough to handle the men under his command but this did not endear him to Göring. On the contrary, the relationship between the two men became steadily worse as time went on. Frustrated by the technicalities of a new sort of air war that he could not master, Göring condemned them all as unnecessary 'black boxes.' He sought out men who could share his memories of the Red Baron and the wind in the wires. And he gave them jobs.

Ernst Udet, although no close friend of Göring, was just such a flyer. Udet was an amiable, much-travelled man who lived only for flying. Germany's second most successful fighter ace (after von Richthofen), Udet had continued to fly after the war. He had got finance for an aircraft factory that bore his name, took one of his products – a U.4 – to South America, and won an air race from Rosario to Buenos Aires. He severed his relationship with the Udet factory, and lived by giving stunt-flying demonstrations round Germany. He flew for an expedition filming African wildlife, and went so low that one of the aircraft was damaged by a lion that jumped at it. He made an impressive showing at the National Air Races in Cleveland, Ohio, where he stunted his old Flamingo biplane. He flew in Hollywood and in Greenland, where he worked with Leni Riefenstahl, the famous German woman film-maker.

In the USA, in September 1933, Ernst Udet watched a flying demonstration of Curtiss F8C biplanes. These were rather old by American standards and the Americans had no objection to Udet's buying them. The Curtiss company called this design a 'Helldiver' and gave the same name to all their subsequent dive-bomber designs. Although the exact way in which Udet found enough money to buy two such machines has not been established, it seems virtually certain that on Udet's recommendation, Göring paid money into Udet's bank account, and the aircraft, when shipped

Figure 3

War hero, stunt-flyer, and bon vivant, Ernst Udet made this self-portrait in 1933.

to Germany, were tested for the new air force. The concept of aircraft using machine guns and small bombs against front-line infantry had been discussed by German theorists since the First World War. Now Udet demonstrated his Helldivers, and the accuracy of this sort of bombing attack – within 30 yards of the target was not unusual for an expert pilot – persuaded the German Air Ministry to ask Junkers and other companies to design such a machine. The Junkers Ju 87, the famous Stuka, was the result. It became the world's most successful dive bomber.

Many times Udet was offered a job with Göring, but he was unable to decide what he wanted to do. And yet during these years, when the air force was being created, Udet always had access to the top levels of command. It was a memorandum of Udet's in 1933 that first considered the military application of the glider. This idea eventually brought far-reaching changes to military operations. And Udet kept in touch with the aircraft industry too, and could prove as suspicious of new ideas as Göring was. In August 1935, 39 years old and still a civilian, he sat in the cockpit of the Bf 109 prototype.[1] Professor Messerschmitt said that Udet looked uneasy as the mechanic closed the canopy over his head. The prototype was not yet ready to fly but Udet pronounced on it. 'When he got out, he patted me on the back and said, "Messerschmitt, this will never be a fighting aeroplane. The pilot needs an open cockpit. He has to feel the air to know the speed of the aeroplane." '

There was no argument but Messerschmitt knew that his arch-enemy, Professor Ernst Heinkel, was his most serious rival for the new fighter contract, and that the Heinkel prototype had an open cockpit.

No wonder that there were so many criticisms and misgivings when 'the flying clown' joined the Luftwaffe in

[1]The Messerschmitt 109 and 110 designs were started when the company was named Bayerische Flugzeugwerke and thus were abbreviated Bf 109 and Bf 110. In July 1938 the company became Messerschmitt A.G., so that the abbreviations for the later designs were Me 210, Me 410, Me 163, etc.

January 1935, and one month later was named as Inspector of Fighters and Dive Bombers. By June of that same year, Udet was chief of the Development Section of the Luftwaffe's Technical Department.

Some said that Udet's quick promotion was Göring's way of limiting the fast-growing power of Milch. The workings of Göring's mind have to remain conjecture but Udet was temperamentally and intellectually unsuited for this vitally important job. Milch, in spite of all the outward gestures of friendship for Udet, despised him and resented his appointment. He did not like having to consult the overmanned and disorganized department that Udet headed, and Milch resolved to get control of it. Eventually, as we shall see, he did.

Udet was an unusual combination of noisy Bohemian wit and sensitive timidity. In the First World War, having returned from air combat without having fired his guns, he said he couldn't be sure whether it was a reluctance to kill or fear of being shot down.

As a flight commander with *Jagdstaffel 15*, he had once gone alone on a balloon-bursting expedition, only to find himself in a dog-fight with another lone machine. As they looped, dived, and circled, looking for an opening, Udet read the words 'Vieux Charles' painted on the enemy fighter. He knew he was fighting Charles Guynemer, the French ace. During the combat Udet's guns jammed. Seeing this, the Frenchman flew over Udet inverted – and waved to him before flying away.

It was suggested to Udet that Guynemer's guns had also jammed but Udet rejected this idea emphatically. He insisted that even modern warfare could find a place for chivalry. Such a lonely romantic would find little in common with the hard-eyed ambitious men who were jockeying for power in the huge Air Ministry building in Berlin.

Ernst Udet's critics pointed out that he smoked too much, drank too much, and had the disconcerting habit of scribbling acerbic caricatures of his friends and colleagues.

Yet Udet's love of flying gave him an advantage in the matter of assessing new aircraft designs. He liked to describe himself as the Luftwaffe's chief test pilot, and when he got a chance to see the Bf 109 in flight he was magnanimous enough to change his mind about Messerschmitt's new fighter.

Initially there had been four fighters from which to choose. The Arado was eliminated because it had a fixed undercarriage, and so was the Focke-Wulf prototype (which had a parasol wing supported by struts). Its wheels retracted into the fuselage, and this complicated mechanism was never satisfactory. This left the Heinkel He 112 as the only rival for the Bf 109. German engine development, or rather the lack of it, forced both manufacturers to use a Rolls-Royce Kestrel engine in the prototype.

At first it seemed certain that Heinkel would get the contract. His fighter was based upon the beautiful He 70. It was strongly made, with a top speed only marginally less than its rival. The structure was rather complex, but its wing loading (that is, the weight per square foot of wing area) was calculated to appeal to the biplane protagonists, and so was its open cockpit.

Messerschmitt's fighter was radically new. Its wing loading was so high that it needed 'gadgets' such as slots, and the wings were incredibly thin compared to the Heinkel's. But once in the air the Messerschmitt was supreme: rolling, diving, and excelling in all the tests that the Air Ministry specified. And although the aerodynamics were advanced, the slab-sided, square-tipped wings and very narrow but otherwise orthodox fuselage would give no production problems. It would be superior in cost, in man-hours, and in materials.

Heinkel's readiness to compromise with the aerodynamics of the biplane had resulted in a prototype that was heavy and unresponsive to the controls. Heinkel took his sluggish prototype and changed it, not once but many times, until eventually it was comparable to the Bf 109, but Udet took Professor Heinkel aside and told him that, now the Bf 109 was in full-scale production, there was no place in his building programme for the He 112 fighter. Stick to bombers, he told Heinkel.

The Messerschmitt Bf 109 was Udet's most important contribution to the Luftwaffe. His decision came at a time when the unconventional Udet was at the height of his influence. Hitler described him as the world's greatest pilot. Sourly Milch added, 'But he also saw him as one of our greatest technical experts, and here he was very mistaken.' But Milch was not yet ready to get into conflict with one of Hitler's favourites and Udet became a member of Milch's group of influential cronies who dined regularly at Horcher's famous restaurant in Berlin.

Neither did Udet have much to fear from Göring. As elected chairman of the Richthofen Veterans Association, Udet had expelled Göring, the unit's last commander. Udet accused Göring of falsifying his First World War record and victory claims and said he could prove it. Milch said that Göring admitted it was true, and was frightened of Udet.

By now Milch had few friends. Heartily disliked by Göring, he found little support from the Luftwaffe General Staff. In spite of this, the irrepressible Milch, working like a beaver, consolidated his authority, and in certain areas increased it. When the Spanish Civil War started and Franco asked for Hitler's aid, Milch instantly recognized it as a chance to increase his power. He took charge of the intervention.

The Spanish Civil War

By early 1937 Milch had a small experimental air force unit operating in Spain. One of its first missions had been the air-transporting of 10,000 fully equipped Moorish infantry from Tetuan, in Spanish Morocco, to Seville. They used Junkers Ju 52/3m aircraft, and the movement went almost without a hitch. In some respects it was as significant as any of the Condor Legion's combat actions.

The Condor Legion's commander was Sperrle, who later became an Air Fleet commander in the Battle of Britain. His Chief of Staff was Wolfram von Richthofen, a dive-bombing and close-support specialist. (He was a cousin of the First World War ace.) The Luftwaffe's first taste of combat was a terrible disappointment for Göring, Milch, and the High Command. The Junkers Ju 52/3m proved unsuitable for bombing, and most bombing turned out to be far less accurate than had been hoped. The Heinkel He 51 biplane fighters were inferior to the I-16 fighters (supplied to the other side by the USSR) in speed, climb, manoeuvrability, and armament. Reluctant to believe this, the German flyers often misidentified them as 'Curtiss fighters.' But as German skill improved and newer German aircraft arrived, things got better: Berlin's apprehension turned into equally wrong complacency. When Dornier Do 17 and Heinkel He 111 bombers proved faster than enemy fighters the *Schnellbomber* concept seemed vindicated. Rashly the men in Berlin concluded that bombers would never require fighter escort.

The Junkers Ju 87 dive bomber also exceeded expectations, and its small bomb-load was more than compensated for by the fast turn-around time at its bases: some of the units completed half-a-dozen missions per day. And von Richthofen's close-support techniques proved decisive in some actions, even though the war's front line was notoriously difficult to see. There was a shortage of aircraft radio but the airmen relied on signals spread out on the ground. They did little to improve air-to-air or air-to-ground radio. This, too, was to prove a grave error.

The Messerschmitt Bf 109s arrived to take over the fighter combat tasks. Heinkel He 51 biplanes were already adapted to carrying 10-kg high-explosive bombs and improvised petrol bombs. This flat-trajectory bombing in support of infantry attacks became a specialized technique of German (and Allied) light-bomber squadrons. It was one of the few new methods to evolve in the Spanish fighting.

The Luftwaffe's first building programme had begun in

January 1934; it went to war in September 1939. By 1937 there was clearly little time left for redesigning the Luftwaffe's aircraft. These aircraft types that fought in Spain – Bf 109s, He 111s, Ju 87s, Ju 52s – remained the basis of the Luftwaffe's strength right up until the end of the Second World War.

Milch sent Hugo Sperrle's Condor Legion to Spain to assess the aircraft already in production. With this in mind, many different aircraft types were sent there, including even float-planes. The flying personnel were rotated after six months to provide combat experience for as many crews as possible. All ranks were encouraged to send reports to a specially constituted department of the Air Ministry.

Just as men from von Seeckt's Defence Ministry provided the Luftwaffe with its staff and its Air Fleet commanders, and Lipetsk (the secret training school in Russia) provided its field commanders, so now did Spain provide combat specialists. Men such as Adolf Galland and Werner Mölders came back from leading a fighter *Staffel* in Spain to revolutionize the formations and tactics of the fighter arm.

Adolf 'Dolfo' Galland was an outstanding personality of this period. Born in 1912, of Huguenot ancestry, Galland, like so many other Luftwaffe aces, was attracted to the sport of gliding while still a teenager. Accepted by the Air Transport School at Brunswick, Galland was soon selected for the secret Luftwaffe. At 22 years old he was an instructor at the famous Schleissheim Fighter Pilot School. Galland went to fight in Spain but, flying a Heinkel He 51 biplane, deliberately avoided combat with the far superior Russian- and American-made enemy monoplanes.

The poor performance of the He 51s caused them to be relegated to the infantry support role. Galland pioneered these experiments and produced a considerable body of written material about the use of aircraft in support of ground forces. This fitted very well with the dive-bombing theories of Udet, which were by now enthusiastically received by senior officers, including General von Richthofen, Chief of Staff of the Condor Legion, who would soon command the Junkers Ju 87 Stuka units in the Battle of Britain.

And so Galland found himself trapped into the role of ground-support air specialist. As the Bf 109s were shipped to Spain, Galland handed his command over to a young man who was to become his rival as the most famous fighter pilot in Germany – 'Vati' ('Daddy') Mölders. As Mölders began to use the monoplane fighters to win victories, Galland returned to Berlin and a job in the Air Ministry.

In September 1937, as the Condor Legion fighter units near Santander, Spain, flew seven sorties a day against crumbling resistance, senior Luftwaffe officers paid an official visit to Britain. Milch and Udet were invited to inspect RAF Fighter Command at Hornchurch, a key airfield in the defences of London. The aircraft there were Gloster Gladiator biplanes which, like the Hawker Fury fighters also in service, were slower than the Luftwaffe's *bombers*.

There were virtually no monoplanes of any sort in RAF service at this time. The Hurricanes and Spitfires were suffering new delays caused by a modification to the nose that an engine improvement demanded. It is sometimes said that this was part of a nicely timed deception plan, for the RAF's first Hurricanes reached 111 Squadron during the following month. Why such a provocative deception would have been desirable is not explained.

The German Navy

Although by tradition subordinate to the army as a fighting force, the German navy was independent of it in a way that the Luftwaffe was not. In the spring of 1940 the German navy fought a brilliant and daring campaign in Norwegian waters. This had to some extent been made possible by the navy's *B-Dienst* cryptanalytic department which, by the time war began, was able to read even the most secret of the British Admiralty's messages, having broken the codes and ciphers.

In the spring of 1940 the German navy's prestige was high. Its strategists demanded more steel for submarines and were preparing a surface fleet that, with Italian help, might control the Mediterranean by 1942.

But the navy needed time to recover from the grave, but worthwhile, losses that the conquest of Norway had caused it. So the Admirals had little enthusiasm for hasty and dangerous invasion plans that would hazard their few remaining ships in the Straits of Dover.

In Norway it had lost ten destroyers and three cruisers. The *Scharnhorst* and *Gneisenau* had been put out of action by torpedo hits. Of the three 'pocket battleships' with which Germany had entered the war, the *Lützow* had been damaged by torpedoes, the *Admiral Scheer* had engine trouble, and the *Graf Spee* had been scuttled after the naval action off Montevideo, Uruguay. The new battleships, *Bismarck*, *Tirpitz*, and the cruiser *Prinz Eugen*, would need until the following year to train their crews and work up to combat readiness.

To cover the Sea-lion invasion, face the Royal Navy's Home Fleet, motor torpedo boats, coastal batteries, submarines, minefields, and the combined air units of the Fleet Air Arm and the RAF, the Germans had only one heavy cruiser, *Hipper*, two light cruisers, half-a-dozen destroyers, and some U-boats.

No wonder that the German navy had sent motorized naval commandos with the panzer armies that invaded France, as part of an attempt to seize French warships. But the French sailed away. Even the incomplete battleship *Jean Bart* had escaped just before the Germans got to St Nazaire.

Churchill, afraid the Germans would still be able to barter armistice terms for the warships they badly needed, ordered the Royal Navy to persuade the French crews to sail beyond German reach or scuttle. In July at Oran in French North Africa units of the French navy came under the gunfire and bombs of the Royal Navy. The blood of 1,300 French sailors spattered all over the British, for two or three generations.

Sea power still decided the fate of nations. In the USA nothing worried Roosevelt and his advisers more than the threat to their eastern seaboard that would come if Germany controlled the Royal Navy's ships. All American decisions were based on this fear, and Churchill tried unsuccessfully to play on it.

Operation Sea-lion

Undoubtedly Hitler – and most of his advisers – would have preferred a negotiated peace with Britain after France fell. Count Ciano, Mussolini's son-in-law, wrote in his diary, 'Hitler is now the gambler who has made a big scoop and would like to get up from the table risking nothing more.'

So confident was Hitler that the game was over, and Britain had lost it, that he disbanded 15 divisions and put 25 divisions back to peacetime footing. But the British were gamblers too. They wanted double or nothing.

By the middle of July, Hitler issued Directive No. 16. 'Since England, in spite of her hopeless military situation, shows no signs of being ready to come to a compromise, I have decided to prepare a landing operation against England, and, if necessary, to carry it out.' Many historians have italicized the final half-dozen words of that sentence, claiming that it shows he was never in earnest. A more powerful indication of the unreality of Directive No. 16 is its timetable: all preparations were to be ready by the middle of August.

The Directive was so secret that it was sent only to the Commanders in Chief. But Göring passed it on to his Air Fleet commanders, and did so by radio. To put such an important message on the air was an unnecessary risk but the Germans had great confidence in their coding machines. At all levels of command, the Luftwaffe used the Enigma

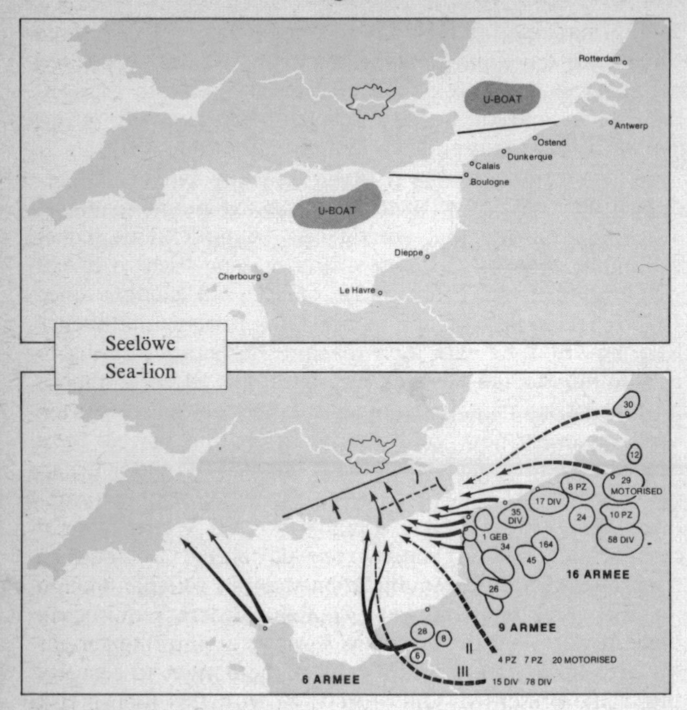

Figure 4

TOP The German navy submitted an invasion plan that would have created a narrow sea-lane, protected on each side by minefields. This plan was compatible with the very small naval force still available after the Norwegian campaign. On the other hand it would call for concentration areas in the Pas de Calais that would become targets that even RAF Bomber Command would be able to hit.

BOTTOM The German army envisaged landings all along the south coast. They wanted the speed and convenience of using the great ports and harbours of northern Europe, from Rotterdam and Antwerp to Le Havre and Cherbourg. This was particularly important to the armoured and motorized divisions.

coding machine, at this time changing keys two or three times each day. The Enigma was a small battery-powered machine not unlike a portable typewriter. Rotors changed the cipher, and the receiving machine lit up each letter. This was then written down by one of the code clerks.

When war began the British staged a big cloak-and-dagger operation to get their hands on an Enigma machine. This was hardly the intelligence triumph that recent claimants suggest, as the company making them had had virtually identical Enigmas on sale to all comers since 1923. Having left things rather late, British intelligence were now fiddling with their machine desperately trying to decode intercepted German messages. It was very much a hit-or-miss affair. (In spite of all the nonsense written about it, very few vital messages of this period were decoded, and it wasn't until the 'Colossus' computer began its work in 1943 that there was a regular flow of information.) When reading about Enigma it must be remembered that armies and air fleets received orders by landline teleprinter. Radio communication was not reliable enough for the very long and very complex orders required in modern war. And the Germans – whose monitoring service was excellent – were well aware of the danger to security that radio presented. Only rarely, as with this foolish risk taken with Directive No. 16, did the Enigma intelligence pay such a dividend. It gave the British the German code word 'Sea-lion' and was a shot in the arm for the code-breakers. Some claim that this decoded message prompted Churchill to make his 'fight on the beaches' speech.

When the German naval Commander in Chief received Hitler's Directive No. 16, his response was immediate. The Admirals were agreed that no date could be determined until the Luftwaffe had air supremacy over the Channel, but they produced a draft plan and on 28 July the army looked closely at it. The navy planners proposed a beach-head near Dover. By using the narrowest section of the Channel they could lay minefields to protect the invasion fleet corridor. Submarines would be assigned to the Channel, in spite of the difficulties these shallow waters presented to submarines, and more to guard the North Sea flank. It was estimated that the navy would require ten days to put the first assault ashore. The army was horrified.

For the attack westwards through France in May, the German army command's objectives had proved ridiculously modest, in the light of its panzer Generals' achievements. Now the army was determined to show more ambition. It told the navy that it wanted landings all along England's south coast, from Folkestone to Brighton, with a separate crossing from Cherbourg. The army would need tanks and wheeled vehicles which meant all the car ferries must be employed, together with the other cross-Channel tourist facilities. The first wave must be ashore within three days. The primary objectives were massive areas of southern England almost as far as London. And, in case you are still taking all this seriously, the first wave was to consist of 260,000 men, 30,000 vehicles, and 60,000 horses! Having looked at the navy's proposal, Walter von Brauchitsch, the army's Commander in Chief, and his Chief of the General Staff, Franz Halder, stated unequivocally, 'We cannot carry through our part of the operation on the basis of the resources furnished by the navy.'

On 31 July Hitler summoned his army and navy chiefs to the Berghof, his chalet in the Bavarian Alps near Berchtesgaden. *Grossadmiral* Erich Raeder explained the navy's position first. Preparations were going as fast as possible. The navy was scouring occupied Europe for suitable barges, but the work of modifying them for military use and getting them to the Channel ports could not be completed before 15 September. In view of the army's demand for a wider front for the landing, and with the prospect of autumn storms, it might be better to plan for an invasion in May 1941, said Raeder.

Hitler did not get angry at this suggestion but he pointed out that the British army would be better able to deal with an invasion by the following year, and suggested that the weather in May would be little better than that in September.

Having put the navy's point of view, Raeder left the conference. Hitler continued to discuss 'Sea-lion' with his army commanders. At one point he went so far as to say that he doubted whether it was 'technically feasible.' However no such doubts intruded into the Directive of the following day. It was signed by *Feldmarschall* Keitel and came from the OKW, the High Command of the combined armed forces which Hitler personally controlled. Preparations were to continue, and all would be ready by 15 September. Meanwhile the Luftwaffe would begin a large-scale offensive and, according to the effects of the air raids, Hitler would make a final decision about the invasion at the end of August.

The most significant aspect of all this top-level discussion was the absence of Luftwaffe chiefs. At the Berghof meeting, where the ball was passed to Göring's Air Fleets, there had been not even one representative of the Luftwaffe.

And so Göring's so-called Eagle Attack (*Adlerangriff*) was born in the same bungling, buck-passing muddle that had left Guderian at Sedan without objectives, and then halted him while the men in Berlin thought about it. It was the same mess of contradictory orders that had stopped the German armour at Dunkirk. The top brass of the Wehrmacht were learning that it was safer to equivocate. 'Sea-lion was contemplated,' said the jokers afterwards, 'but never planned.'

There was no proper training for the highly specialized amphibious assault and no staff officers with enough experience to plan one. But, having passed the immediate problems to Göring, the army engaged in a series of energetic invasion rehearsals, and propaganda units filmed them for release to cinemas on the actual day. Even more diligently, the German navy searched the rivers and canals of Europe, and crammed the northern ports with barges from all over Europe. Countless men with saws and welding torches fitted each with crude ramps for sea-sick horses under fire. The barges were to be towed across the channels in pairs, by tugs, at a speed of five knots. The lines of barges were expected to be at least twelve miles long. When they neared England, the plan said the barges were to be sailed into lines from which one unpowered barge would be lashed to a powered barge. Together they would assault the beaches.

Not even the initial assault boats (*Sturmboote*) were armoured. They were tiny vessels, some held only six infantrymen plus two crew. They were designed for river crossings and modified so that they could be launched from minesweepers that would take them as close as possible to the British coast. And the barge crews included Dutchmen,

ILLUSTRATIONS

6 Robert Watson-Watt He didn't invent radar (the Germans were way ahead long before he even drafted his memo about it) but with his motto of 'second best tomorrow' he put together an adequate system in record time.

7 Chain Home radar aerials The aerials of a typical Chain Home radar station (called Radio Direction Finding stations in 1940) were too tall to be disguised or hidden. However, they proved difficult to destroy by bombing because the open girder work was not vulnerable to blast effect, and the height of the towers made dive-bombing attacks hazardous.

8 Inside a 'receiver hut' This photograph was taken in 1940 at Dunkirk, Kent, and shows the interior of the small 'receiver hut' that was positioned at each set of transmitting and receiving aerials. The sloped desk at which the man with headphones sits holds the cathode-ray tube. The WAAF corporal seated on a raised box oversees the tube and plotting table (foreground). At the extreme left background a sergeant near the switchboard holds the telephone that conveys the plots to the Filter Room at Fighter Command HQ. Notice the Auxiliary Air Force badge – a small A beneath the main badge – on the shoulders of the WAAFs at left and centre.

9 Operating the cathode-ray tube This photograph shows more detail of the cathode tube seen in Plate 8. Women operators proved exceptionally suited to this very difficult and tiring work, and were used in spite of warnings from many quarters that the women would panic when the installations came under attack. This proved untrue.

6

7

8

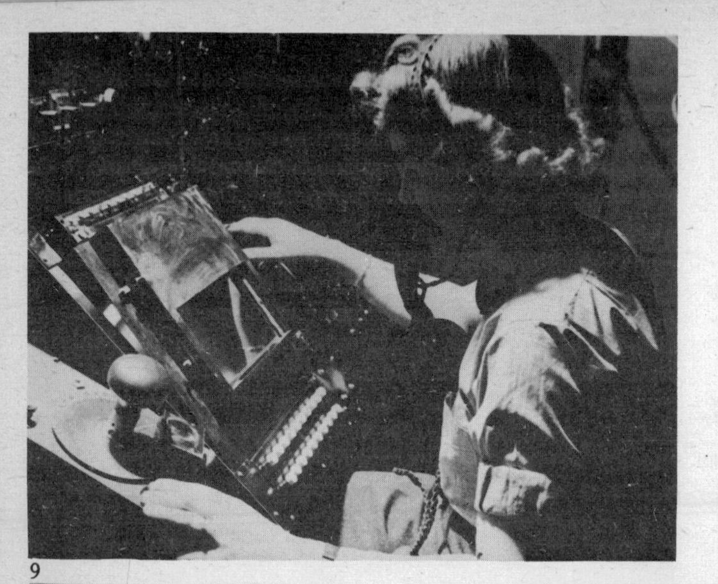

9

10

11

12

13

Belgians, and Frenchmen with no vested interest in the operation's success.

Even if one is generous enough to equate the modified German barges with what were later called LCTs (Landing Craft, Tanks), the Germans still had nothing to compare with the two vessels that the Allied armies were later to find indispensable for seaborne invasion. First, the LST (Landing Ship, Tank) that could survive a heavy sea, and

10 The German view of Dover radar station Technically one of the most impressive photos of the whole war. A35-mm camera was set up by the Germans to photograph across the Straits of Dover. Although not in itself a difficult feat, in this case the shutter speed was fast enough to capture the Messerschmitt fighters too. But even more interesting is the proof that the Germans could actually see the towers of the Dover radar station (and yet they did so little to destroy it). From that station the RAF operators could watch the German aircraft getting into formation deep inside France.

11 Fighter Command's underground Operations Room at Bentley Priory (Dowding's HQ) The girl plotters use headphones to hear the reports of enemy raiders from the Filter Room next door. They then use their rakes to move coloured counters across the map table. Note the special clock with coloured triangles to show which raids are freshly reported (see text). The officers on the balcony decide which Sector will be assigned to attack the raiders and that Sector's Operations Room will look very much like this one. But on this balcony there are men who decided about sounding public air-raid warning sirens and switching the BBC programmes between transmitters so they could not be used as a homing signal by the German bombers.

12 A typical Observer Corps post After the German raids had crossed the coast there were no other means of tracking them except by the eyes and ears of these volunteers. The man in the centre is using a sight to measure the angle of the enemy raiders but to convert this into a map reference requires an accurate estimate of their altitude. This was guesswork, and it was this element of error that caused the plots on the tables to look as if the raids were zig-zagging.

13 A British army 3.7-inch anti-aircraft gun site on the south coast in 1940 At this stage of the war the guns scored few hits and were used to force the raiders up higher and make their bombing less accurate.

Lacking the sophistication that came later in the war, these gunners had to depend upon the shells arranged in racks according to the fuse settings which were also chalked on to the base of each shell.

yet had shallow enough draft to put tanks directly onto a beach. Secondly, the DUKW, which was a two-and-a-half-ton truck, with a hull and propeller fitted to it. Groups of them brought supplies from supply ship to beach very quickly, so releasing the ship for another trip.

Churchill did not take the threat of invasion seriously. On 10 July he told the War Cabinet to disregard Sea-lion. '. . . it would be a most hazardous and suicidal operation,' he said. It is in the light of this that one must see Churchill's boldness in sending tanks to Egypt in the summer of 1940. It also explains why he backed up Beaverbrook, the new Minister of Aircraft Production, when he poached personnel and commandeered property that built more fighters but caused delays and shortages in other war industries.

At this stage of the war, any German invasion – seaborne or airborne – would have been cut to pieces. British experiments with setting the sea ablaze were fearsome, and Bomber Command were secretly training their squadrons in the use of poison gas. A cover story about spraying beaches to destroy vermin had been prepared for release should the Germans object to this form of warfare. RAF Medical Officers assigned to the poison gas units were being fortified with copious draughts of 'captured' champagne.

All this has encouraged some to suggest that there was no real danger of invasion in 1940, and conclude that Fighter Command did not fight a decisive battle. This is a specious argument. Had the Luftwaffe eliminated Fighter Command, its bombers could have knocked out all the other dangers one by one. Given the sort of command of the air that the Luftwaffe had achieved in Poland in only three days, German bombers, guided by radio beams, could have destroyed everything from Whitehall to the units of the Home Fleet. There would have been no insurmountable problem for invasion fleets and airborne units if the air was entirely German.

The Douhet Theories

Like many high-ranking airmen, and manufacturers of bombing aircraft, Göring subscribed to the theories of General Giulio Douhet, an Italian who believed that armies and navies were best employed as defensive forces while bomber fleets conquered the enemy. Just before he died in 1930, General Douhet wrote a futuristic story called 'The War of 19—.' Often quoted but seldom read, Douhet's words had such profound effects upon the German and the RAF High Commands that they are worth examining. Written in the documentary manner of H. G. Wells, Douhet's story described how an 'Independent German Air Force' fought great aerial battles against the Belgian and French air units. 'There was no doubt that the enemy's purpose was to make the mobilization and concentration of the Allied armies as difficult as possible,' said Douhet's imaginative fiction. The Allies replied with 'night-bombing brigades' that attacked German cities with explosives, incendiaries, and poison gas.

Douhet's fiction continues with the Independent German Air Force dropping leaflets telling the citizens of Namur, Soissons, Châlons, and Troyes that their cities are to be obliterated, and that Paris and Brussels will go the same way unless they sue for peace. The tale ends when those towns are obliterated, and the governments do sue for peace. It was the pressure that civilians under air bombardment would put upon their own government that formed the basis of Douhet's theories. At the end of his story he writes:

> Impressed by the terrible effects of the bombings and the sight of the enemy planes flying freely and unopposed in their own sky, though they cursed the barbarous methods of the enemy, they could not help feeling bitter against their own aeronautical authorities who had not taken enough protective measures against such an eventuality.

Douhet believed that any nation devoting a large part of

its air force to air defence, was risking conquest by a nation that spent everything on bombing fleets. Totally disregarding all the advantages that the defence enjoys in any form of warfare, Douhet smoothly concluded that 'No one can command his own sky if he does not command his adversary's sky.'

The German Army Air Service's tactics in the First World War had already proved that this was nonsense, but Douhet provided abundant quotes for ambitious bomber theorists. Such men, in Germany, France, Britain, and the USA, had long since decided that in war the importance of an air force (and its commanders) would be judged by the amount of damage done to the enemy, not by skill in defence. Douhet was important because he reinforced illusions about the effectiveness of the bomber and reduced still further the influence of the fighter pilots.

Although he had been a fighter pilot, Hermann Göring found Douhet's ideas easy to accept. He was not sympathetic to the complex technical devices which had converted air warfare from armed barn-storming to crude science. Like many of his contemporaries, he found it convenient to stick to von Richthofen's simplistic dictum that shooting down enemy planes was 'the only important thing' and that 'everything else is nonsense.' And Göring's Luftwaffe was dedicated to the offensive, designed for close co-operation with the invading German armies. It lacked long-range bombers, but – argued its leaders – what did that matter if the invasions were so successful that you could leap-frog forward with your medium-range machines from each new lot of captured airfields. It seemed to make sense.

By 1940, some were already claiming that Göring had proved Douhet right. The capitulation of Poland and the Netherlands had followed quickly after the bombing of Warsaw and Rotterdam respectively. Even sceptics were beginning to believe that this was cause and effect. Certainly it seemed to provide Göring with a trump card. If his overall programme of air attacks against military targets in southern England failed, he had only to switch his whole attack to London itself and the British government would seek terms. Douhet said so, and history proved it.

Unfortunately for Göring there were, in Britain, some young flyers who had never read Douhet, and an elderly disbeliever named Dowding.

PART TWO

Air Chief Marshal Sir Hugh Dowding, Commander in Chief Fighter Command

[illegible]

[illegible]

[illegible]

As the eldest son of the school's head-master, Inigo [illegible]

[illegible] within the Army Class [illegible] in South Africa. [illegible]

[illegible] the Royal [illegible]

'A difficult man, a self-opinionated man, a most determined man, and a man who knew, more than anybody, about all aspects of aerial warfare.'

GEN. SIR FREDERICK PILE, G.C.B., D.S.O., M.C.
(General Officer Commander in Chief) Anti-Aircraft Command, 1939–45), of Dowding

It is difficult to imagine a man less like Hermann Göring than was Hugh Dowding. In 1914, already 32 years old, Dowding qualified as a pilot. His father heard about it and forbade him to fly because it was too dangerous. Hugh Dowding obeyed his father.

Both his parents came from the sort of upper-middle-class families that supplied senior men to the Church, India, and the armed forces. His father, a kind and conscientious man, had founded a successful preparatory school in Scotland. There were four children, three boys and a girl.

As the eldest child of the school's head-master, Hugh Dowding was expected to set an example of duty, manners, patriotism, and industry. Like his father, he went to Winchester, a public school reputed to produce inscrutable intellectuals. Dowding's subsequent career did little to change the Wykehamist reputation.

At Winchester he found that joining the Army Class was a way to avoid Greek verbs. Later Dowding said that he went into the army rather than learn Greek, but in 1899 – when he entered the Royal Military Academy – Queen Victoria's scarlet-coated soldiers were just about to fight the Boers in South Africa. The British, after many years of widespread contempt for men and matters military, were undergoing a bout of hysterical jingoism.

In response to the crisis, the army shortened its Royal Military Academy course to one year. Dowding's family could not have afforded the private income that their son would have needed in a smart regiment. Instead Hugh

Dowding went to Woolwich but failed to get the exam results necessary for a commission in the Royal Engineers. He had to be content with gunnery. Second Lieutenant Dowding, of the Garrison Artillery, graduated but never fought the Boers. Instead he served in Gibraltar, Ceylon, Hong Kong, and with the Mountain Artillery in India.

By the time he returned to England the world had fundamentally changed: the Wright brothers had built their flying machine, and a Frenchman, Louis Blériot, had flown the Channel. The idea of learning how to fly attracted Dowding, in the same way that polo and skiing did. By getting up in the early hours he was able to have flying tuition at Brooklands before arriving at the Camberley Staff College each morning. The Royal Flying Corps had been formed the previous year, and anyone who could fly and was accepted by it could get the cost of his flying tuition refunded. Dowding persuaded the flying school to teach him on credit until he got the refund. It was on this 'fly now, pay later' arrangement that Dowding was able to afford his Royal Aero Club certificate. The school assigned a mechanic to be his instructor and he got his 'ticket' after a total of one hour and forty minutes in the air.

After a further three months' instruction at the Central Flying School, Upavon, Dowding received his wings. Until then he had considered flying as a sport, or at best a help to his army career. But his short time with the men of the Royal Flying Corps – still a part of the army – made him think that he would like to stay with them. His father's veto did no more than delay matters. It was 1914. Within weeks of getting his wings, war with Germany began. Dowding's qualification as a pilot required him to serve with the RFC.

Dowding went to France. By 1915 he was a squadron commander. Dowding was considerably older than the average wartime pilot – ten years older than von Richthofen, for instance – and, as the RFC expanded and became the RAF, his military background brought him rapid promotion. By the time the war ended, Dowding was a Brigadier-General. Many rungs lower on the promotion ladder were three young squadron commanders. They were all to play vital roles in the Battle of Britain almost a quarter of a century later.

Commanding an army-cooperation squadron, there was Major Leigh-Mallory, who was to continue with this speciality in the peacetime air force. Leigh-Mallory, who later became Dowding's severest critic, was ten years younger than Dowding. He had taken an honours history degree at Cambridge before becoming a soldier and, in 1916, an airman. Trafford Leigh-Mallory was a thick-set man with heavy jowl and a small, carefully trimmed moustache.

Major K. R. Park, M.C. and bar, D.F.C., was an astounding New Zealander who had fought at Gallipoli, been wounded on the Somme, and then, by losing his medical records, transferred to the air force and shot down twenty German aircraft.

Keith Park was a popular and persuasive man. He had quelled a near mutiny in 1918 by assembling the airmen and talking to them on random subjects and in such a monotonous voice for so long that all rebelliousness was destroyed by fatigue.

Thirdly there was Major W. Sholto-Douglas, D.S.O., M.C., a fighter pilot credited with five victories. In another example of post-war *Angst*, Dowding was instructed by the Air Ministry to court-martial Sholto-Douglas over something that was in no way the young officer's fault. In spite of a rather delicate situation that obtained between Dowding and the Air Ministry over his own retention in the RAF, Dowding refused to take any action. For this, Sholto-Douglas seemed suitably appreciative.

Dowding was an enigmatic man. His inability to make intimate friends will probably keep him so. It is difficult to reconcile a man who put on his hat before stepping into the next office, with a ski champion who seldom missed a season on the slopes, and eventually became president of the Ski Club of Great Britain. There was Dowding the diligent administrator, and Dowding the impatient technician; Dowding the devout and courteous, and Dowding of whom the Air Ministry was afraid. If Dowding remains an enigma there can be little doubt that that is exactly what he wished.

Already an abstemious and dedicated man, his social life virtually disappeared upon the tragic death of his wife after only two years of marriage. He was left to care for an infant son. Withdrawn and reflective, Dowding now devoted himself entirely to his work. Some mistook this attitude for ambition.

In the early 1930s Dowding was appointed to the Air Council as Member for Supply and Research. One of his first dicta was that wood must no longer be the structural base of combat aircraft. During Dowding's time in this vital job, the RAF changed from biplane fighters to metal monoplanes. It was not done without strong opposition from the biplane lobby. In 1935 the first Hurricane flew, and the prototype Spitfire came a few months later.

It was on Dowding's authority that Robert Watson-Watt of the National Physical Laboratories demonstrated the way in which an aircraft could reflect a radio beam (in this case a BBC overseas programme). They watched a pinhead of light on a cathode-ray oscillograph stretch to a tiny green line. It was the crude beginning of Britain's radar.

Boldly Dowding assumed that radar would work, and went ahead with plans for a control system, and fighter tactics, on that assumption. Until radar was ready, the fighters emitted radio signals like echoes, so that plotting could be set up.

Because the original (10-metre) radar network could not detect low-flying aircraft, Dowding took the navy's more complex 1.5-metre radar that were designed to detect ships. These sets had aerials that revolved, to scan the whole horizon. Adapted for the detection of low-flying aircraft, these sets became Chain Home Low (CHL). By 1940 Dowding was devoting a great deal of his time to the development of airborne radar fitted into night fighter aircraft.

In 1936, with the growth of Göring's air force more and more in evidence, the RAF decided to reorganize into specialist Commands. All of the bombers in Britain would come under Bomber Command, sea reconnaissance units would be organized as Coastal Command, and Training would be done by Training Command.

In March 1936, as the Spitfire prototype took to the air for the first time, and the radar he had nursed into being made rapid strides, Dowding ended his job as Member for Research and Development (the supply part of his original task had been given to another member of the Air Council). With a neatness usually only found in the pages of fiction, Dowding was now appointed to prepare these weapons and take them to war.

This appointment, to Commander in Chief of Fighter Command, was not due to any friends that Dowding had in the Air Ministry. On the contrary, plans were afoot to deprive Dowding of the promotion to Chief of Air Staff which had already been promised to him.

In July 1936 Dowding made a first visit to Bentley Priory, HQ of the newly created Fighter Command. Bentley Priory was an old Gothic house on a hill to the extreme north-west of London. At one time it had been a girls' school. It was typical of this idiosyncratic man that instead of arranging the ceremony that would normally take place, he arrived at nine o'clock in the morning, unannounced and all alone. The guard was extremely reluctant to let him through the gate but after inspecting his papers, he handed him over to the most senior man there, a sergeant from the Orderly Room. The two men wandered through the grounds and then through the empty rooms. Selecting a room with a southerly view, Dowding asked the sergeant to put his name on the door, thanked him, and left.

By this time Dowding was 54 years old, a tall, thin, rather frail-looking widower. He set up house with his sister, just along the road from his office. Dowding's son was preparing to go to the RAF College at Cranwell. In 1939 he would graduate and come under his father's orders, as a Spitfire pilot in Fighter Command, just in time for the Battle of Britain.

Meanwhile there was the gigantic task of reorganizing the fighter defences of Britain. Working with Dowding, as his Senior Air Staff Officer, there was a man who was perhaps the RAF's foremost expert on fighters. Keith Park, now a 44-year-old Air Commodore, had followed his success as an ace fighter pilot of the First World War with time at the staff college and a short spell commanding a fighter station. Park was a tall, neat New Zealander of Scots origin. Thin-faced, with a military moustache, he had the springy step and confident manner of a bank official. He liked flying and never missed a chance to use his personal Hurricane. During the Dunkirk evacuation – where Park had special responsibility for air cover – he had logged more than 100 flying hours, in order to see what was happening to his men. One fighter pilot of the pre-war days at Tangmere remembers him as an austere man who was never heard to utter a damn or a blast. Park is also remembered for his curious habit of wearing a steel helmet over his flying helmet when flying his plane.

Trafford Leigh-Mallory commanded the fighter squadrons of 12 Group and so was responsible for defending one of the large areas into which Britain had been divided by the new Fighter Command system. Leigh-Mallory's Group, in central England, was vital for the defence but not so vital as 11 Group, which covered south-east England and London, a region which would undoubtedly bear the brunt of enemy attack, and which contained the greatest number of fighter squadrons.

In the spring of 1940, as the war began to heat up, Dowding changed his Group commanders. Many would have said that Leigh-Mallory, who had commanded 12 Group since 1937, must be a prime choice for command of the more vital 11 Group. Instead, Dowding assigned his SASO, Keith Park, to this command. If Leigh-Mallory felt himself slighted it is possible to understand why.

The separation of the RAF's resources into specialized Commands was partly a response to the political atmosphere that Hitler's aggressive speeches had generated. The senior ranks of the RAF remained convinced that Bomber Command was the key to victory, but after the Munich crisis the inadequacy of the defences gave some priorities to Fighter Command.

And the Munich crisis gave Dowding an importance that had not been foreseen by the Air Ministry. He was the Commander in Chief of a command that included not only the fighter squadrons but the control network, the balloon barrage (steel cables suspended from balloons to impede low-flying attackers), and anti-aircraft guns. Although technically the latter were under army orders, Dowding's suggestions were never ignored. Now he pressed for money to be spent on the Observer Corps (volunteer skywatchers who reported aircraft movements across the whole of Great Britain). He also asked for Operations Rooms at all levels of Fighter Command and all-weather runways at the fighter airfields.

It was in this year of the Munich crisis that Dowding received the first of a series of official letters, terminating his service with the RAF, and then at the last minute, extending his service. To what extent these letters were the result of muddle and inefficiency, and to what extent they were the work of cruel and spiteful rivals, is still argued. Certainly Dowding, a desiccated old widower, was totally devoid of charm and made no attempt to be diplomatic to men who questioned his judgments. Dowding showed an old-fashioned correctness when dealing with senior officers.

They were all junior to him in both rank and service and many of them had once been his subordinates. That did not make their jobs easier. But such a man as Dowding could never deserve the years of uncertainty that the sackings and reinstatements caused, nor the final curt dismissal that told him to clear out of his office within 24 hours.

But Dowding was no paragon. Too often he resorted to caustic comments when a kind word of advice would have produced the same, or better, results. And it was during Dowding's time that the RAF was equipped with the egregious Fairey Battle bombers and Boulton Paul Defiant fighters that were totally inadequate against the Luftwaffe. Dowding was the responsible officer when the R.101 airship flew to its doom. Dowding was too ready to defer to the advice of his specialists. He did not challenge the men who told him that self-sealing fuel tanks were too heavy for fighters (they showed him the calculations for crash-proof fuel tanks).

Dowding was indifferent to the boardroom politics of higher office, impatient and abrasive to men who failed to understand his reasoning. When he told an Air Ministry conference that he wanted bullet-proof glass for the Hurricanes and Spitfires, everyone laughed. 'If Chicago gangsters can have bullet-proof glass in their cars I can't see any reason why my pilots cannot have the same,' he said, and was irritated by their laughter. He delegated authority readily and seldom interfered with subordinates he trusted. Not unreasonably – but unrealistically – he expected the same treatment by the men in the Ministry.

Although Dowding's concern for the fighter pilots was central to every decision he made, he seldom met them or talked with them, believing that the presence of the Commander in Chief would merely provide an extra burden for them. But it is an attractive aspect of this reserved man's character that his staunchest supporters should be low-ranking subordinates who worked at his HQ, including his personal assistants and his office staff.

Dowding understood men well enough to issue an order that his fighter squadron commanders could not continue in that job after reaching the age of twenty-six. In the same way it was logical that his fighter pilots would take orders more readily from Sector Controllers who were experienced fighter pilots, and so many of them were. His icy logic was expressed in the order that German air crews descending over Britain were prospective prisoners and therefore must not be shot at, while RAF pilots parachuting were potential combatants, and therefore fair targets for German guns. What Dowding failed to understand is that although men might revere logic to the point of death, few revere it to the point of admitting their mistakes.

Captain Basil Liddell-Hart – whose theories of military strategy are often expressed in social terms – spoke of the importance of leaving your opponent a line of retreat. This Dowding failed to do. Perhaps his ethics would have considered such 'scheming' bad form. Bad form or not, he was to confront Churchill in such a way that he made an enemy of him, and so was deprived of Churchill's aid at a time when he desperately needed it. The freedom Dowding gave his Commanders, and the high morale of his pilots, were the two greatest contributions to victory. Ironically it was these same two factors that brought Dowding's downfall.

Flying Training

It would not be true to say that the Battle of Britain was decided by flying training. And yet it would not be very far from the truth. Just as the all-metal monoplane had to be created from scratch, so was the new sort of fighter pilot like no other aviator.

One of the worst set-backs suffered by the pre-war RAF was the repeated refusal of Mackenzie King, the Canadian

Prime Minister – from 1935 onwards – to discuss the Empire Air Training Scheme. By denying the British government a chance even to submit their proposals, he was able to claim later that no peacetime training scheme was ever suggested to him. Australia and New Zealand had responded warmly. But in wartime these distant training schools would not be as useful as the relatively nearby Canadian ones. South Africa and Rhodesia were willing to assist the RAF but it was not until war began that any of the flying schools trained men other than their own nationals.

So in 1936 the British government announced the formation of the RAF Volunteer Reserve. It provided a chance for civilians aged between 18 and 25 to learn to fly at the tax-payer's expense. These spare-time flyers were made sergeants. Weekend flying instruction was given by local flying schools (fees paid by the RAF), and there were compulsory evening classes in armament, signals, and navigation.

University Air Squadrons were created for part-time training of student volunteers. Another source of spare-time air crews was the Auxiliary Air Force. Starting in 1926 with four squadrons, by 1939 twenty squadrons had been recruited from various districts and bore their names. There was 601 (County of London) Squadron, 610 (County of Chester) Squadron, from Yorkshire 609 (West Riding) Squadron, and so on. By August 1940, one quarter of RAF fighter resources were AAF squadrons, although casualty replacements had brought many VR men and regulars into them.

In theory the AAF was to the RAF as the Territorial army was to the British army. These squadrons were essentially spare-time local formations with regional support. But no Territorial regiment wore bright scarves, and lined their jackets with red silk, as did so many of the AAF's exclusively officer pilots. And none of the Territorial regiments had reputations to match that of the 'millionaires' squadron' that was to carve such a name for itself during the Battle. At the outbreak of war the 'millionaires' were concerned about the prospect of petrol rationing and how it would affect their private transport. An officer was assigned to the task of buying petrol. He came back having bought a service station but announced that the pumps there were only half-full. This situation was remedied when another pilot remembered that he was a director of Shell. His secretary arranged a delivery.

More than one pilot was less than enthusiastic about the AAF squadrons. Skilled RAFVR Sergeant pilots, such as 'Ginger' Lacey, posted to an AAF squadron, sometimes found them 'a rather snobbish preserve of the rich.' 'Johnnie' Johnson, another of the RAF's top fighter aces, remained convinced that he had failed to get into an AAF squadron when the interviewing officer discovered that he was not a fox-hunting man. On another AAF squadron there was always 'a social test' in which a prospective officer candidate would be given Sunday lunch, and 'several glasses of sherry' to discover 'if his parlance was no longer that of a gentleman.' Said one of them, 'Auxiliaries are gentlemen trying to be officers, Regulars are officers trying to be gentlemen, VRs are neither trying to be both.'

Many AAF recruits had sports flying experience before joining but there were service instructors for these squadrons. These included men to teach recruits to become spare-time ground tradesmen: fitters, riggers, armourers, etc. 'There was no shortage of recruits,' said the Commanding Officer of 609 (West Riding) Squadron, after they received three Avro Tutor trainers and three Hawker Harts, 'the difficulty was choosing them.'

When war began, the AAF squadrons were incorporated into the RAF. They became full-time units and each was attached to a parent RAF squadron. Many of the AAF bombing and army-cooperation squadrons became fighter units as – in the second half of 1939 – the Hawker Hurricanes arrived. The AAF pilots were almost all well-educated, intelligent young men with a high morale and peak physical fitness. They adapted almost effortlessly to the new fast monoplanes but many hours of flying experience were needed to make these part-time pilots into professionals. And they did not have many flying hours to go before facing the battle-hardened veterans of the German Air Fleets. It was also true that many Auxiliary flyers were far older than their adversaries, and older than RAF Regular pilots too. One AAF squadron had pilots on average five years older than the RAF Regulars with whom they shared the airfield.

Dowding was concerned about the flow of trained pilots from the flying schools. Even after war began, the intakes were still based upon peacetime establishments. Dowding reminded all concerned of the suddenness with which war inflicted casualties, and the long training that was needed to produce a skilled fighter pilot.

It took a year to complete basic pilot training, followed by another year of squadron service to get flying experience. So how long would it take to get the additional instructors they would need to increase the flow of fighter pilots? The outbreak of war not only underlined the shortage of trained pilots but it caused RAF fighter squadrons to be taken away from defence duties and sent to France. Dowding objected.

The Air Ministry chose to ignore Dowding's suggestions and so was directly responsible for the shortage of skilled fighter pilots during the Battle of Britain. This, more than any other factor, brought the Luftwaffe close to air mastery.

The war began, but it did not begin with the great air attacks upon London and the two million casualties that the theorists had predicted. In fact air-raid casualties for Great Britain in the whole war totalled under 300,000 and about half of them were 'slight injuries.' But the experts could not believe they were wrong. On 3 September 1939 air-raid warnings were sounded only a few minutes after the declaration of war – the 'attack' proved to be a small liaison aircraft carrying the Assistant French Military Attaché and an interpreter. In the early hours of the next day, a hoaxer caused the central London air-raid sirens to be sounded, simply by telephoning Scotland Yard from Guildford and saying that a large bomber formation had just passed over him, heading for London.

If, when war began, anyone in Britain's air defences believed that the system was functioning well, the events of 6 September should have changed their mind. According to Dowding it all began when a 'refugee aircraft from Holland' was reported. Since there had been no notification of this incoming flight, RAF fighters were sent to intercept.

Like the aerial of any cheap transistor radio, the radar aerials produced a strong signal when at right angles to the aircraft (or radio station). Only by electrical screening could the radar distinguish seaward aircraft from those behind the aerials. On 6 September the screening failed, said Dowding, and the fighters sent up from British airfields to intercept appeared on the screens as blips out to sea. More RAF fighters took to the air, and each one looked like another incoming raider.

How the fighting began is still unknown but as the Spitfires from Hornchurch met the Hurricanes from North Weald, a battle began and two Hurricanes were shot down. One pilot died.

At Dowding's HQ the movements of the coloured counters were being watched by King George VI, who had chosen that day to pay a visit. 'I fear I was a most distrait host,' said Dowding, who realized that something had gone terribly wrong.

The 'sense-finding screen' at Canewdon was checked and found to be working perfectly. Afterwards Watson-Watt insisted that all the fighters had been seawards of the aerials and the radar had reported accurately.

The rights and wrongs were never settled but there began an urgent reassessment of the radar and reporting network. Electronic sets that would enable RAF aircraft to identify themselves were ordered immediately. These IFF sets were crude and imperfect devices but, in September, 500 of them were put together by hand, so that the fighters could have them. And from the fiasco came an instruction that enemy raids should be confirmed by a visual sighting by the Observer Corps, before the fighters went in. As we shall see, this rule brought new difficulties.

Meanwhile the Luftwaffe were busy elsewhere, providing intensive air bombardment for the German army invading Poland. There was little air fighting, for the Polish air force had been almost destroyed by attacks upon the airfields. While the fighting continued, the governments of Britain and France worked hard at the task of convincing themselves that the Luftwaffe would not attack western cities unless provoked to it. The Anglo-French air forces were forbidden to drop anything more lethal than propaganda leaflets over German towns. RAF Bomber Command was allowed across the North Sea with bombs but only to attack German warships. Trying this in daylight, without fighter escort, they suffered heavy casualties. As 1939 came to an end RAF Bomber Command's operations had proved disastrous. The raids had suffered a loss rate of 9.5 per cent (never again, in any year of the war, did losses reach even half this rate). Instead of adding fighter escort to their raids, they simply abandoned daylight bombing, which had been the basis of all their pre-war planning.

At night, the RAF contented themselves with leaflet dropping, and few of the attacking airmen ever found the designated targets. Replying to a proposal that the German forests could be set afire with incendiary bombs, Sir Kingsley Wood, Britain's Air Minister, a one-time insurance consultant, revealed the official attitude: 'Are you aware it is private property? Why, you will be asking me to bomb Essen next.'

Dowding and the 15 May Cabinet Meeting

On 10 May 1940, lacking such respect for property, panzer groups crossed the frontier without customs formalities. They were heading for the Meuse. The great blitzkrieg of 1940 had begun. The French asked the British to employ their heavy bomber force against the German columns. By 15 May panzer forces had bridged the Meuse. At a meeting of the War Cabinet on that day it was agreed that RAF Bomber Command should be authorized to attack.

In accord with the same theories that so impressed Göring, the RAF mounted the largest air bombardment the world had yet see, and sent it off that same night. It was not sent to attack the bridges on the Meuse. Complex reasonings of strategy and the influence of Douhet selected oil industry targets in the densely populated Ruhr, and under cover of darkness 100 Whitley, Hampden, and Wellington bombers tried to find them.

The French had argued desperately that air attacks upon the Ruhr could have no effect upon Guderian's armoured invasion of France. The French were entirely right. The RAF official history admits that the bombers 'achieved none of their objects. Industrial damage was negligible,' and goes on to explain that the greatest benefit expected from this opening shot of the strategic bombing of Germany was 'an informal invitation to the Luftwaffe to bomb London.' By this means it was hoped to divert the German air offensive away from the French ground forces. To what extent this motive was arrived at, after the raid failed to be anything better than a provocation, can only be guessed.

That particular War Cabinet meeting on 15 May was as important as any in the nation's history. Dowding, alarmed by the numbers of his precious Hurricane fighters being sent to fight in France, had asked for permission to talk to the Cabinet. To his surprise he was invited along.

It is important to record the nature of Dowding's

objection. His upbringing, training, and his character would forbid his commenting upon the strategic advisability of moving fighter aircraft to France. Such a decision would, rightly, be that of the War Cabinet, advised by the Air Ministry. Dowding argued that, since the Air Ministry had long since decided that 52 squadrons would be needed for the defence of Britain, fighters sent to France must be written off as an overseas force, and separated from home defence. The force remaining in Britain must then be expanded to 52 squadrons.

Technically Dowding never argued his case before the Cabinet, and for entirely new information throwing light on this mysterious incident I am indebted to Professor A. J. P. Taylor who has most generously passed his research to me.

Dowding argued his case to Churchill, Archibald Sinclair (the new Air Minister), Beaverbrook (newly appointed Minister of Aircraft Production), and Sir Cyril Newall (Chief of Air Staff). He told them his 52 squadrons were already reduced to 36 and that at the present rate that Hurricanes were being shot down in France, there would be none left anywhere within two weeks. He produced a graph to support this contention and placed it in front of Churchill.

Dowding stayed on for the subsequent Cabinet meeting (it was not unusual for the room to be crowded with people in spite of its small permanent complement). However, Dowding didn't speak before the Cabinet, neither did anyone else refer to Dowding's plea. After the Cabinet meeting, Newall insisted that Sinclair should have raised the matter but by then it was too late. Orders were given that four more fighter squadrons should be sent to France.

Dowding went back to Fighter Command HQ and described the situation – just as he had put it to Churchill – in an official letter to the Under Secretary of State for Air. It proved a sound precaution, as we shall see.

The next day, 16 May, Churchill flew to Paris to hear

Paul Reynaud, the French Premier, plead for still more RAF fighters to stem the German flood. Churchill phoned London (using two officers speaking Hindustani to preserve secrecy) and asked the Cabinet to agree that another six squadrons should be sent to France (additional to the four taken from Dowding on the previous day). The Cabinet met late that evening to consider it. Without Churchill's commanding presence they wavered. The ineffectual Sinclair was emboldened enough to tell them about Dowding's argument. Newall added that lack of suitable French airfields was another factor. (For it must be remembered that the Hurricanes would need a complex retinue of men and a considerable amount of equipment and spares to operate from France – and France was now in chaos.) Newall referred to 'the figures laid before us by Air Chief Marshal Dowding yesterday,' meaning not the Cabinet but the meeting beforehand. The Cabinet did not dare to defy Churchill but they compromised. They agreed that six more Hurricane squadrons could operate from French airfields, providing they returned to bases in England each night.

In two days Dowding had lost another ten fighter squadrons, and was now down to about half of the strength that was considered a dangerous minimum. It is in the context of these events that the bitter accusations of French High Commanders (that Churchill betrayed the alliance by denying France RAF fighters) must be considered.

Undoubtedly Churchill was extremely moved by the pleas of the French politicians and by the great and sudden tragedy that France was suffering. To what extent he wanted to reassert his command of the War Cabinet, and whether he took an instant dislike to Dowding – as he had to certain other military commanders – or what other motives he had, remains unknown. Churchill's memoirs only add to the mystery. He does not refer to Dowding's attendance at No. 10, and did not acknowledge any urgent warning. On the contrary, Churchill wrote, 'Air Chief

Marshal Dowding, at the head of metropolitan Fighter Command, had declared to me that with twenty-five squadrons of fighters he could defend the island against the whole of the German Air Force, but that with less he would be overpowered.'

This was nonsense. There were witnesses, there was the graph of Hurricane losses, and there was the letter that Dowding – ever distrustful of politicians – wrote immediately after the meeting. Without these, history might have recorded another instance of a politician being badly advised by his experts.

Dowding's fears about fighters sent to France proved well founded. When the final figures came in, the losses caused to the 261 Hurricanes sent to support the British army were grave. Only 66 of these got back to England.

With German bases facing the British coast from north-western France to southern Norway, Dowding arranged his fighter squadrons to meet the inevitable attack.

Military experts were still incredulous that *Panzerkorps Reinhardt* had moved tanks through France forty miles in one day. Now began a battle in which units would move at 300 mph.

To fight such battles Dowding had quartered Britain into Fighter Groups. Each Group had a commander and a staff who worked at a large operations table, over which girls, using croupier's rakes, moved coloured counters.

Depending on the generalship of these commanders, and their Operations Room staff, the battles would be lost or won. They would have only minutes – seconds sometimes – in which to decide which coloured counters might be a feint attack. Ordering fighters into the air too late made them easy prey for the Germans above them. Scrambling too few squadrons might lose a battle, scrambling too many meant undefended towns or, worse still, fighters refuelling so that a second wave of bombers destroyed them on the ground.

To all these calculations were added the problems of

cloud that hid the raiders at certain heights and weather that might shut in British bases while leaving cross-Channel ones operative. Anti-aircraft gun batteries and balloon barrages had to be deployed so that they played their part against the enemy.

And while these great battles raged across the tables of the Operations Rooms, the Sector Controllers spoke with their fighter pilots 20,000 feet above. They watched the counters converge and heard the pilots as they wheeled and fired and cursed and died. Never before had there been battles like these.

PART THREE

Weapons: The Metal Monoplane and Radar

'Take the piston rings out of my kidneys,
The connecting rods out of my brain,
Take the cam-shaft from out of my back-bone,
And assemble the engine again.'

TRADITIONAL AIRMAN'S SONG

The history of invention often shows a pattern of acceleration, in the later stages of which inventors take it for granted that some other element they need will miraculously appear. This is particularly true of inventions applicable to warfare, stimulated as they often are by politics, economics, or predicament.

Before the First World War, for instance, the oil-fired boiler, the turbine, the fifteen-inch gun, and armour had together produced a revolution in battleship design: the *Queen Elizabeth* class.

In the nineteenth century, percussion caps, bolt action, and a needle firing device contributed to a new kind of infantry rifle that then remained virtually unchanged for a hundred years. And Hiram Maxim evolved a design for a machine gun that would never have functioned except that in the final stages a new explosive was developed. Only then did he have enough bore and chamber pressure for a practical gun.

So it was with the metal monoplane fighters that fought on both sides during the Battle of Britain. In the 1930s, two-gun, wood-and-fabric biplanes – not very different from the aircraft of the First World War – suddenly gave way to a totally different sort of flying machine. Three designers: Willy Messerschmitt, Sydney Camm, and Reginald Mitchell led the radical change. The result was the Bf109, Hurricane, and Spitfire.

Biplanes and Monoplanes

The biplane was as old as the history of powered flight. The Wright brothers had chosen two wings, one above the

ILLUSTRATIONS

14 Feldmarschall *Erhard Milch (left)* He was also *Staatsekretär* of the German Air Ministry. Apart from Göring, his boss, he was the only man to have complete power in the civil as well as the military sphere of aviation. Ambitious, ruthless and completely without scruple, Milch kept files of information that he could use against his enemies and rivals. Although almost universally hated, his skill, diligence and unquestioning loyalty to Hitler helped him to increase his power at the expense of men around him, including Göring. Here, on the cover of the Luftwaffe magazine which was a part of Milch's empire, the short, fat, pop-eyed Milch is depicted in the most flattering of photos. On his right is Albert Speer, the Armaments' Minister.

15 Professor Hugo Junkers Few men contributed as much to the history of aviation as did Junkers. As one of his senior men he chose the dynamic young Erhard Milch. In return he was hounded, arrested, bankrupted and eventually driven to his death.

16 Reichsmarschall *Hermann Göring, chief of the Luftwaffe, with* Generaloberst *Ernst Udet* This photograph was taken about the time of the Battle, when Udet was head of the Luftwaffe's Technical Department. The easy-going but hard-drinking First World War fighter ace was often called to account for the mess and muddle of his department. But he was usually able to deflect the *Reichmarschall*'s wrath by turning the conversation round to old times when they flew together in the 1914–18 war.

17 Oberst *'Onkel Theo' Osterkamp* An ace of the First World War who continued flying and became an ace of the Battle of Britain too. He was ordered off combat flying at the age of 48 and became *Jafü 2* (commander of all the fighter units of Air Fleet 2). At his neck he wears the 'Blue Max' and the Knight's Cross, respectively the highest awards for valour in each war. This photograph was taken when 'Onkel Theo' went back to spend an evening with his old unit, JG 53 *Pik As* (Ace of Spades) *Geschwader*. By this time he had crossed swords with Milch, something from which few men recovered.

18 Feldmarschall *Hugo Sperrle, commander of Air Fleet 3* Of him Albert Speer said, 'The Field Marshal's craving for luxury and public display ran a close second to that of his superior, Göring.'

19 Major *Werner Mölders* A serious and reflective man, Werner Mölders was nicknamed 'Vati' ('Daddy') by his men. In a regime which suppressed all religions, Mölders made no secret of his Roman Catholicism, and thereby made enemies. He got to Spain just as the new Bf 109 all-metal monoplane fighters arrived. He became an ace and pioneered the techniques of air fighting that the Luftwaffe used in 1940. By 12 October 1940 Mölders had added 45 victories to those of the Spanish

14

15

16

17

18

19

21

22

23

fighting. He became the Luftwaffe's General of Fighters when aged only 28, an extraordinary achievement for a man who failed his first aircrew medical because of air sickness and continued to suffer from this all through his short life. This cover of a German magazine (Dutch edition) shows, too, the way German fighter pilots painted their accredited victories on the tail of their fighters. Each bar is surmounted by the national marking of the victim and a date. By the end of 1940 Mölders was credited with fifty-five victories.

20 A Messerschmitt Bf 109E crash-lands in England This Bf 109E bears (behind the cockpit) the personal markings of the Adjutant of a *Geschwader*. Dated 28 July 1940, the censor has marked his insignia for deletion, also requesting that 'south-east coast' be changed to 'south-east England'. This was the day when the German ace Mölders led JG 51 as *Geschwaderkommodore* for the first time. The South African ace 'Sailor' Malan attacked the leading flight of the German formation and got one victory before fighting Mölders himself. Probably this is the aircraft that Malan shot down from that Staff Flight. Notice that the cockpit cover remains on the aircraft, showing that the pilot remained in the aircraft for the forced landing. It would certainly have been worthwhile for the British to conceal the fact that they had captured a pilot of such importance. The segmented paint pattern of the spinner is unusual, and the way in which the gun troughs on the cowling have been picked out in a different colour even more unusual. Notice too the hole in the spinner which still today persuades experts to believe, quite wrongly, that there was a cannon housed there. In fact it provided cooling for the generator. This Messerschmitt hood has been equipped with armour behind the pilot's head and over it. Such protection worsened the visibility. The inverted vee-shaped engine meant that the exhausts were low on the side of the cowling. The square-shaped intake above it is for the super-charger.

21 Oberleutnant *Werner Baumbach* He flew with 5/KG 30 (*Adler-Geschwader)* during the Battle. On 15 August these Junkers Ju 88s flew from Aalborg, Denmark, to attack England across the North Sea. Cut to pieces, they were then moved to Eindhoven, Netherlands. Here Baumbach is wearing the special rank badges designed for use on flying overalls. The *Feldwebel* on the right is not wearing any aircrew badge. The Iron Cross first class on his pocket might have been one of those sometimes awarded for periods of intensive work by ground crews.

22 Hauptmann *Helmut Wick* He flew Messerschmitt Bf 109E fighters with I/JG 2 *(Richthofen)*. On 27 August 1940 he was awarded the Knight's Cross, or what the pilots called the 'tin-tie' after shooting down 20 enemy aircraft. Soon after this photograph was taken in September 1940 the 25-year-old Wick became the youngest *Major* in the whole German armed forces and one of only three Battle of Britain pilots who got the oak leaves that went to men with forty victories. By the time the Battle of Britain was ending, Wick was the most successful fighter pilot on either side, and had become *Kommodore* of the *Richthofen Geschwader.*

23 Major *Adolf Galland* Smoking one of the black cigars for which he had installed an ash tray in the cockpit, he clambers from his Messerschmitt fighter. The cloth bag hanging at his knee is dye that would colour sea water if the pilot ditched. The life-vest is of a pattern issued during 1940 when the 'sausage-type' proved too bulky for fighters. The square super-charger intake shows this to be a Bf 109E, while the chevron marking suggests that this photograph was taken at Caffiers, France, while Galland was commanding III/JG 26. Notice the Mickey Mouse, which in this version was Galland's personal emblem. Partly hidden by the fitter's head is the S symbol of the *Schlageter* (Strike) *Geschwader* (JG 26). Notice the other man waiting with Galland's peaked cap at the ready.

other, for the same reason as the other experimenters: it gave double the amount of wing for any given size of machine, and the wings could be braced together to form a lightweight but rigid box. But doubling the wing area, by making a biplane, did not produce double the amount of lift. Wingtips were a primary source of drag. There is also an effect called 'biplane interference' which is the way that each wing's airflow disturbs that of its neighbour. In the 1920s and 1930s aircraft designers built curious-looking machines in which little leg-like struts held the fuselage above the lower wing. But, no matter how far apart the designers placed the wings, these troubles remained.

Mankind discovered the secret of flight as soon as he stopped flapping his home-made wings long enough to understand that it was all a matter of decreasing the air pressure upon a wing's upper surface. This realization came long before the Wright brothers. The most important work was that of a German, Otto Lilienthal, who made more than a thousand flights in gliders of his own design and studied the way in which certain curved wings – aerofoil sections – gave better lift than others. By the end of the nineteenth century, man still could not build a powered flying machine but the theory was defined, wind-tunnels were in use, and airflow had been photographed. It became more and more obvious that the problem was to get enough air flowing fast enough across the wing to decrease the air pressure there and so lift – or one could almost say suck – the wing upwards.

The Wright brothers went to live at Kitty Hawk, North Carolina, because there was a constant wind off the sea. This gave them an effective airspeed of about 20 mph, even when their glider was not moving forward. This was exactly the benefit they needed while they perfected a glider design suitable to hold an engine. They could not use a motor-car engine, because all contemporary ones were too heavy by far. It was their assistant, an unsung hero named Charles Taylor, who took only six weeks to build a lightweight petrol engine from scratch. He even made the camshaft, from a solid block of metal. His engine was based upon an earlier gas-engine design by Lenoir but that does not alter the fact that Taylor was more important as a pioneer of powered flight than were the Wright brothers.

There had been other aircraft that flew. As early as 1848 John Stringfellow had built a steam-powered flying machine, and demonstrated it with enough success to win a prize. But Stringfellow's machine could not take the added weight of a man.[1]

The invention of the petrol engine had enabled Charles M. Manly to design a radial engine many years ahead of its time for a flying machine built by Professor Samuel Pierpont Langley. This machine crashed just a few days before the Wright brothers' famous flight, and the US authorities officially recognized Langley's aircraft as the first one capable of sustained man-carrying free flight. This so angered Orville Wright that he put his 'Flyer' into London's Science Museum. When war began, to safeguard

[1]Steam-powered flight was not an unfulfilled dream. Nowadays a Boeing 707 jet airliner at the moment of take-off is largely powered by steam. Three times as much water is sprayed into the engines' burner cans as kerosene (156,000 lbs water per hour compared with 45,000 lbs kerosene), a technique whereby the super-heated steam provides take-off power and the water keeps the temperature from rising above 1,600°F.

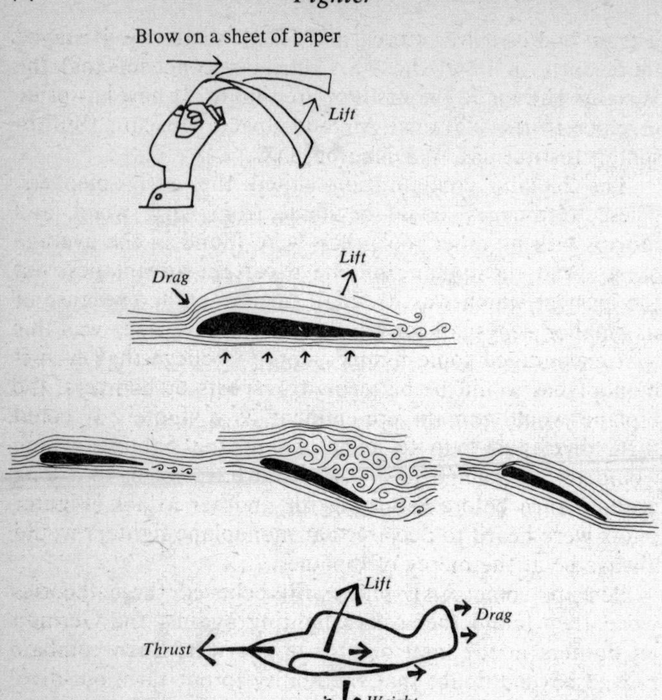

The Secret of Flight

Figure 5

If you blow across a sheet of paper the speed of the airflow causes a decrease in air pressure. Since the air pressure below the paper is not decreased the paper must rise. This is the secret of flight and it took mankind thousands of years to discover it.

But even a well-designed aerofoil section causes the airflow to build up at the leading edge and this is called 'drag'. Another problem is the break up of the airflow as it eddies behind the wing. As the wing is tilted upwards the eddying increases until (as in the diagram) there is no lift. Now the aeroplane will fall from the sky like a stone. However, the use of a leading-edge slot (as Messerschmitt had on his Bf 109) smooths the airflow and makes the wing more efficient.

it from bombs it was stored in a London subway. It stayed there until, in 1942, the USA officially conceded that the Wrights had made the first powered flight. It now has pride of place in the National Air and Space Museum (Smithsonian Institution), Washington, D.C.

The biplane configuration suited the early pioneers. These 'bird-cages' could be made from wire, wood, and fabric, with no other tools than were found in the average home. And the biplane did have certain advantages, not the least of which was its small turning circle (because of its smaller wingspan for any given wing area). It was this that encouraged some fighter pilots to believe that even if monoplanes would be better as transports or bombers, the biplane would remain pre-eminent as a fighter. It could turn, dive, and loop to avoid monoplane fighters, which would just go racing past them, and have to make a long gradual turn before returning for another attack. Fighter pilots were heard to declare that monoplane fighters would always be at the mercy of biplanes.

Perhaps some RAF pilots still believed these theories when they found themselves fighting against the German jet fighters in the final months of the war. Such combats proved beyond doubt that the ability to out-turn, out-dive, or out-loop one's opponent counted for nothing against superior speed. The very-high-speed jets could literally fly rings round their slower opponents, and simply place themselves in a favourable position to shoot them down. And so it would have proved had the RAF gone to war in biplanes against the monoplane-equipped German air force.

One of the limitations of the wood-and-fabric biplane fighters had been the positioning of the armament. Only the engine was mounted firmly enough to support machine guns (guns positioned over the upper wing were usually braced from the engine cowling). Because of this, the armament of the Hawker Fury biplane fighter was just two Vickers machine guns. But the new sort of metal monoplane was to have wings strong enough to hold guns. Instead of the Fury's two guns, the Hurricane had eight.

Now the fragile biplane's manoeuvrability counted for nothing, for a two-second burst of fire could shatter it to pieces.

But in spite of the better aerodynamics that the monoplane promised and its ability to carry heavier armament and all sorts of other equipment, it would fail unless it had an engine that could provide enough thrust.

Thrust: the Power Unit

Right from the beginning, the pioneers of flight understood that they were engaged in a contest between weight (plus drag), on the one hand, and thrust (plus the lift provided by the aerofoil) on the other. So the experimenters jumped to the conclusion that lightness was the secret of success. They were wrong! Only gradually did it become obvious that power was the key to flight. Men realized that they could build aircraft of almost any size and weight, providing that the power of the engine was *high in proportion to the aircraft's weight.*

Blériot, the first man to fly across the Channel, climbed out of his machine saying, 'More power, more power . . . I'm going to get a Gnome [engine].' The same motor-car engines that had seemed too heavy to power the Wrights' Flyer were now dismissed as too small.

The internal-combustion engine was a German invention, but the French were the first to build engines specifically for aircraft. The remarkable Le Rhône Gnome rotary, to which Blériot aspired, set a pattern for aircraft engines, and – like many other French aeronautical inventions – was used by German, British, American, and French air forces throughout the First World War. The progress of aviation was no longer centred upon lightness. Even the refinement of the aerofoil was set aside. By the end of the First World War, aviation became a race for horsepower per unit of weight. (See Table 1.)

In spite of many other scientific factors, it has been calculated that streamlining so improved the performance

Table 1

The Development of Aero-engines, 1848–1960

Power Unit	*Year*	*Horse-power*[1]	*Weight (lbs)*	*Weight per hp*	*Remarks*
Stringfellow (steam)	1848	25	600	24	Unmanned
Manly radial (Langley)	1903	52.4	187	3.6	A remarkable achievement. Five cylinders, water-cooled. Crashed on take-off
Original Wright bros. (Flyer 1)	1903	12	152[2]	12.7	The first heavier-than-air, sustained, powered flight
Wright bros. improvements (Flyer 2)	1904	16	180	11.4	The first circle in the air. Longest flight – 5 min. 4 sec.
Wright bros. improvements (Flyer 3)	1905	19	180	9.5	The first practical aircraft. Flights of more than half an hour
Wright bros. improvements (Flyer 32)	1908	35	182	5.5	Enabled Flyer 3 to take a passenger
Gnome rotary	1909	50	165	3.3	French engine. Later versions powered Sopwith Camel and Fokker monoplanes
Liberty V-12	1918	420	882	2.1	American. Finest engine of WW I and one of the first designed for mass production
Rolls-Royce Condor	1920	650	1,310	2.6	
Daimler-Benz 601A	1937	1,100	1,344	1.2	
RR Merlin Series II	1938	1,030	1,335	1.3	The most outstanding piston engine of its time (see note on p. 12)
RR Tyne Turboprop	1960	6,000	2,000	0.3	For rough comparison only. Jets and turboprops cannot be accurately compared with piston engine performance

[1] Horsepower ratings of the early engines can only be approximate.

[2] This is the most commonly accepted figure, but in a conversation with H. Peartree, 7 March 1911, Wilbur Wright described this engine as weighing 'more than 200 pounds.' This would have given it a power ratio of 16.7 lbs per hp. The Science Museum, which once housed the engine, says it weighed 240 lbs. This would give it a power ratio of 20 lbs per hp and has led many people to believe that the Wrights' 1903 flights were assisted by catapults or other means of launching.

of aircraft that it required four times the power to push a 1920 biplane as was required to push a streamlined 1950 aircraft of the same size and weight.

It was natural that British engineers aimed for an engine that would produce one horsepower for every pound of weight, although designers using metric measures had no such convenient target. The remarkably successful American 'Liberty' engine of 1918 had shown what a vee-shaped twelve-cylinder design could do. And this was the type of engine that Rolls-Royce had ready for the Supermarine S.6. In 1931 this engine and airframe combination won the Schneider Trophy outright[1] with a speed of 340.8 mph. The engine had produced one horsepower for each eleven ounces of weight (that is, 0.68 of a pound per horsepower). But this had been done with the aid of special chemical fuels, in a machine designed – like that of the Wright brothers – solely for brief flights. Moreover it was designed for highly skilled pilots. The new fighter would have to be an entirely different machine.

The original designation of the Merlin engine was PV 12, for 'private venture.' Its name came from that of the pigeon-hawk, a small falcon, at a time when Rolls-Royce were naming engines after birds of prey.

The design was made possible only by the large number of technological breakthroughs from research in the 1920s. The development of fuels in the USA resulted in the discovery that tetraethyl lead suppressed detonation. In 1925 came the iso-octanes. From now on, fuel quality was

[1]Britain's socialist government refused to finance this RAF entry for the Schneider Trophy, in spite of the two previous RAF wins. The Supermarine company could not afford to build the two new seaplanes without subsidy, to say nothing of the cost of the engine and of sending the team to Italy. The problem was solved by the intervention of Lady Houston, with a gift of £100,000. This enabled the British team to win the Schneider Trophy for the third time and keep it. The aircraft used was the Supermarine S.6B with a Rolls-Royce R engine. This in turn gave Britain the Spitfire and the Merlin engine (which powered Spitfire, Hurricane, Mosquito, Lancaster, and P-51 Mustang – some of the finest aircraft of the war).

Figure 6 **Power Units**

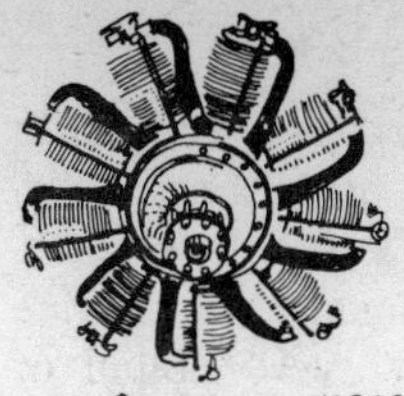

LE RHÔNE ROTARY (1913)

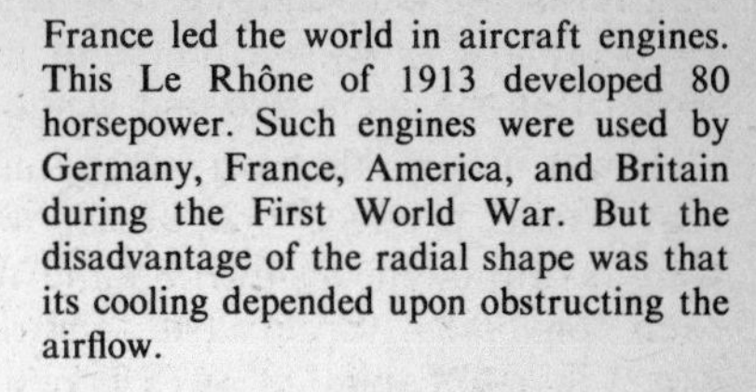

France led the world in aircraft engines. This Le Rhône of 1913 developed 80 horsepower. Such engines were used by Germany, France, America, and Britain during the First World War. But the disadvantage of the radial shape was that its cooling depended upon obstructing the airflow.

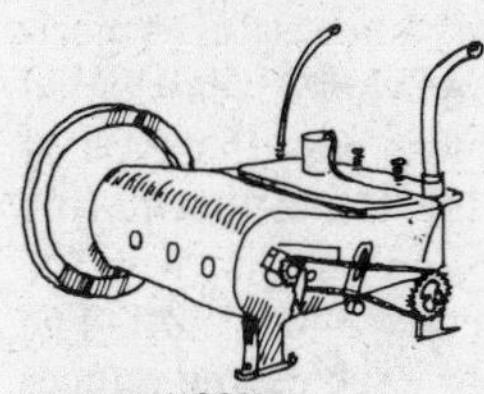

WRIGHT (1903)

This engine powered man's first successful flight. It was built from scratch by Charles Taylor, assistant to the Wright brothers. Even the camshaft started as a solid block of metal. Petrol was vaporized by passing over a heated water jacket. The pipes are for fuel and water circulation.

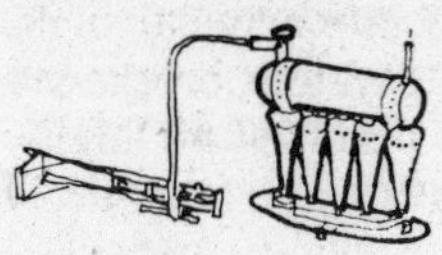

STRINGFELLOW
STEAM ENGINE (1843)

This steam engine was constructed by John Stringfellow and William Samuel Henson in 1843 to power a model aircraft, as a prototype for a man-carrying version. The inverted cones are the steam generators feeding into the steam drum.

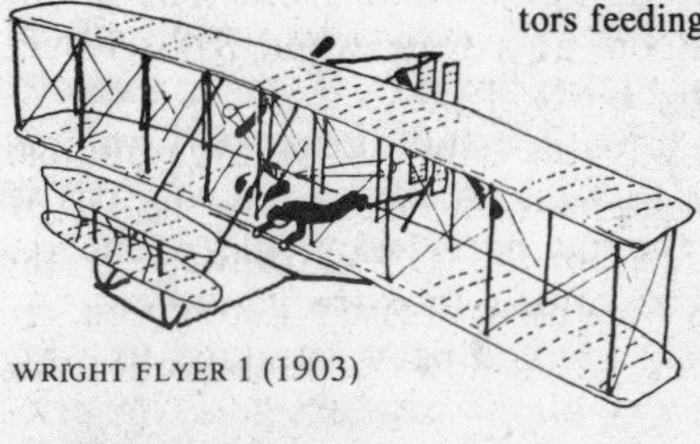

WRIGHT FLYER 1 (1903)

The world's first powered, sustained, controlled flight was made in this 'Wright Flyer 1' on 17 December 1903. The best flight that day lasted only 59 seconds, but this was not equalled in Europe until November 1907.

ROLLS-ROYCE MERLIN (1940)

The vee-shaped in-line engine made possible a truly streamlined, high-speed fuselage. However, it needed coolant, which proved a vulnerable target during the 1940 battles.

measured by means of an octane scale. In the late 1930s came all the work on blending agents, so that by 1939 most military aircraft were using 100-octane fuel (compared to the earlier 87 octane).

Fuel development – mostly done in the USA – spurred engine designers to improve super-chargers (to use the engine's hot, high-pressure exhaust gas). Now it was the exhaust valve seatings (which became overheated) that most concerned the engine designer, and soon the use of sodium-cooling and stellite valve seatings enormously improved performance.

While the engine designers were concentrating upon power, and chemists upon detonation, the metallurgists were making significant changes in the weight of the power units. Not only was the range of alloy steels extended to chromium, nickel, manganese, tungsten, silicon, etc., but new lightweight alloys were made. A Duralumin crank-case, for instance, was not only one tenth of the weight of aluminium alloy, but almost twice as strong.

The super-charger was vital to the high-performance fighter. It blew air into the engine and increased combustion as does blowing into a fire. A luxury on motor cars or for the low-level flying of racing aircraft, it was a necessity for aircraft that must have constant peak performance while climbing high into thin air. A typical engine lost 45 per cent of its power in the low pressure air of 15,000 feet but with a super-charger it gained an extra 5 per cent.

At first the engine designers had been attracted to using the otherwise wasted energy of the exhaust gases to drive the blowers. But by the end of the 1920s these turbo-super-chargers had given place to a more conventional design driven from the crankshaft.

The New Metal Airframes

The new power units were the heart of the all-metal monoplanes but there were a thousand new airframe problems that would also have to be solved. The mono-

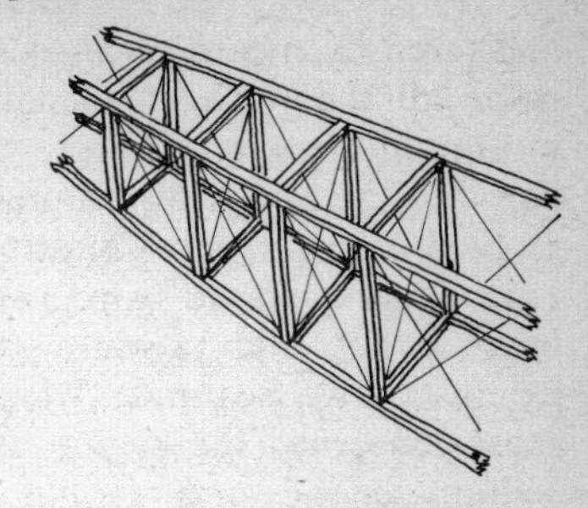

Airframe Structure

Figure 7

No longer would fighter airframes be braced by interior cross-wires. Now the metal fuselages would have space for additional equipment.

plane's wings had to be designed to take all stresses and buffeting of high-speed flight and centrifugal force without tearing off at the roots. Biplanes had bracing wires and struts to hold wings and fuselage together, but the monoplane's wings had to have enough internal strength to withstand the strain, while providing enough space inside the wing to take not only the retracted wheels and undercarriage but also machine guns. The guns could not be in the thick roots of the wings, for they must fire outboard of the propeller (so that they could fire at the maximum rate, rather than be slowed by synchronizing gear).

The RAF experts wanted speeds in the region of 300 mph and a ceiling of 33,000 feet. Such speeds meant streamlining, and wheels that retracted into the wings meant all the complications of a hydraulics system. The cockpit had to be completely enclosed, without loss of visibility, and the hood must be made so that the pilot could slide it back easily, even at high speeds. Yet these new machines would not be handled just by record-breaking experts. The average service pilot must be able to fly them, and land on a grass field no more than 1,250 yards long. That called for a slow landing-speed, without danger of stalling, and there would have to be reliable brakes on the wheels.

At the sort of speeds the new monoplanes would fly, there could be no more wing-waggling, and hand-waving, to tell the formation what the leader wanted. The pilots must be able to talk to ground control, and talk to each other. Two-way radio meant high-frequency signals. There were other sciences too. Low landing-speeds meant split flaps on the wings. High ceiling meant oxygen for the pilot, and super-charging for the engine. And high-speed combat would grant pilots only a glimpse of the enemy. They would need better gun-sights, and guns that could deliver a fatal burst in just two seconds.

And the guns must be reliable, for if they were in the wings, the pilot would no longer be able to hammer a jammed round out of the breech. The RAF tried all the world's machine guns and then selected the Colt-Browning. It proved an excellent gun, with a stoppage rate averaging once in 15,000 rounds. When installed alongside seven other guns this stoppage rate was entirely acceptable.

Having decided to put eight guns into each fighter, the RAF required enough bullets to provide for a total of fourteen seconds of firing. So there had to be space enough, and strength enough, to carry 2,660 rounds.

The aircraft factories would have to retrain workers in the new skills of lightweight metal alloys, and they needed designers who understood the theories of stressed-metal construction. No longer would fighter airframes be braced by interior cross-wires: the strength had to be in the shell. This was the definition of monocoque, and this type of airframe became more and more necessary as ancillary equipment was packed into the fuselage.

Metal aircraft were not a new idea. Professor Hugo Junkers – perhaps the greatest genius of his period of aircraft design – had built an all-metal, cantilever-wing monoplane as early as 1915. In 1917, Dornier had built a metal seaplane and then a biplane fighter. The British designer Oswald Short progressed from the box-like German designs to a streamlined – circular-section – Silver Streak in 1919. But these isolated examples were not much help with the new designs. There was nothing in America that would help either. American all-metal monoplanes were large, passenger-carrying aircraft, such as the magnificent Boeing 247, a twin-engined design that set the pattern for such airliners for the next quarter century, including the remarkable Douglas DC1 which followed shortly afterwards. But high-speed monoplane fighters needed extreme altitude, extreme speed, and an ability to withstand the G of tight turns and steep pull-outs. The British and German designers were on their own.[1]

The Hurricane

Like the Spitfire, the Hawker Hurricane began with Air Ministry specification F.7/30 for a fighter to replace the Bristol Bulldog biplane fighter then in RAF service. Sydney Camm was Chief Designer of Hawker Aircraft Ltd, which had evolved from Sopwiths, one of the world's most famous manufacturers of First World War fighters. Camm submitted a design for a biplane and a monoplane. Both were rejected. Of the monoplane, an official historian wrote, it 'was too orthodox even for the Air Ministry.'

Sydney Camm was a tall, dark man, slightly bent in posture from years of working at drawing boards. His nose was patrician and he had the sort of prominent chin that is said to go with determination.

[1]The navy's aviation requirements dominated US fighter design. The navy wanted lightweight, short-take-off fighters suitable for carrier operations. And that meant biplanes with air-cooled radial engines.

The only comparable fighter designs anywhere in the world in January 1940 were the French Dewoitine 520S and the Japanese Mitsubishi A6M2 Zero-Sen but less than ten of the former had been delivered by this time, and the latter had not even been officially accepted.

Even less in evidence was any power unit that could compare with the Daimler-Benz 601 or the Rolls-Royce Merlin. That's why the British purchasing commission that went to the USA in 1940 had to specify its own requirements to US airframe manufacturers, and have Merlins built there under licence. In time, this combination became the P-51 Mustang fighter.

Now, given full support by Hawker's, he began to design a fighter monoplane as a private venture, ignoring the Air Ministry specification. For reasons of economy, he used as much as possible of Hawker's tools and jigs. And all the time, he was keeping one eye upon the work that Rolls-Royce were doing on their new engine PV 12.

So by the time the Air Ministry had decided to issue a more advanced specification, Camm was ready with his design, and about to build a prototype of what he called a 'Fury Monoplane' – a development of his very successful Hawker Fury biplane fighter.

It was a project he had long talked about. In the summer of 1935, Camm, now 38 years old, and with ten years as Chief Designer of Hawker's, received Air Ministry specification F.10/35. The major remaining difference between this specification and the fighter he was building was the number of machine guns. Rather than delay the first flight of his prototype, he had another pair of wings made. When these new wings were fitted, in the summer of 1936, the Hawker Hurricane was born.

So the Hurricane was a monoplane version of the Hawker Fury. It used the same patent construction: a wire-braced framework of metal tubes. Round this was built a wooden frame, of formers and stringers. Fabric was stretched over the outside. At first not even the wings were of stressed-metal construction, but metal ones were designed before full-scale production started.

The Hurricane was not a monocoque construction. It was an old-fashioned wood-and-fabric machine, stiffened by a metal-tube framework. It was a half-way house between the old biplanes and the new Spitfires and yet there were certain advantages to such construction. The exploding cannon shells, which did terrible damage to metal skin, had less effect upon any sort of girder work (in the same way that bombs so often failed to topple the radar towers). And the RAF had very few men who understood the complexities of stressed-metal construction, but its airframe fitters and flight mechanics had spent their lives

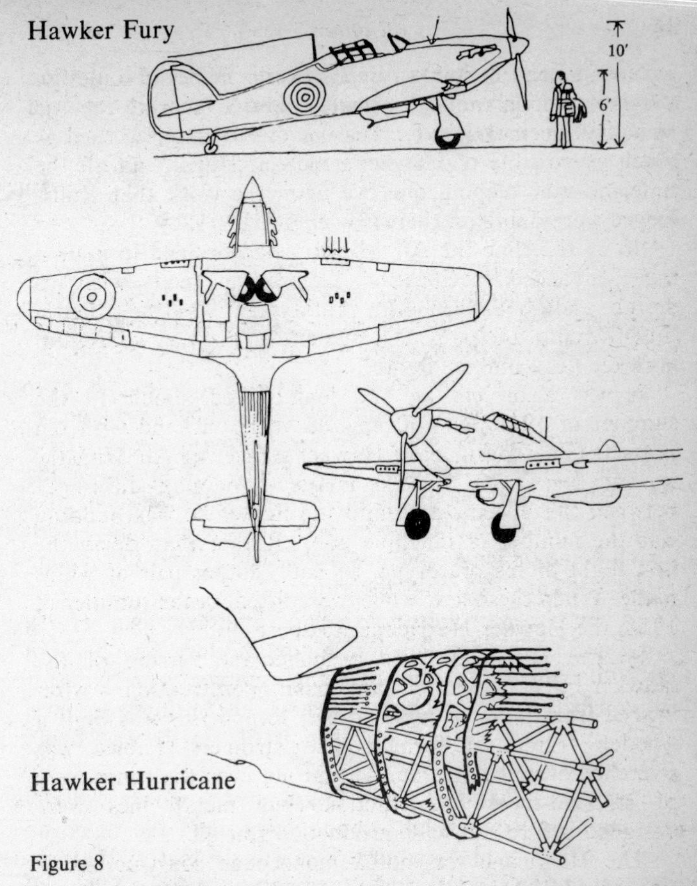

Figure 8

TOP The Hurricane was a very large aircraft by the standards of the day, and although many of the parts were identical to the same manufacturer's Fury biplane, the monoplane was much larger.

CENTRE Sydney Camm solved the problem of placing the retractable undercarriage in the wings quite differently than did Mitchell or Messerschmitt. The Hurricane's wheels retracted inwards. Its wide, stable landing gear made it easy to land. The machine guns were grouped very closely together and as close inboard as was possible. The slots under the wing are for the spent cartridges.

BOTTOM The strong metal framework is shown in red, the rest of the fuselage construction – formers and stringers – is wood. The covering is fabric.

servicing, and rigging, aircraft like this. When the fighting started, many seriously damaged Hurricanes were repaired in squadron workshops.

The Messerschmitt Bf 109

Willy Emil Messerschmitt was born in 1898, the son of a Frankfurt wine merchant. He had been obsessed with aviation since, as a small child, he had seen a Zeppelin flying. It was Messerschmitt's good luck that, as a schoolboy, he was permitted to give a hand to the famous flyer Friedrich Harth, and help with his gliding experiments. Harth was the second man in Germany (after Otto Lilienthal) to experiment with flying machines. When Harth went into the army, in 1914, he gave the plans of a glider to Messerschmitt, who was still a schoolboy. Harth came home on leave and was astonished to find that young Messerschmitt had built the glider.

When Messerschmitt came of military age, Harth arranged for him to join him at the military flying school at Schleissheim. In spite of being eighteen years younger than Harth, Messerschmitt became his business partner. The two men worked together until Harth was badly injured in a crash.

Eventually Messerschmitt raised enough money – partly through his wife's wealthy family – to buy the Bavarian Aircraft Works at Augsburg. This was the factory that was started by the First World War fighter ace Ernst Udet.

Messerschmitt's contribution to aviation was very great. Perhaps it was genius, but if so it was an erratic genius, ranging too far, through too many aspects of aviation. His early record-breaking glider designs were far ahead of the times, but they left a legacy of frailty that continued even as late as his 1940 fighter. After that came an amazing collection of machines, from the disastrous Me 210 twin-engined fighter, and the aptly named *Gigant* six-engined transport, to the only rocket-powered fighter to see operational service – the *Komet* – and the most effective fighter of the war – the Me 262 jet.

Like most other things about Willy Messerschmitt, his relationship with the Nazis was ambiguous. Hess, the deputy leader of the Nazi Party, was an old customer and a life-long friend, but Erhard Milch, Göring's right-hand man, was an implacable enemy. Milch's hostility can be traced from 1931 when two Messerschmitt M 20s crashed, killing the passengers, one of whom was a great personal friend of Milch, head of Lufthansa, purchaser of the machines. He blamed Willy Messerschmitt but the enquiry said that the specification was at fault. The specification was altered but the enmity remained. Milch cancelled the order for ten more M 20 aircraft and demanded the refund of money already paid. This bankrupted Messerschmitt's company and he had to start again almost from scratch.

When the Nazis took power in 1933, Milch made sure that Messerschmitt did not share the contracts and subsidies that other German aircraft manufacturers enjoyed. It was part of Milch's vindictiveness that when political pressure (due to Messerschmitt's having secured a foreign contract) forced Milch to give him a German government contract, Milch ordered him to build Heinkel biplanes under licence. Messerschmitt hated Heinkel almost as much as he hated biplanes.

Even Messerschmitt's early gliders had been monoplanes, for his credo was lightweight, low-drag, high-speed, simple design. Biplanes were everything that Messerschmitt detested. But as Milch's power grew, so his influence in departmental decisions weakened. Udet became the Luftwaffe's Inspector of Fighters and Dive Bombers and then chief of the Development Section of its Technical Department. And when Messerschmitt's Bf 109 met his rival's He 112 in comparative trials, it was the flying demonstration that was the deciding factor at a time when the Heinkel still had wide support. But when Messerschmitt's chief test pilot came to the spinning test (considered very important by the German Air Ministry), instead of doing the ten spins to port and ten to starboard that the specification demanded, he did seventeen and twenty-one respectively. The aircraft gave no sign of developing the flat spin that many on-lookers predicted. Then he took the plane up to over 24,000 feet and did a terminal velocity dive that flattened out almost at ground level. At that moment the Heinkel team must have guessed that their cause was lost.

Just as at Hawker's Sydney Camm had taken his Fury biplane fighter as the basis for his Hurricane, so Willy Messerschmitt used his previous design as a basis for his fighter. But Messerschmitt's Bf 108 *Taifun* was a civil monoplane, a lightweight four-seat 'tourer,' so far ahead of its times that a company was formed to rebuild the same design in 1973. But Messerschmitt had no engine that could compare with the Rolls-Royce Merlin. German

ILLUSTRATIONS

24 A Messerschmitt factory In its original conception the Messerschmitt's Bf 109 fighter was a superb aircraft. Only when more guns were added did the troubles start and none of the Bf 109s of the war years was really satisfactory. However, the need for aircraft kept it in production until the end of the war. Here is a typical assembly hall, building the 109Es that fought in the Battle of Britain. (They can be recognized from the tail strut of the machines in the left background.)

25 Professor Willy Messerschmitt (right) briefs a test pilot Behind them there is a Bf 109, and just visible beyond that, Messerschmitt's personal Bf 108 with the registration D–IMTT. (This test pilot is Fritz Wendel, who broke the world airspeed record in April 1939 in a specially prepared Messerschmitt that was described as a Bf 109 for propaganda purposes.)

26 Spitfires under construction In the foreground are Rolls-Royce Merlin engines. Near the nose of the Spitfire is a fuel tank that will be fitted into the section immediately in front of the cockpit. These aircraft are on trestles so that the retracting undercarriage can be tested.

27 (Inset) *Reginald Mitchell, chief designer of Supermarine, and the man responsible for the Spitfire* He was convinced that there would be a war and that his fighter design would play an important part in the British victory but he died before the machines started coming from the production line.

24

25

27

26

1
4/3

29

engine design had concentrated on the reliability that civil airliners needed. All such engines were heavy. He chose the Jumo 210D to go into the production models of his fighters but it proved difficult to modify. While the Merlin was being pushed from 720 hp to 990 hp (in 1936), the Jumo, even in 1938, was still delivering a miserable 670 hp.

Knowing the limitation of German engines, Messerschmitt designed the smallest, lightest, and most aerodynamically efficient airframe that would fit round the Jumo engine. He used the lessons of his Bf 108 to evolve a very sophisticated all-metal, semi-monocoque airframe. To offset the inevitable high wing loading he employed Handley Page leading-edge slats for extra lift (an unprecedented device for a fighter), as well as slotted ailerons interconnected to the flaps.

28 Messerschmitt pilots waiting for instructions The aircraft type (109E – recognizable from the strutted tail) and the trees in full leaf show that this was in the late summer of 1940. The German crews had the advantage of knowing their flying schedule in advance, while the RAF fighter pilots had to be ready to fly and fight all day every day. At this stage of the war the Luftwaffe marked its aircraft in accord with its radio-telephone codes. This enabled the British radio monitoring service to recognize which units were in the air and where they were based.

Much later in the war a German pilot escaped from internment and having guessed from his interrogation what the RAF had achieved, brought the news back to Germany. Then German aircraft markings and codes no longer tallied.

29 Salvaging wrecked German aircraft Wrecked German aircraft were assembled in England in vast dumps. The parts were sorted and salvaged and the alloy was melted down so that many German aircraft eventually flew again as RAF aircraft. Here workmen pose happily: the man with a Thermos of tea occupies the bomb-aimer's position and the workman on the right the pilot's seat of a Heinkel He 111 bomber. The nose was entirely glazed providing wonderful visibility but a terrible feeling of vulnerability too.

The way in which aircraft crashes were recorded by the civil police and then provided with an armed guard by the nearest RAF unit shows how simple it would have been for the British authorities to have accurate records of the British victories. Instead the RAF allowed the pilots to inflate their claims to provide better propaganda.

The new speeds to which the designers of the monoplanes aspired meant that a highly efficient very thin wing was needed. But the wing sections that gave the aircraft its top speed were not efficient at low speeds, that is, during take-off and landing. Slats and slots were ways to change the effective shape of the wing for those lower speeds.

Messerschmitt kept to the German Air Ministry specification, which wanted only two machine guns. To this end, he inverted the vee-shaped engine so that there was room for guns along the top of the cowling. Within the engine there was also room for a 20-mm cannon, firing through the airscrew hub. This was an attractive idea because, it was reasoned, the mass of the engine would buffer the recoil. Messerschmitt took full advantage of a specification that left the wings free of guns, and concentrated upon making them totally functional as a means of lift.

The news that the RAF was putting eight machine guns into their new fighters came as a terrible blow to the men who had nursed the Bf 109 through its trials. Messerschmitt's wings were simply not suitable for guns. But now they had to be made suitable. The problem of wing armament is that the ammunition must be at the centre of gravity (otherwise firing guns will upset the trim). This means that the gun breeches must be at the centre of gravity. So the positioning of any gun is dictated to the designers.

As an interim measure they were given a redesign job that found room in each wing for one 7.92-mm MG 17 – a development of the infantry's light machine gun. But there was no room for the boxes of bullets so the new wing was given an incredible ammunition feed. It took the belt of bullets all the way out to the wingtip, over a roller and all the way back to the wing root, and then over another roller and out to the machine gun. It was absurd, but it worked.

Soon, another wing was designed. It had one 20-mm Oerlikon MG FF cannon (in each wing) but there were large bulges for the drums of cannon shells and it was obvious that the airframe could not take much more such tampering.[1] But the Messerschmitt Bf 109 was the Luftwaffe's only single-seat monoplane fighter. The redesigned wing had become more and more vital to all concerned as the failure of the engine-mounted cannon became undeniable.

By the time of the Battle of Britain, cannons had replaced wing machine guns but the engine-mounted cannon – although its muzzle seems evident in many photos – was not fitted. But by then the lightweight wings had created new problems that had nothing to do with guns.

In 1938 Messerschmitt started to produce the Bf 109E, popularly called the Emil because of the German phonetic alphabet. The basic change was the fitting of a Daimler-Benz 601A engine. This provided another 400 hp for its additional 400 lbs of weight. But the new engine needed more cooling than the Jumo of the previous models. Just to enlarge the air scoop under the nose would create so much drag that much of the extra power would be lost. The only solution was a whole new cooling system, with proper ducted radiators, that is to say, radiators with controlled airflow to minimize drag. There was only one place they could go – under the wings. Again the wing was changed so that at least some of the cooling equipment could go aft of the centre of gravity, to make up for the extra weight of the new engine.

There were many redesigned Bf 109s still to come after the Battle of Britain. It stayed in production until the end of the war and was produced in greater numbers than any other combat aircraft of the Second World War. Because the Bf 109 was such a fine aircraft, the butchery done to its airframe was not fatal. In 1940, it was still marginally better than the Hurricane and as good as the Spitfire, but changing the initial specification, for a two machine-gun

[1]A shortage of MG FF cannons meant that, although, from the G-3 model onward, the Bf 109 had wings suitable for the cannon, machine guns were fitted at the factory.

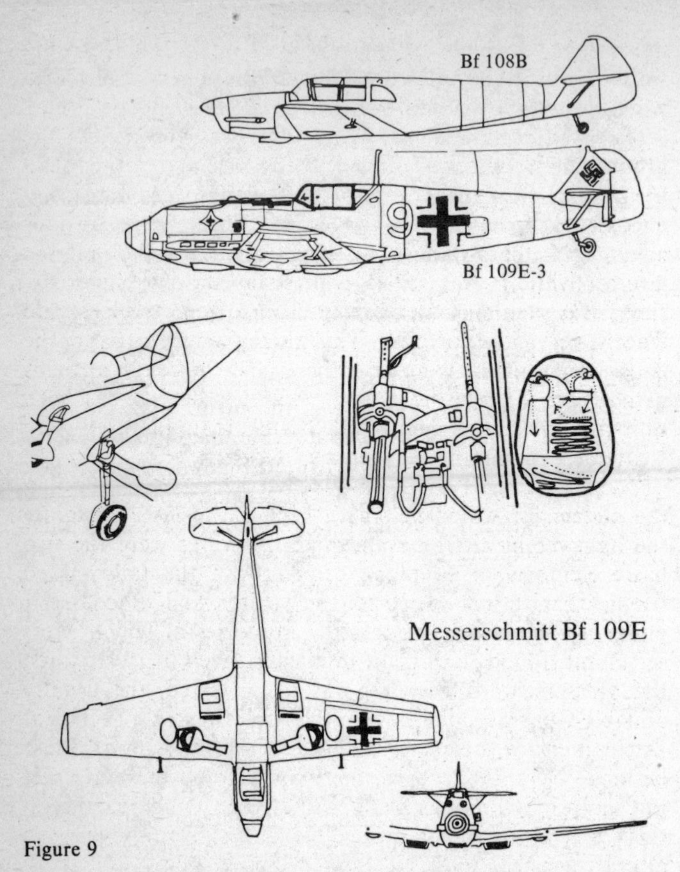

Figure 9

TOP A Bf 109E-3 compared with Messerschmitt's civil 'tourer' from which it was to some extent derived (not to scale).

CENTRE LEFT The undercarriage legs took the weight to the fuselage (not to the wings) and the wings could be removed without other support, but the narrow undercarriage caused many landing and taxiing accidents.

CENTRE RIGHT Two machine guns were installed above the inverted vee engine. They were staggered so that each ammunition box could fill the whole fuselage. Additionally there were wing guns.

BOTTOM Note the ducted radiators, the undercarriage and the cannon-gun installation with bump for ammunition. The twin machine guns are above the engine. There was no engine-mounted cannon used in 1940.

monoplane, crippled it. The problems of the Bf 109 wing were never solved. After the Emil, the designers reverted to wings without armament *for all the later variants*!

The undercarriage was of an ingenious design. On the ground the weight was carried by the fuselage, rather than by the wings as in other aircraft. The wings were not strong enough to take the Emil's weight. There were obvious advantages: for instance, the wings could be taken off the aircraft while it was still supported by its own undercarriage. But such an undercarriage had to keep the legs, and wheels, very close together. This narrow undercarriage, the extra weight of the wing armament, and the rough airfields of northern France did not go well together. It has been estimated that 5 per cent of all Bf 109s manufactured were written off in landing accidents.

Messerschmitt's enemies said that he was still building the gliders for which he was a keen enthusiast. Certainly the lightweight airframe and high-lift wings were the two basic elements of sailplane design. And the tail was so fragile that it was supported on struts. And of course a glider had no undercarriage, the mysteries of which Messerschmitt found so difficult to master. Even in 1941, when the Messerschmitt Me 210 was being tested, the usually amiable General Udet, now in the Air Ministry's Technical Department, wrote: 'One thing, dear Messerschmitt, must be made clear between us, there must be no more aircraft lost in normal landings as a result of faulty undercarriages: this can hardly be described as a technical novelty in aircraft construction.'

Willy Messerschmitt was not the only manufacturer who had difficulties with the design of undercarriages. At Heinkel's they actually harnessed an engineer to hang in the wheel bay of an He 70 so that the retraction could be studied in flight.

By the time of the Battle of Britain, the Luftwaffe's High Command was anxiously watching the tests of a new fighter – the Focke-Wulf FW 190 – which had so obviously been designed to avoid the weaknesses of the Messerschmitt Bf 109. Perhaps there was intended irony in making the FW 190's undercarriage wider than had been seen on any other similar aircraft.

The Spitfire

In 1928 the Supermarine aircraft company had been bought by the giant Vickers-Armstrong concern. Some said that the Vickers decision had largely depended upon securing the services of the design department.

Born in 1895 Reginald Mitchell, Chief Designer of the Supermarine company, had designed the S.6B seaplane which in 1931 won the Schneider Cup race, and later that year did 407 mph. Now he wanted a chance to use some of this expertise on a new fighter. As a starting point for a revolutionary aircraft, this record-breaking seaplane design was far more liberating than the military biplane specification of the Hawker Fury, or the strict economies of the Bf 108 'tourer.'

It has been written, many times, that the Spitfire was a privately developed machine that impressed the Air Ministry so deeply that they wrote a specification to fit it. This is not true. The true story is less dramatic and more complex. It begins with Air Ministry specification F.7/30,

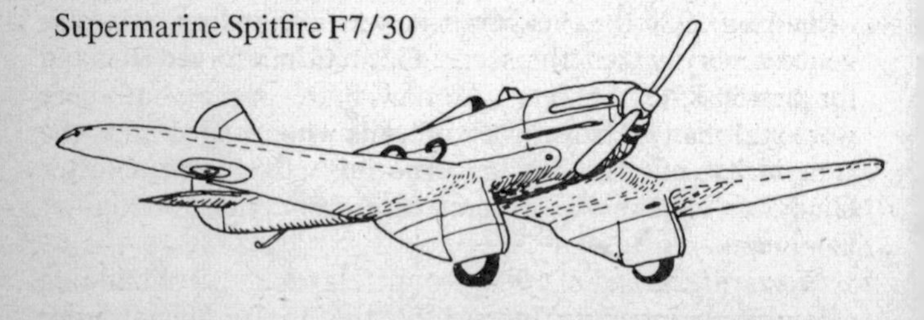

Figure 10

A curious-looking gull-wing monoplane with an open cockpit.

which had been issued in 1930 (and was also the beginning of the Hawker Hurricane).

First Mitchell submitted designs and a report. By March 1932 the Air Ministry agreed to one prototype being manufactured. But Reginald Mitchell was a sick man. In 1933, while the prototype was being built, he had an operation on one lung. He took a continental holiday to convalesce. During that holiday he talked with some young German aviators, and he returned to England convinced that war would come soon. With a prescience sometimes given to the very old or the very sick Mitchell began to believe that his fighter design could influence the outcome of the war, and from that time onwards he refused all medical advice about resting, devoting his life entirely to his aeroplane.

He looked again at his prototype, which began flying by the end of 1933. It was a curious-looking gull-wing monoplane with an open cockpit and a spatted fixed undercarriage. (It looked more like a Junkers Ju 87 than like a Spitfire.) The unsatisfactory Goshawk II engine gave it a top speed of no better than 238 mph. No one had to tell Mitchell that it wasn't good enough. Even while the prototype was under construction Mitchell had been scribbling radically different shapes on the drawing board: closed cockpit, outward-retracting undercarriage, and smaller wings with split flaps.

During 1934 the Air Ministry was responding to intelligence reports about the secret German air force. Demand for better RAF fighters was now more urgent but there were still many Air Ministry officials who insisted upon the superiority of the biplane. In July 1935 the Gloster Gladiator biplane was ordered into production for Fighter Command.

Towards the end of 1934 – while Hawker's were building a Hurricane mock-up and still waiting for an official order – Reginald Mitchell prepared detailed drawings of his entirely new fighter. This time he ignored the unsuccessful Goshawk engine and designed his fighter around the PV

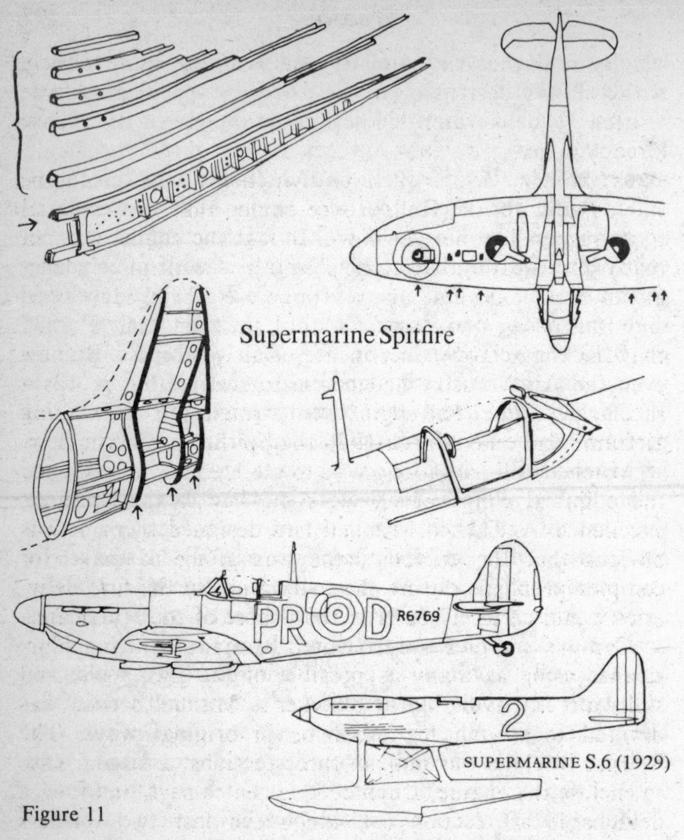

Figure 11

TOP LEFT The main spar, built from layers, had the resilience of a leaf-spring.

TOP RIGHT The elliptical wing provided space for the eight machine guns. Arrows show muzzles; rectangles are hatches for two ammunition boxes; slots are for ejected cartridges.

CENTRE LEFT Rearmost two fuselage formers continue upwards to become tail fin, providing great integral strength.

CENTRE RIGHT Spitfire's clearview canopy provided excellent all-round visibility. Note armour-glass front panel and rear-view mirror.

BOTTOM A Spitfire Mark IIA, as used in 1940 with the markings of 609 (West Riding) Squadron.

BOTTOM RIGHT For comparison, one of the racing seaplanes from which the Spitfire evolved (not to scale).

12. By now the Air Ministry was working more closely with the two designers, and as the new specification was written it deliberately incorporated much of the work already done.

In January 1935 work on Mitchell's new prototype started, and yet the Rolls-Royce engine that was essential to its success had not yet flown. In fact the engine was not ready. Overheating had to be solved by means of ethylene-glycol coolant. Engine and airframe were being developed simultaneously, and it wasn't until the very end of 1935 that the engine got its certificate of airworthiness. By now even the Air Ministry had begun to realize that it was a race against time. The engine went straight into the waiting airframe and on 5 March 1936 the Spitfire prototype flew.

Mitchell still had a long way to go. He had not designed the elliptical wings which were the key to the Spitfire's excellence. And when Mitchell had designed them, it was obvious that the curved shape was going to make for complex problems during the tooling-up, so the first deliveries would certainly be later than those of the Hurricane.

Camm's energies were devoted to manufacturing Hurricanes using as many as possible of the jigs, tools, and skills already available at Hawker's. Mitchell's time was devoted to solving his problems in original ways. The Spitfire fuselage was built in three sections: a tubular case to enclose the engine, a monocoque centre part, and then a detachable aft section (of which the last two formers extended upwards to become the tail fin).

The spar – the large structural beam upon which the wings were built – was made up of box-like girders that fitted one inside the other. Each was a different length, so that although the girder had five layers near the wing root where the stress was greatest, it was hollow at the wingtip where there was less strength needed. The spar was like a huge leaf-spring.

Forward of the wing spar the wing was covered with heavy-gauge metal, so that the whole leading edge of the wing was, in effect, a box. This gave the wing immense strength. Aft of the spar the wing was clad in thinner metal.

The Supermarine factory wasn't big enough for even the first modest order of 310 aircraft, so they had to subcontract the pieces. One company made wingtips, another made wing leading edges, another made engine mountings, etc. At Supermarine's they put the pieces together and tested them. There were many teething troubles but considering how much finer were the tolerances for this sort of aircraft, it was a miracle that such a method worked at all.

The Spitfire's curved wing is said to have been influenced by the Heinkel He 70. Whether or not this is specifically true, Mitchell, along with the rest of the world of aviation, must have found Heinkel's superb combination of aesthetic line and aerodynamic efficiency inspiring.

It was in the spring of 1935 that the demand for four extra machine guns forced Mitchell to abandon the orthodox tapering wing. The new elliptical wings that made the Spitfire so distinctive in the air were a logical response to keeping the machine-gun breeches in line while still having space to house the wheels without bumps or bulges.

The production difficulties caused by the subtle wing shape were more than outweighed by the advantages. Not only did the curved shape provide maximum area – and low wing loading – for a given span, but the long cord gave strength at the wing roots where it was fixed to the fuselage. All the time the wing was kept as thin as possible. By the standards of the day the result looked more like a racer than a military plane. Amazingly Mitchell's Spitfire wing, housing four big machine guns, was thinner than that of the Messerschmitt. It was an inspired achievement, for only long after Mitchell's death, as speeds went up and up, did research show how far ahead of its time Mitchell's wing design had been. Vickers suggested to the Air Ministry that the name Spitfire – used for the previous gull-wing prototype – should be kept. Mitchell was not consulted on this point, but neither was he surprised. Told of the decision, he said it was 'just the sort of bloody silly name they would choose.'

But Mitchell was proud of his aeroplane. The two test pilots, flying it at Eastleigh during the early summer of 1936, often noticed Mitchell's old Rolls-Royce motor car parked alongside the hangar. He had come to watch it fly. It was just as well, for he never lived to see his fighters coming off the production line. In 1937 he died aged 42.

Machine Guns and Cannon

Both the RAF fighters had eight Browning machine guns. The Bf 109E was equipped with two 7.92-mm machine guns and two 20-mm cannon. Although exact comparison is difficult (because in combat the 20-mm cannon were firing thin-shelled 'mine type' missiles that exploded on impact), it is reasonable to say that a three-seconds' burst of gunfire from the Messerschmitt Bf 109E weighed 18 lbs. The RAF fighter fired nearly 13 lbs in the same duration of shooting.

The Bf 109E's 20-mm Oerlikon cannon (one in each wing) was a Swiss anti-aircraft gun drastically modified for use by aircraft. This meant making it smaller and lighter, with a faster rate of fire. The German experts shortened the barrel and redesigned the 20-mm shells, reducing the amount of powder inside them. This allowed the breech-block mechanism to be lightened.

In some respects the modification was brilliant: the gun was very light and very compact, but the design of the breech-block did not incorporate anything to lock it when the shell fired. The explosion in the breech that fired the shell also opened the breech for the next one. All of this resulted in a very poor muzzle velocity. However, the experts reasoned that since all air combat takes place at close range, and because the missile would actually explode, muzzle velocity was not very important. As we shall see, this proved to be a major error.

Its other shortcoming was the rate of fire (see Table 2).

The Fighter Armament

Table 2 During the summer of 1940 the Hurricanes and Spitfires carried eight Brownings. The Messerschmitt Bf 109E usually had two machine guns on top of the engine cowling and a 20-mm cannon in each wing. Sometimes machine guns were substituted for cannon. Most cannon shells were thin-walled and contained explosive, but incendiary and armour-piercing rounds were also used.

The German pilots could select their fire: on a stick-like control column a thumb button on top fired the wing guns, and a finger-trigger fired the guns on the cowling. The latter were considered very useful by pilots who sighted along the stream of bullets, while still looking through the gun-sight. The German fighters were equipped with indicators to show ammunition supply. The RAF pilots usually had a couple of dozen tracer bullets at the bottom of the box to warn them that their ammunition was expended.

	Browning (RAF)	*Oerlikon MG FF*	*Rhein metall-Borsig MG 17*
Calibre	7.7 mm (0.303 in)	20 mm	7.92 mm
Supply carried (rounds)	300	60	1,000[1]
Gun weight (lbs)	22	53	28
Gun length (inches)	44.5	52.8	47.2
Muzzle velocity (f/sec.)	2,660	1,800	2,450
Rate of fire (rds/min.)	1,200	520	1,100
Projectile weight (ounces)	0.344	4.82	0.45

[1]When fitted as wing armament only 500 rounds per gun.

Fast in comparison with an anti-aircraft weapon, it was slow by the standards of the fighter pilot, who could seldom hope to have a target in his sights for more than two seconds (seventeen shells from each of the two cannon). And such a two-second burst consumed well over a quarter of the supply of shells, for even with Messerschmitt's wings modified by bumps, there was only a 60-round drum on each cannon.

In fighter-to-fighter combat, the two sides were not far apart in firepower, but the structural strength of the larger aircraft, that is, the German bombers, made it very difficult to bring them down with bullets. This is illustrated by an incident in the Battle when six Spitfires of 74 Squadron expended 7,000 bullets in attacks on a Dornier Do 17 but did not bring it down.

Although the rival merits of machine gun and cannon were much argued at the time, the RAF had secretly concluded that the cannon was far better. In 1940 (at the Royal Aircraft Establishment), a series of tests was carried out against an old Blenheim airframe (incorporating armour). The eight machine-gun configuration was fourth in a list in which two cannon were top.

As an experiment, the RAF used a few Spitfires equipped with cannon during the 1940 battles. However the RAF had trouble with its cannon guns, and the few pilots given them during the Battle of Britain for the most part cursed their luck and were re-equipped with machine-gun fighters.

One of the problems of the Browning machine gun, in RAF use, was the fact that it had to fire the army's rifle bullets. The British army persisted in using nitro-glycerine – cordite – propellant at a time when virtually every other army had changed to the nitro-cellulose type. Whatever the rival merits of the two types of ammunition – cordite, for instance, was more stable in tropical conditions – the cordite bullets were apt to detonate in the breech of hot guns. There could hardly have been a graver disadvantage from the fighter pilot's point of view. The Browning was modified to overcome this problem (by holding the breech-block open, with empty chamber, at the end of each burst). It was also modified to suit large-scale mass production, and again for a problem that arose with the feed. By this time there was hardly a component of the gun that remained unaltered. The Colt-Browning gun used in the Battle was virtually a British gun: a rare event for a nation that had used so many foreign-designed weapons, from Lee-Enfields, Maxims, and Lewis guns to Brens, Bofors, and Besas.

Only in 1939 was it decided that the RAF fighters must be able to fire a continuous burst of 300 rounds (from each gun). This required a complete redesign of the muzzle attachment. This modification was not available to all units until as late as May 1940. It was almost too late.

The RAF incendiary bullet was almost too late for the Battle of Britain too. In January 1939 the De Wilde bullet design was purchased for £30,000 in spite of its defects (which were not mentioned to the Belgian inventor for fear of telling the Germans about the test results). Modified by British experts, this De Wilde bullet (its name was unchanged) was the best of its type and contributed to RAF success in 1940.

Wing armament, in fighter aircraft of all nations, usually gave rise to two major problems: the positioning of the ammunition (and its feed to the gun) and the cold condensation of high-altitude flight. This was particularly troublesome when aircraft climbed through cloud to heights where the condensation froze. These problems had not been solved by 1939, because in peacetime the RAF seldom did much flying in bad weather. The first winter of war was severe enough to make the freezing Brownings a major problem. As an emergency measure, oil diluted with paraffin was applied to the guns, to cure the problem of dry cold. However, it gave the armourers a great deal of work, for it was ineffective as a rust-preventative.

The problem of wet cold – encountered in cloud – was solved, up to the moment of the first shot, by sealing over the gun muzzles with stretched pieces of fabric. As a longer-term solution, engine heat was fed to the guns.

Other Comparisons

Any comparison of the Merlin engine and the Daimler-Benz DB 601A must begin by mentioning the latter's fuel-injection system. The work of Rudolf Diesel, with Karl Benz, Gottlieb Daimler, and Nicholaus Otto, had made the modern internal-combustion engine virtually a German invention. Diesel's work gave German designers a big start when they applied the fuel-injection method to petrol engines.

Fuel injection, which puts a measured amount of fuel into each cylinder according to temperature and engine speed, etc., was demonstrably superior to the carburettors that the Merlins used. Carburettors are, at best, subject to the changes of temperature that air combat inevitably brings. At worst they bring a risk of freezing or catching fire. And with such large, high-performance engines, the carburettor system seldom delivers exactly the same amount of fuel simultaneously to each cylinder. Worst of all, the carburettor was subject to the centrifugal effect, so that it starved, and missed a beat or two, as it went into a dive.

The RAF pilots learned how to half-roll before diving, so that fuel from the carburettor was thrown *into* the engine instead of out of it, but in battle this could be a dangerous time-wasting necessity.

It was a legacy from the biplane age that pilots, feeling defensive about their equipment, claimed that they had the advantage of manoeuvrability. Pilots of Spitfires, Hurricanes, and Bf 109s all claimed that their aircraft had the tightest turning circle, but the 32-foot wingspan of the Bf 109 gave it the advantage over its rivals. In spite of its high wing loading, it had a turn radius of only 750 feet (Spitfire 880 feet and Hurricane 800 feet), and this could be a vital factor in air fighting.

German fighter pilots envied the sheet of armour plate that was behind the seat of the RAF fighters. Seat armour for fighters had been rejected by British officialdom because it would 'spoil the balance' of the aircraft. Ignoring this, 1 Squadron, in France early in the war, took a sheet of back armour from a wrecked Fairey Battle light bomber and fitted it to a Hurricane. To convince all concerned that it didn't spoil the balance, one of the pilots returned to England and performed a hair-raising series of aerobatics before an audience at Farnborough. After that it became a standard fitting. As we shall see, this proved a vital factor in the 1940 fighting.

Another semi-official modification that had an important effect on the Battle resulted from a phone call to de Havilland's propeller division. It came from Flight Lieutenant McGrath and it came as late as 9 June 1940. He asked if it would be possible to try out a constant-speed propeller on a Spitfire 'without a lot of paperwork and fuss.' The propeller added 7,000 feet to the service ceiling and so transformed the aircraft's performance that the Air Ministry authorized all Hurricanes and Spitfires to be changed to constant speed props (which the Bf 109 had as standard equipment). Each squadron selected its finest fitters, and the de Havilland experts went from airfield to airfield demonstrating the first conversion, supervising the second conversion, and watching the third, before handing over to the home-team and travelling on to the next squadron. A test pilot followed them. A total of 1,050 props were fitted by 15 August. All without a price being agreed, a contract written, or any paper signed. More than one de Havilland executive was convinced that they would never get paid for the work but they continued with it anyway.

Considering that the constant-speed unit was a British invention, it was remarkable that the Air Ministry sent its Hurricane and Spitfire to war with fixed-pitch, two-bladed wooden props, or at best with two-pitch (variable-pitch) propellers. The constant-speed unit was a simple governor that kept the propeller's speed (and the engine's speed) constant by varying the angle at which propeller blades bit into the air. For take-off, the blades were turned to bite very little air which, with the engine at full power, gave take-off thrust. For full speed, the constant-speed unit took over to give the maximum size of bite and so maximum forward speed. The angle of the old fixed-pitch prop was a compromise for all these situations. The constant-speed propeller's value to the squadrons was not only in the improved performance it conferred but in the much reduced wear and tear on the engines.

Messerschmitt and Spitfire – What Were They Like to Fly?

The flying characteristics of the Spitfire and Bf 109E-3 were only marginally different, and some of the differences were simply a matter of personal preferences. Both machines came off the ground very quickly – the Messerschmitt had a very short run. Both swung on take-off, but in straight and level flight the Spitfire could be trimmed to fly feet off. The Messerschmitt required a boot on the rudder bar all the time. The German pilots tolerated it and soon got used to it, but Allied pilots who flew captured machines usually complained about this.

Visibility – life and death for combat flyers – was incomparably better in the Spitfire. The bubble-shaped hood gave head room and a chance to see down, up, and around. The 109 hood had thick bars like a prison and it sometimes touched the top of the helmet. (Later this hood was changed on the advice of Galland.) The 109 cockpit was very small indeed but there again it was what one got used to; some German pilots liked it. Both aircraft were light and delightful to fly at medium speeds but both became hard work at high speeds. This was a telling fault because in a diving attack this meant a great deal of muscle was required to bring the target into the gun-sights. Eventually both air forces discovered that this problem was

Turning Circles
(Drawn to Scale)

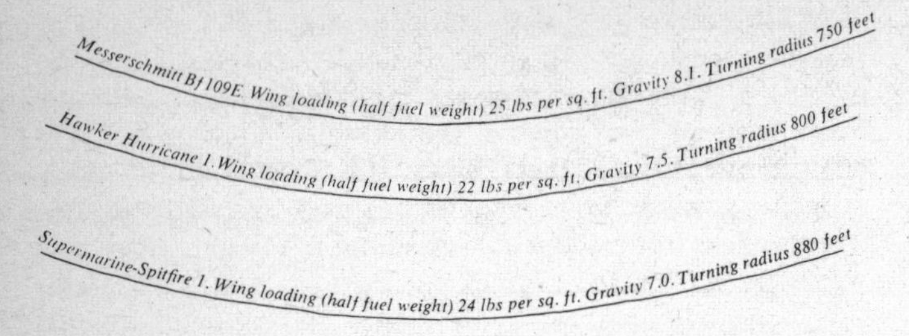

Figure 12

These curves are drawn to scale for the three single-seat fighters flying at 300 mph at 10,000 feet. This is for a vertically banked turn, in which there is no aerofoil providing lift. Such a turn is theoretically possible by inclined thrust (tilting the nose slightly skywards) but more or less impossible in practice, which is why all dog-fights moved downwards (and fighting at low altitudes carried a real risk of aircraft hitting the ground by accident).

A tight curve is a great test of a pilot's skill because as G increases, so does the stalling speed. In a tight turn, the aircraft is on the threshold of stalling and will teeter as the pilot loses and then regains control. Note the gravity exerted. A pilot of average fitness begins to black out at only 4G or 5G. At 9G the average airframe begins to break up, for the wings are taking the strain of nine times the weight of the aircraft. And the stalling speed is by then very high: for example, a Spitfire will have a stalling speed of over 250 mph.

Note the way in which neither wingspan nor wing loading is decisive in the matter of the tightest turning circle.

due to the effect of high-speed airflow over the fabric-covered ailerons. When the ailerons were metal covered, like the wings, high-speed flying became much lighter.

Some of the Spitfires were lost in spins, so pilots were told to avoid this manoeuvre. The Messerschmitt suffered no such vice; there was no problem getting out of a spin and it never went into a flat spin.

On the ground the Messerschmitt was 'a pig'. It had

terrible forward vision, and whereas you could slide the Spitfire's hood back, the cumbersome hinged cover of the Messerschmitt had to be closed for taxiing. The lightness of the airframe made the Messerschmitt dance all over the place when running over uneven ground. It was easy to put a wingtip onto the grass.

Spitfires seldom broke up in the air. In those rare cases where too much stress was put on the airframe, those beautifully thin Mitchell wings were the first part to go. The Messerschmitt wings were also a weak part structurally but the tail was even weaker.

In 1940 a pilot was expected to judge the amount of stress he was putting on his airframe; there were no instruments to tell him how near he was to break-up. In practice this meant that most pilots were very careful to keep well within the limits, and few aircraft were stressed to breaking point. The arguments about which type could out-turn which are usually no more than a reflection of the recklessness of the opponents a man had flown against.

And just as every squadron had pilots who would fly to 'ten tenths' of their aircraft's structural strength, so every squadron – on both sides – had dud aeroplanes that were to be avoided and unusually good ones that were often claimed by those with rank or influence. And these pilots got the best riggers, fitters, and armourers too. The green pilots got the slack and inferior ground crews, and the inferior aircraft, and they were shot down. The squadron diaries record the way in which men who scored a victory or two dramatically increased their chances of survival.

Radar[1]

As the 1920s became the 1930s, the politicians who had pursued a popular course of denying tax-payers' money to the military now found it politically expedient to spend a

[1]At the time this was called RDF, Radio Direction Finding, then it was Radio-Location, and eventually the name was changed to radar.

little money on defence against the bomber. Pacifism as a way of cutting taxes was one thing, but getting bombed was something else. Bombing killed voters; precision bombing killed politicians.

In 1934, a vast sound-location device was built on Romney Marshes. It was 25 feet high and 200 feet long. It did not detect approaching RAF bombers until they were eight miles away, and could give no information about altitude or bearing. And it did not work at all unless the aircraft were on the axis of its fixed curve. As a final absurdity, this expensive manifestation of official lunacy faced France, Britain's closest military ally.

Grasping at straws, a newly formed scientific committee under Henry Tizard asked Robert Watson-Watt (a plump, pedantic radio expert of the National Physical Laboratories) whether there was any chance of developing a 'death-ray' that was a popular ingredient of spy fiction of the period. That meant a weapon that would emit damaging radiation to stop engines, or kill, maim, or disable air crews, or perhaps weaken an aircraft structure. The answer was an unequivocal no, but reasoning that even if a death-ray was possible, the defences would still need to know where to aim it, Watson-Watt added a final paragraph on the subject of detection. He wrote:

> Meanwhile attention is being turned to the still difficult but less unpromising problem of radio-detection as opposed to radio-destruction, and numerical considerations on the method of detection by reflected radio waves will be submitted if required.

So, at the committee's first meeting in January 1935 they asked Watson-Watt to submit his 'considerations.' Air Marshal Hugh Dowding (at the time the Air Council's Member for Research and Development) called for a demonstration of this reflection theory. Using existing equipment, an ordinary BBC broadcast as the beam, and an RAF Heyford bomber as the enemy aircraft, the experiment was set up immediately. In spite of a thousand cautions from Watson-Watt that this makeshift arrangement might well prove a fiasco – or perhaps because of them – the cathode-ray tube's flickering response was far beyond expectations.

The demonstration was set up in a field, using mobile apparatus. Watson-Watt – an opinionated Scotsman in baggy suit and granny glasses – took his nephew along for the ride but because the experiment was such a closely guarded secret he left him at the roadside nearby.

The successful demonstration generated great enthusiasm and moved the conversation immediately from long-distance detection – which now seemed well within their grasp – to the possibilities of precision radar accurate enough for aiming anti-aircraft guns. Watson-Watt remembers no excitement or elation but he admitted driving his car a considerable distance towards London before remembering that he had left his nephew behind.

The Radar Theories

Between 1876 and 1903, three inventions changed the world more drastically than man had ever done before. First, Dr Nicholaus Otto built a gas engine that was improved by Daimler in 1885 so it could propel a wheeled vehicle. Only two years later, Heinrich Rudolf Hertz made sparks into an electric wave, and by 1897 Guglielmo Marconi used those electric waves to send a wireless message nine miles. Now the world had only to wait until 1903 for the Wright brothers to combine an internal-combustion engine with a glider.

The internal-combustion engine, the aeroplane, and wireless transformed war even more than gunpowder or steam-power had done. But during the twentieth century only one great battle has been fought and decided by these three inventions alone, and that was the Battle of Britain.

Hertz's invention had been developed into radio-telephony, with which the fighter pilots spoke to ground control and to each other, into HF/DF (high-frequency direction-finding) for friendly fighter location but, most vitally, into the technique of radar. Hertz himself had been aware of the way in which his radio waves reflected from solid objects, and had even demonstrated it. Very soon afterwards, a German engineer proposed this technique as a way for ships in fog or darkness to 'see' each other and avoid collision.

But there were great problems still to be overcome. If the radio transmission is likened to a shout, and its return to an echo, it was not known how to make the shout loud enough to carry very far, or short enough to separate shout from echo.

The Americans Gregory Breit and Merle Tuve contributed short-pulsed transmissions, and showed how they could be bounced back from layers of the ionosphere. Curiously, it was six years before Professor E. V. Appleton, the distinguished English physicist, used radio to establish the height of the ionosphere, and of another layer that was named after him. Appleton was showered with honours and, along with at least a dozen other people, he is often named as the father of radar. However, Appleton's radio probes of the ionosphere were based upon a frequency-change method, and had no resemblance to the later radar techniques. Nor was he able to measure the distance from earth of any *selected part* of the ionosphere. His approximations were good enough for physicists but not accurate enough for gunnery.

The all-metal aircraft gave new impetus to radar research, both because of the metal's radio-reflecting quality and because of the new threat that high-speed metal bombers presented to the defences. During the 1930s many countries carried out experiments with radio-detection devices. In Japan, the Yagi short-wave directional aerial was invented. In America, the army's Signal Corps Laboratories worked on radio-detection, and the US navy sought the co-operation of American industry. The Yagi aerial's wide use, and the US navy's name 'radar' that was adopted by all concerned, gave chauvinists in those countries an opportunity to claim that it was a national invention. In fact the Germans had an even better claim.

Dr Rudolf Kühnold – head of German naval signals research – was prompted by early work on sonar (underwater detection) to rig up a crude radar set, using a brand-new powerful valve from Philips. By 20 March 1934, before Watson-Watt in England had even proposed experiments, Kühnold's apparatus was beamed across Kiel Harbour and obtained a 'picture' of the battleship *Hessen.* By October of the same year, a test was arranged to show that his apparatus could detect a ship at seven miles. Aircraft flying through the beam provided an unexpected demonstration of the application of radar to air defence.

By the end of the 1930s Germany was producing detection equipment that was superior to the equivalent British sets. The German battleship *Graf Spee* had a gun-ranging radar, *Seetakt*, as early as 1937. When the *Graf Spee* was scuttled in Uruguay in 1939, after the Battle of the River Plate, a British radar expert took a rowing boat out to the half-submerged ship and climbed up to examine the aerial. He reported on it as a gun-laying radar but so reluctant was anyone in Britain to admit that the Germans might have such a device that the report was filed away and forgotten.

By July 1938, the Germans had the Freya, a good early-warning radar, in action. It detected a Junkers Ju 52 transport aircraft at 90 kilometres, although it had no altitude-finding ability. However, the German anti-aircraft guns had radar accurate enough for gunnery. Their Würzburg-A – demonstrated in July 1939 – was very sophisticated. A Telefunken product, it used 8 kilowatts on 50 cm and had the same parabola for sending and receiving. Its initial range was 30 kilometres, and when afterwards it was equipped with a rotating dipole to give an overlapping beam, it was accurate to half a degree and 100 metres.

And German radar sets proved excellent in use. In the winter of 1939–40, Freya radar units on the German islands of Wangerooge and Heligoland had detected incoming RAF raids so efficiently that Bomber Command formations were decimated. In May 1940, an anti-aircraft battery at Essen-Frintrop used a Würzburg radar, and was able to shoot down an RAF bomber which they could not see. This so impressed Göring that he made a public announcement that no enemy aircraft would ever fly across Germany. It was a remark he was never allowed to forget.

After the Dunkirk evacuation there was great consternation in Whitehall when it was realized that some British mobile radar units had been left behind in France. Furthermore, British radar secrets had all been shared with their French allies. There was considerable relief when the crews who had abandoned the radar sets all swore that the equipment had been totally destroyed.

In fact, the French armed forces proved faithful to their British friends even in those years of misery. No such secrets, of radar or anything else, were passed to the Germans. However, at least one British radar set, more or less in working order, was captured during the German advance. But the British need not have worried. German experts gave it no more than a perfunctory look before declaring it rather primitive by German standards, which it was.

Berlin and London shared a determination to believe that the other side knew nothing of radar technology, even though there existed plenty of evidence otherwise. And Milch had shown a German radar set to a visiting French air force delegation in August 1938. In the autumn of 1937, during an official visit to England with Udet and other officers, he had boasted about German radar to an astonished audience of high-ranking RAF officers during a formal lunch held in Milch's honour.

In the ante-room of the Officers' Mess at Fighter Command HQ Milch suddenly addressed a loud question to the assembled officers. 'Now, gentlemen, let us all be frank,' he said. 'How are you getting on with your experiments in the detection by radio of aircraft approaching your shores?'

There was some embarrassed laughter, and an attempt to change the subject, but Milch persisted. 'Come' gentlemen, there is no need to be so cagey. We've known for some time that you were developing a system of radiolocation. So are we, and we think we are a jump ahead of you.[1]

Perhaps, in technical terms, Milch was correct but radar could never be a practical warning system for any frontier except a coastline. But the system itself was born out of a unique British ability to compromise.

It has been said that the motto of the team at Bawdsey, Suffolk, where practical radar was developed, was 'Second best tomorrow.' This meant that they could not afford to spend a year or two in search of perfection but must get radar working soon, even if its performance was below peak. Although an egoist, Watson-Watt never promised more than he knew he could deliver.

It was this restraint that caused Watson-Watt to name their experiments RDF (Radio Direction Finding). It was a deliberate attempt to deceive the curious, because although they believed they could crack the problem of range-finding, they thought the problem of direction-finding would be difficult or even impossible.

Watson-Watt's original memorandum of 27 February 1935 is a remarkable document. It not only set out the alternative paths of research but guessed rather accurately what might be achieved. At the end it noted the importance of identifying aircraft, and suggested a radio method by which friendly aircraft could give a coded reinforcement of the reflected radio wave. He added a note about the need that all this would bring for really good radio-telephone communication with the fighter pilots, realizing that his

[1]This at least is the story Milch told his biographer. But the RAF officer who arranged that visit told me that the delegation did not go to Fighter Command Headquarters, and radar was not mentioned by anyone, British or German, during those visits.

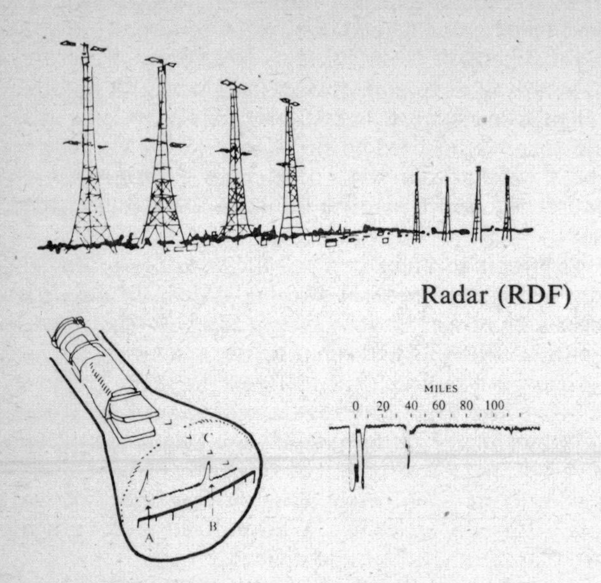

Figure 13

The Germans could see the Dover radar masts from France. There was no way of hiding or disguising the huge girder-work towers upon which radar (then called Radio Direction Finding) depended. In any case, the stations were all emitting radio signals.

At the base of the two sets of towers (receiver towers and transmitter towers) there was a 'receiver hut.' Here the operators, often women, watched the cathode-ray tubes.

BOTTOM LEFT As the signal went from the transmitter, a blip (*see A*) came on the screen. That short pulse of energy either disappeared, never to be seen again, or hit something, bounced back, and was received by the second set of tall masts. It made another blip (*see B*) on the screen. By measuring the time between the blips, the operator could estimate how far away the aircraft reflecting it was. However, this was more difficult when there were formations of aircraft.

BOTTOM RIGHT A screen registering 24 twin-engined aircraft.

OPPOSITE PAGE, LEFT The map shows coverage of the ordinary CH (Chain Home) stations for aircraft flying below 15,000 feet. Aircraft higher than this could be detected at a greater distance, although the radar coverage was very poor for aircraft above 20,000 feet.

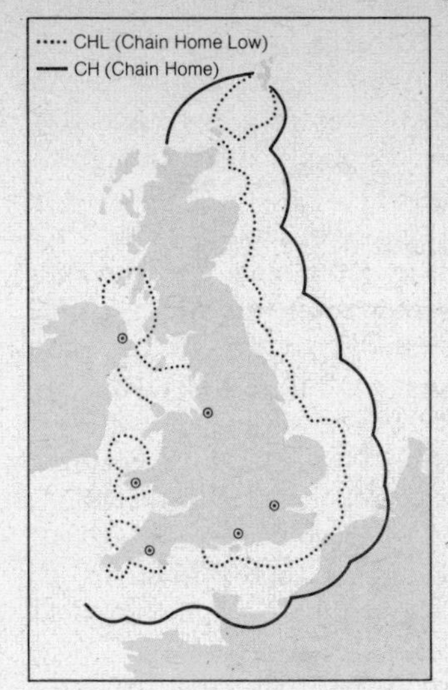

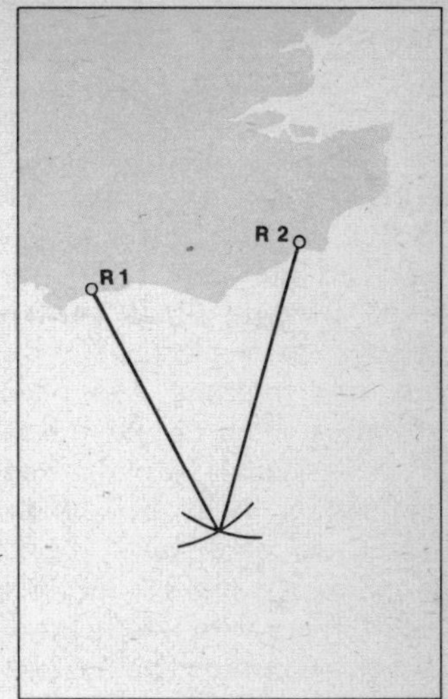

To prevent aircraft coming in under the radar at sea level, CHL (Chain Home Low) sets were used (*see* dotted lines). These rather more sophisticated sets, with rotating aerials, transmitted at 1.5 metres (compared with 10 metres for the CH) and had been developed by the navy for detecting ships. Notice the way in which the coverage at this stage of the war gave priority to ports (*marked with* dot in circle).

Note. The radar coverage only faced seawards. Aircraft that had crossed the British coastline could not be plotted (except by the Observer Corps) while flying over the land.

RIGHT By measuring the time it took the pulse to bounce back from an aircraft, range could be accurately assessed. But direction-finding was much more difficult. However, the Filter Room staff could plot the ranges provided by two adjacent radar stations (R1 and R2) and intersect them to get the position of the enemy.

This technique was called range-cutting and was an important part of the work done in the Filter Room. It was because direction-finding was so difficult to do with this kind of radar equipment that the system was called Radio Direction Finding. This was intended to deceive unauthorized enquirers about the purpose of the tall towers.

radar would be measured by how efficiently it placed fighter planes in a position to attack enemy bombers. (At this time the envisaged equipment was very large and few men dreamed that it would ever be made small enough to fit inside even the largest aircraft.)

But the most remarkable thing about radar is that no one had invented it long before Kühnold's experiments. There were hundreds, perhaps thousands, of scientists and experts paid by their governments to advise on such scientific matters. The phenomenon of radio waves re-radiating from distant aircraft was repeatedly mentioned in professional journals, and the Post Office got endless complaints about the way aircraft spoiled radio reception. Yet these were simply treated as problems to be solved. None of the experts was able to link these 'problems' of interference with the threat of the bomber, which continued to get tremendous publicity.

Watson-Watt's first guesses set British radar off to a good beginning. His decision to treat an aircraft as though its wings were a horizontal antenna started him off using a wavelength of 50 metres, calculating this to be twice the wingspan of the average bomber. Almost immediately Watson-Watt changed to half that wavelength to avoid commercial radio signals. His decision to treat the bomber as if it were a horizontal wire led him to horizontal polarization and to stacked aerials. His experience with cathode-ray tubes (which had been improving rapidly at this time) contributed to the presentation. It was essential that only existing parts could be used: there was no time to start inventing new components. It was upon these basic decisions that rapid British progress depended. Britain was an ideal country for a radar defence chain, for the sea provided no obstructions to the signals transmitted.

In fact, progress was faster than any had hoped: a team assembled in May 1935 had 70-foot-high masts erected, and tests started within the following month. By the end of the year, results were far beyond anything Watson-Watt had promised. He had interpreted the fluctuations of a signal to guess that a formation of three Hawker Harts had strayed across the test area. He had measured aircraft heights to within 1,000 feet and had got some way to solving the direction-finding problem. The team mounted directional aerials to face north, south, east, and west and then measured the relative strength of signal. The results were enough to distinguish the British work from anything done elsewhere, and more than enough to provide Watson-Watt with government money for higher masts and to get research started on alternative wavelengths (in case of enemy jamming) and detection of low-flying aircraft. The money was approved by Dowding but the gruff old man never did endear himself to the scientists, and many of them thought – wrongly – that Dowding did not understand the scientific principles of the new device.

There was a unique atmosphere at Bawdsey, to which the researchers moved in 1936. The old manor house was by the sea. It had extensive grounds that included a cricket pitch, peach trees, and the biggest bougainvillaea in the country. The high-grade academic physicists lived and worked in the manor house. There was no red tape and they stopped work for a swim or a bit of gardening as they felt like it. On the other hand, it was not unusual for the laboratory to be in full operation long after midnight. Visitors came from the famous Cavendish Laboratory at Cambridge to sit round the fire and talk shop. These sessions grew into what the Bawdsey men called 'soviets' in which visiting civil servants, Air Marshals – and eventually air crew straight from operations – could say anything they liked to anyone they chose. An Assistant III was often actively abetted in arguing with an Air Marshal, said an unrepentant Watson-Watt, who was often fomenting such excitement.

It was in this atmosphere of middle-class comfort that senior officers met scientists, with no clearly defined division of authority. No visitor to Bawdsey could fail to see its value as a way of applying scientific method to war. From Bawdsey, in 1937, teams went to study the discrepancies between radar tracks and navigators' logs. Another team went to Fighter Command. The name 'Operational Research' was coined by Watson-Watt. He defined this as 'investigation by scientific method on actual operations – current, recent, or impending – and explicitly directed to the better, more effective and more economical conduct of similar operations in the future.' Although it never got the public attention that radar attracted, Operational Research eventually became just as important to the progress of the war.

IFF

By 1938 many airmen were worried that the radar could not identify friendly aircraft. It was typical of the negative attitude of most brass hats when the Commander in Chief Bomber Command said he would do everything in his power to oppose the radar work unless this problem was solved. Eventually it was solved, up to a point. It was called Identification Friend or Foe – IFF – a device for every aircraft. This re-radiated a much more powerful pulse than the one it received (but on the same frequency) so that its blip on the radar screen could be identified as that of a friendly aircraft.

The Reporting Network

The sort of radar defence that Britain had built by 1939 could only have grown out of the informal interaction of scientist, airman, and civil servant. Part of Watson-Watt's genius was knowing what was possible, so that as the government put money into research they found his promises fulfilled. But the great achievement of British radar was not to be found in the rather crude Chain Home RDF stations – or the more sophisticated CHL (Chain Home Low) sets – but in the way its information was interpreted and used. In this respect it was most fortunate that

Dowding, who gave the first go-ahead for radar, then became Chief of RAF Fighter Command.

Bawdsey became the first radar station, as well as the scientific laboratory. Here, too, there were RAF officers planning the training of the personnel needed to man the other stations. Additionally they set up a full-scale experimental Group Operations Room, and experts were already planning the immense network of telephone cables that would be needed to feed all the information back to other such control centres.

By January 1938, Fighter Command aircraft at Biggin Hill airfield were working under radar control from the station at Bawdsey. From this time onwards, civil airliners passing within range of the Bawdsey apparatus had fighters sent to intercept them for practice. When war began, the operators were able to track German bombers mine-laying in the Thames Estuary. Sometimes the radar was so accurate that RN minesweepers could find the mines immediately.

The canny Scotsman Watson-Watt had proved to be the perfect man for the job, in spite of many bitter disputes in which he was involved. His knowledge of pure science gave him the basis upon which to work and his experience with electrical storms stood him in good stead at a time when electrical disturbance was one of the worst problems of practical radar. His career as a scientist for government departments equipped him for the internal politics he now encountered, and above all he was driven by a sense of urgency that made him set time limits to research, after which equipment went into production whatever its state of development.

The scientists realized that the quality of radar would depend upon generating very high power for very short wavelengths. Already the original experiment's 50-metre wavelength had been reduced to 10 metres for the chain of stations that was being erected round the British coast. For a supplementary chain (CHL) the wavelength was only 1.5 metres. The shorter wavelengths provided a narrow beam that was far more directional. So the CHL masts had rotating aerials that swept the horizon to find the maximum intensity of response. These CHL sets were largely due to the work of an Australian named W. A. S. Butement, a War Office scientist who had started such beamed radar experiments as early as 1931 but had been discouraged from continuing with them.

But, even by 1940, it was still very difficult to read the blips on the cathode-ray tubes and height estimation was done by comparing the signals of different aerials. Judging the number of aircraft in any formation just from the wobble of the cathode's glow was even more illusive. And when the operators were reading many blips at once, and trying to distinguish single aircraft from large formations, the results were confused and contradictory.

The Filter Room

From each of the Chain Home stations they phoned the details seen on the cathode-ray screens to a Filter Room at Bentley Priory. (This room also received reports from the Chain Home Low stations that searched for low-flying raids.) The Filter Room exemplified the way in which the whole radar system reconciled man with machine. Here the reports from the radar stations were weighed against the accuracy of their previous reports and against known faults in the apparatus. Only after the reports were compared, judged, and interpreted were they passed on to the Operations Rooms. A good example of the value of the Filter Room was 'range-cutting.' The Chain Home stations were far more accurate at measuring range than finding direction, so the range reports from two neighbouring stations could be intersected to provide an accurate position.

Another important task was comparing the reports of enemy raids with the estimated position of any RAF aircraft that might be seaward of the radar chain. The IFF system that enabled friendly aircraft to characterize the blip they made on the screen was far from perfect. It remained the weakest link in the system for a long time and eventually was radically changed. Meanwhile the Filter Room was responsible for preventing RAF squadrons from attacking friendly aircraft.

Operations Rooms

The filtered reports were plotted on the Filter Room map table. The counters – red for enemy and black for friendly – had numerals to show estimated height and strength, with an arrow to indicate direction, and a reference number for that particular formation. From the Filter Room balcony the whole map table was watched, and a teller passed details of these filtered plots back to Operations Rooms at Sector, Group and Fighter Command HQ. At each place, the map table was identical. On the wall in every Operations Room there was a special clock, marked to give each five-minute segment a different colour. Each raid's coloured direction arrow was changed (to match the clock), and moved as each new report was received. Providing that the reports kept coming, all the plots would be the same colour. But a lost, or neglected, raid would be noticed because its colour remained unchanged.

Also available to the controller and his staff on their balcony was 'the Tote.' This was a board fitted with coloured lights. It showed at a glance which squadrons were available in 30 minutes, which were at readiness (5 minutes) or at cockpit readiness (2 minutes), and which were in the air.

The Observer Corps

Virtually all of Britain's radar stations were near the coast and facing seawards. But as soon as the raiders passed over the coast, the Operations Rooms were forced to rely upon an army of volunteers equipped with only enthusiasm, binoculars, an aircraft recognition booklet, and a simple sighting device (see Plate 12).

As Churchill said, it was like going from the middle of the twentieth century to the early stone age. To cater to this transition there were 'Lost Property Offices' which recorded aircraft reported by the Observer Corps but not by radar. (The Observer Corps were only allowed to track aircraft that had been detected by the radar stations.)

The Observer Corps volunteers devoted much of their spare time to aircraft recognition. The system was wholly dependent upon these men for reports of enemy aircraft that had crossed the coast of Britain. On cloudy days this meant that enemy formations over land were reported only on the basis of the sound of their engines.

High-Frequency Direction-Finding (HF/DF) – 'Pip-squeak'/'Huff-duff'

For the radar system to work, it was essential that the Sector Controllers have an accurate plot of the position of their own fighters, in order to guide them to the raiders.

The direction-finding stations – there were three of them in each sector – took bearings on transmissions from the fighter pilots' radio-telephones. To save the pilots effort, these were automatically switched to transmit for fourteen seconds in every minute of flight. The cross-bearings were translated into a map position in a D/F room, which was usually next door to the Sector Operations Room. There the Sector Controller could watch the movements of the enemy formation and of his own fighters.

Calculating quickly the compass course on which to send the fighter squadrons for accurate interception proved a vexing problem. Not only were pages of trigonometry consulted but a number of small computers were built to assist the calculation. Until one day, watching an exercise, an exasperated Wing Commander said he could judge the interception course by eye alone. He was immediately challenged to do so by the irritated boffins. He picked up the microphone that connected the Operations Room with the fighter pilots and gave them courses, until the two RAF formations taking part in the exercise met in a perfect interception.

The Wing Commander's judgment was greeted by amazed disbelief. Asked to explain how he did it, he said it was a process of imagining an isosceles triangle with the fighters and bombers at each base corner – interception would take place at the summit. He gave the course accordingly. It was a rough calculation but quite good enough to become standard procedure. The most common discrepancy, due to the superior speed of the fighters, was no real problem. The fighters were simply ordered to orbit until the bombers arrived.[1]

The System

First reports of incoming attackers were seen on the cathode-ray tubes inside the 'receiver huts' at the radar stations. Estimates of the strength, altitude, and position of the enemy were phoned from here to the Filter Room at Fighter Command HQ (although 10 Group had its own Filter Room).

On the plotting table of the Filter Room women plotters moved markers showing the reports of aircraft. Here very skilled officers had to decide which were friendly, which hostile, and which 'doubtful.' This 'filtered' information was then passed next door, to Fighter Command Operations Room, and simultaneously to Group Operations Room and to the Sector Operations Room of any sector with raiders. All of the tables in these Operations Rooms

[1]The Royal Navy found a different use for HF/DF when they adapted this method to fix the positions of enemy seaborne radio traffic. 'Huff-duff' stations, first on land and then shipborne, played such an important role in the war against the U-boat that the mast-head site of the radar aerials was used for 'huff-duff' aerials instead, and the radar attached lower.

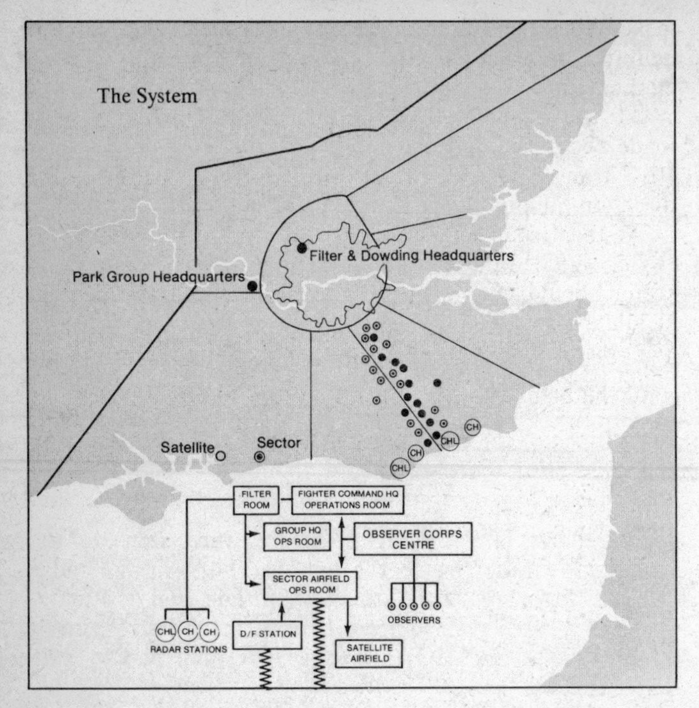

Figure 14

As the German raiders approach the coast they are picked up by two Chain Home radar stations and a Chain Home Low. These reports, together with those from Observer Corps posts (via the Observer Corps Centre at Horsham), go to the Filter Room at Fighter Command HQ.

The Filter Room staff sort out the sometimes conflicting reports and pass what they believe to be the facts.

This information goes to Fighter Command HQ, next door, and also to Group Operations Room and the Operations Room of a sector chosen by Park, the Group commander.

At the Operations Room at the sector airfield the Controller has the 'pip-squeak' reports showing where RAF fighters are. He uses these to vector his fighters to the enemy. He has more fighters at the satellite airfield. These can be put into action only by order of the Group Controller.

looked like the Filter Room tables, except that all the doubtful information and errors had (hopefully) been eliminated.

At the Command Operations Room, decisions were made about sounding the public air-raid alarms and taking BBC transmitters off the air (in case they were used for direction-finding by the German airmen).

At the Group Operations Room the Duty Group Controller watched the plotting table, in order to decide which sector should deal with the raid and how many fighters should be sent to intercept it. It was here that decisions were made about anti-aircraft gunfire, so that RAF fighters could be kept clear of it.

The Sector Operations Room was usually in the Operations Block of the most important airfield in the sector. In the same block there was a D/F room where they received the pip-squeak transmissions from RAF fighters so that these could be shown on the plot too.

The Sector Controller ordered the squadrons under his command to various states of readiness, or 'scrambled' them into the air. As with all the Operations Rooms, girl plotters received the plots over their headsets and used croupier's rakes to move coloured counters on the plotting table. The Controller – or his deputies, often NCOs – spoke with the leader of each of the fighter formations while they were flying and directed them towards the enemy. They employed simple code words intended for brevity and clarity rather than security. 'Angels' meant height, so that 'angels ten' meant 10,000 feet. 'Vector' meant steer, so 'vector 180' meant head due south. 'Pancake' meant come home and land. A 'bogey' was an unidentified aircraft and a 'bandit' an enemy one. From the fighter pilots, 'Tally-Ho!' meant enemy sighted, 'liner' was cruising speed, and 'buster' meant full throttle.

There were, of course, no radar sets of any kind in the Hurricanes and Spitfires. The fighter pilots were guided entirely by the voice of the Controller, who was watching the plotting-table map. In practice it was found that one

Controller could not manage more than two squadrons at a time, so subordinate Controllers assisted.

The importance of the country-wide network of telephone and teleprinter cables is obvious. When the bombing began, it was often only the exemplary courage of Post Office engineers that enabled Fighter Command to continue the interceptions.

Once the enemy had crossed the English coastline the only reports coming into the Operations Rooms were from the Observer Corps posts. They had no radar or detection aids of any kind. Their reports were also filtered (through

ILLUSTRATIONS

30 Waiting for take-off Pilots of 610 (County of Chester) Squadron of the Auxiliary Air Force at readiness near their Spitfires. The flying equipment proved bulky and inconvenient and these pilots preferred to fly in their ordinary uniform plus the inflatable vests that were called 'Mae Wests' to celebrate that buxom lady's figure. This Squadron moved into Biggin Hill in May 1940 and was constantly in action throughout the Battle. The original AAF pilots were all officers, so the presence of so many Sergeant Pilots shows the way in which casualties caused the Squadron to be diluted with new men.

31 Taking a prisoner A captured German NCO pilot (recognizable by the badge worn next to the Iron Cross) is given a drink by his escort. The soldier behind him is still wearing the old pre-war style tunic and the Ordnance Corps man in battledress is carrying an antiquated Canadian rifle, both signs of the depleted resources of Britain in 1940. The man in the dark uniform is a policeman and the W on the steel helmet indicates an Air Raid Warden. This photograph was taken somewhere on the south-east coast (the censor forbade more exact reference) during August 1940.

32 A convoy under attack British coastal convoys passing through the Straits of Dover came under fire from German torpedo boats, coastal gun batteries, and bombers. The British refused to believe that the Germans had excellent radar and so did not suspect that shipping movements were plotted accurately by day and night. Mostly these domestic convoys carried coal: a shifting cargo that was particularly dangerous in rough water (ships listed and continued to list more until they capsized) and one that could easily have been moved by rail. One naval spokesman admitted that the coastal convoys were simply a matter of prestige, but many airmen and sailors died.

30

31

33

34

the Observer Corps Centre at Horsham). These reports then went to Operations Rooms at all levels – Command, Group, and Sector.

Although the system might have managed without the radar units, it could never have worked without the Observer Corps. And yet, on days when the enemy formations flew over cloud, this is exactly what it was asked to do. On overcast days, the Observer Corps men could only report the sound of engines somewhere overhead.

Even on clear days it was possible for an RAF and German formation to pass through the same map square without sighting each other. There had never before been a battle in three dimensions, and never a battle moving at such speeds. Yet, for most of the fighting, the coloured counters on the plotting table were no more than four minutes – about fifteen miles – behind events. It proved good enough.

33 A major air attack on London On the afternoon of 7 September 1940 Göring moved his personal train up into the Pas de Calais so that he could watch about a thousand aircraft pass overhead on their way to attack London. Until now Hitler had forbidden attacks on the capital but he relented and few of the Luftwaffe high commanders doubted that this new tactic would make Britain sue for peace. The formations passed over Göring at about four o'clock that afternoon. This photograph was taken a few minutes later as they neared their target. Notice the curving trails at the bottom of the photograph. These are RAF fighters diving to attack. Only the very highest aircraft made condensation trails and the largest proportion of the aircraft were lower and not visible in this photograph.

34 Ammunition for a Spitfire at Duxford A Sergeant pilot sits at the controls of a Spitfire of 19 Squadron based at Duxford. This Squadron, part of the 'Duxford' wing led by Douglas Bader, had been supplied with experimental cannon-gun Spitfires which had given endless trouble. On 3 September eight of them went into battle and six aircraft had gun stoppages. This ended the experiment and the next day ordinary eight-gun Spitfires arrived, including the one in the photograph. The armourer has all four of the machine gun access panels removed and is sliding a box of ammunition through one of the hinged panels that each took two boxes. Notice the thick armour-glass on the front windscreen and the small 'door' that made it easier to climb into the cockpit in full flying equipment.

The Opposing Air Forces

In spite of the totalitarian authority that Göring and Milch wielded ruthlessly, the Luftwaffe had no proper preparations for the Second World War. Not only were there no stockpiles of such vital imports as rubber, aluminium, and magnesium but there were no proper supplies of bombs. And Milch's crash programme to make bombs from concrete was only marginally better than Hitler's crackpot idea about converting them from old gas cylinders.

The Luftwaffe had been organized as a short-range force for short wars in which it would co-operate with an advancing army. The emphasis was upon the bomber and reconnaissance units. Its theory was that the daylight bomber could wipe out the enemy air force by attacking enemy airfields. So there would be no need for night bombers or night fighters. German anti-aircraft guns were excellent and their crews well trained, but the emphasis was upon defending the advancing army and its installations rather than the homeland.

German radar development had put the emphasis upon mobility. There had been no attempt to organize any fighter defence system linked with radar, for it was considered unlikely that Germany would be threatened by sustained air bombardment. The industry of the Ruhr was an exception. It was protected in the way military objectives were. German anti-aircraft resources were suitably concentrated. It was to prove a dangerous place for RAF raiders.

For the purpose of command, Germany had been divided into four areas. For each there was an Air Fleet,[1] which contained all types of flying units: bombers, dive bombers,

[1]This 'Air Fleet system' has been harshly criticized but it was probably the most suitable system for the Luftwaffe at that time. The RAF had only gone over to the 'command system' for the RAF based in Britain. Overseas, the RAF organization resembled Air Fleets. As the war continued, the Germans modified the Air Fleet system. When Germany came under attack by heavy bombers, the Luftwaffe organized a defence system rather like the Fighter Command system that the RAF had in 1940.

fighters, etc. Each Air Fleet was self-contained to the extent of providing its own paratroops, anti-aircraft units, and administration, supply, and legal departments. Such Air Fleets followed the advancing Armies, so that by the time of the Battle of Britain the four districts of the Luftflotten had expanded into Poland and France. Additionally, a new Air Fleet had been created in Norway and Denmark, and the air space over Great Britain had already been divided into Air Fleet areas.

The system of Air Fleets prevented any German airmen from gaining the sort of political power that the 'bomber generals' later enjoyed in both the USAAF and RAF. But, while inhibiting the influence of high commanders, the Luftwaffe gave much greater power and flexibility to its medium-ranking officers.

A *Staffelkapitän*[1] could be promoted to command a *Gruppe*, and then become a *Kommodore* commanding a *Geschwader*, while continuing to fly. And German flyers had to accept the chances of assignment from bombers to fighters and reconnaissance units. Kesselring himself had been moved from the army to the air force against his wishes!

By the time of the Battle of Britain, the Luftwaffe had modified several aspects of its Air Fleet system. The *Fliegerkorps* had become more and more specialized. Bombing units employ more men – plane for plane – than the fighter units do. Perhaps this has something to do with the way the history of air warfare has shown a marked

[1]To translate the words *Geschwader*, *Gruppe*, and *Staffel* would be wrong and confusing, because the RAF also had wings, groups, and squadrons which bore no resemblance to the German formations.

Simply described, a *Geschwader* was about 100 aircraft, give or take twenty according to circumstances. It consisted of three *Gruppen*, always designated by Roman numerals I, II, or III. Finally there was the *Staffel*, about twelve aircraft. *Staffeln* were numbered from 1 to 9, in arabic numerals, to make a *Geschwader*. Thus, III/JG 26 means the third *Gruppe* of *Jagdgeschwader* (fighter *Geschwader*) number 26. While 8/KG 76 is the eighth *Staffel* of *Kampfgeschwader* (bomber *Geschwader*) number 76.

tendency for bombing specialists to dominate High Command decisions. So, in 1940, the voices of the fighter pilots were stifled at *Fliegerkorps* level. The low importance given to the Luftwaffe fighter arm contributed to the German failure in 1940.

Into the already too complex Luftwaffe command chain was now inserted a *Jagdfliegerführer* (fighter-aircraft leader). This *Jafü* had tactical control over all fighter *Geschwader* in an Air Fleet, and was responsible directly to the Air Fleet commander. It is easy to describe this as a way of concentrating the fighter strength, but the reality was somewhat different. Rather than rely upon the *Geschwader-kommodore* of each fighter and bomber unit to work out details of the fighter escort work, the new *Jafü* issued directives about formations, radio procedures, flight discipline, and tactics, so as to be sure that the bombers got the co-operation they wanted. The creation of the *Jafü* (significantly made subordinate to *Fliegerkorps* for discipline and administration) was certainly not a way of giving more authority to the fighter arm.

Comparisons – the Machines

It is difficult to compare the opposing air forces. In its simplest terms it was a battle between the RAF – which possessed 2,913 aircraft – and the whole German Luftwaffe – with 4,549 aircraft – but such comparisons are misleading. For example, the aircraft of RAF Bomber Command played only an indirect part in the Battle of Britain. Of Coastal Command's squadrons only three came under Fighter Command control to help in the air fighting. The hundreds of RAF transport and liaison aircraft were useful toys for the brass hats but they could not change the Battle's fortunes.

Even within the resources of Fighter Command, one must distinguish between an aircraft classified as 'serviceable' (which means a pilot can sign for it and fly it away) and an aircraft classified as 'available' (which might mean

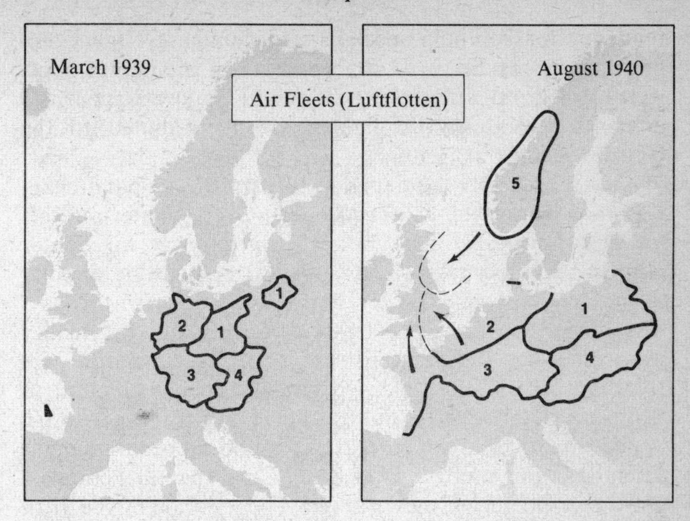

Figure 15

Germany was divided into four areas, for each of which there was a self-contained Air Fleet. These had their own communications system, command, and administration with separate signals and even legal departments. The map at the left shows the Air Fleets in March 1939 after Czechoslovakia had been annexed.

By the summer of 1940 the Air Fleets had been expanded to cover the newly conquered lands. The conquest of Poland had joined East Prussia to central Germany. With the air war against England in progress, Air Fleet 2 had become more important than Air Fleet 1. And a new Air Fleet – Air Fleet 5, based in Norway and Denmark – had been added after the conquest of Scandinavia.

anything from needing a tyre inflated to needing a major overhaul). On 20 July, Dowding had 531 fighters serviceable, out of a total of 609. In reserve he had another 289 fighters.

But while all bureaucracy is devious, military bureaucracy is conspiratorial. And so the effectiveness of the opposing forces cannot be judged by numbers alone. For instance, the RAF measured the efficiency of its squadrons (and its commanders) by the percentage of aircraft that were kept 'serviceable.' So there was a great emphasis, if not to say an obsession, on keeping this figure high. But all aircraft require inspections, checks, and replacements, according to how many hours they fly. So some of the squadrons with the highest percentages of aircraft serviceable had the lowest number of flying hours (a squadron could get 100 per cent aircraft permanently serviceable if it never flew at all).

The 1940 battles forced all the squadrons to maximize their flying hours. In combat, pilots are permitted to use 'panic boost' for a few minutes, which causes immense wear on engines. All this resulted in a dramatic fall in serviceability percentages. Eventually 'serviceability percentages' were seen to be a very misleading indication of efficiency, and squadrons were encouraged to find optimum serviceability percentages instead of maximum ones.

A comparison of aircraft totals is even more misleading when applied to the German air force. It also had a large proportion of transport and liaison aircraft that would play no direct part in the Battle. Neither would the squadrons based in Poland, southern Germany, and Austria nor the single-seat fighters in Norway with not even range enough to get across the North Sea.

The German air force had no reserve of aircraft, in the way that the British did, but the Luftwaffe did draw upon units that were not, at first, engaged in the fighting. The all-important Messerschmitt Bf 109 single-seat fighters were being made at the rate of 140 per month. British industry, newly galvanized by Beaverbrook, were by the time of the Battle turning out Hurricanes and Spitfires at the rate of nearly 500 a month.

The quality of the aircraft designs is of more importance than totals. There were four types of bombers in use by the German Air Fleets in the summer of 1940, and it must be emphasized that the descriptions that follow refer to these alone, and not necessarily to subsequent models of the same aircraft.

Dornier Do 17Z and Dornier Do 215

The oldest type still in operational use in 1940 was the Dornier Do 17, the 'Flying Pencil,' which still equipped about a quarter of the bomber and reconnaissance units facing Britain. During the Battle production ceased and the type was being phased out.

In 1934, when this design was on the drawing board, civil airlines still cherished the idea that there was big money to be made from air mail. But those hopes, and the cramped Dornier prototype, were put into storage as times changed and airlines counted their success in passenger miles. Resurrected by the Luftwaffe, the Do 17 enjoyed a brief moment of glory at the Zürich Air Show in 1937, when it was equipped with Daimler-Benz DB 600A motors and proved faster than any fighter anywhere in squadron service.

But Willy Messerschmitt won the battle for Daimler-Benz engines (to put in his Bf 109s), and the '*Schnellbomber*' had to make do with whatever power-plants Dornier could get. And while the Dornier's speed decreased, fast monoplane fighters came into service. In an effort to put new life into his 'Pencil,' Dornier called his export Do 17Z a Do 215, and later variants (some of which got the coveted DB 601 engines) were expressly designed for reconnaissance duties. For photographic flights, its very small payload did not matter. In spite of its comparatively low speed and a complete absence of protective armour, it was popular with crews, who considered it strong and reliable, and stable in flight.

Heinkel He 111

This was the most numerous of the Air Fleet's bombers. It was a robust airframe that readily adapted to considerable modification. Since the Spanish Civil War it had been given a whole new glazed nose section. It could carry almost double the bomb-load of the Do 17. But Heinkel, too, had sacrificed his Daimler-Benz engines to Willy Messerschmitt. The He 111P (with DB 601A engines like the Bf 109E) had now been followed by the He 111H, with Jumo 211A engines. It was now the slowest of the twin-engined bombers, even slower than the Do 17. To sweeten the pill for the crews assigned to them, the new Heinkels were being given a great deal of protective armour (up to 600 lbs of it) and extra machine guns. But the He 111 proved inadequate against a determined defence and although it continued in use on other fronts, Heinkels in the west were relegated first to night bombing (by mid-September 1940), and then to anti-shipping and transport work.

Figure 16 Inside a Heinkel He 111

A German war artist's version of the Battle of Britain as it might have been seen from the flight deck of a Heinkel He 111 attacked by RAF fighters.

Junkers Ju 88A

Not only the best bomber in service with the Luftwaffe, this was probably the best one in service anywhere at the time (entirely comparable with the later RAF Mosquito). It was produced at an astounding speed, going from drawing board to first flight in the single year of 1936.

Too late for the Spanish Civil War, it had service trials in the spring of 1939. Although its bomb-load was much less than that of the He 111, the Junkers bomber was much faster, and unit war diaries of 1940 showed that men of the German bomber force had a better chance to fight and survive in this bomber than in any other.

The decision to add a dive-bomber requirement to the Junkers Ju 88's role brought problems of over-stressed airframes. Crews were given cautionary instructions about aerobatics, and this gave rise to rumours and doubts about the bomber's airworthiness. This situation was not improved by the high casualties that bomber fleets suffered in 1940, and was compounded by *Feldmarschall* Milch, who, motivated by spite and ambition, conducted a campaign against the Junkers Ju 88. It was a campaign from which this fine Junkers aircraft never completely recovered.

Junkers Ju 87B

Developed from an early Junkers design after Udet saw a demonstration by Curtiss Helldivers, the Ju 87 was in a quite different category from the medium bombers of the *Kampfgeschwader*. This single-engined machine, with its massive cranked wings, spatted undercarriage, and screaming sirens, had earned sole title to the generic word 'Stuka' (dive bomber).

For the Luftwaffe High Command the Ju 87 seemed to provide precision bombing in a way that was very cheap in money, materials, and manpower. Delicately balanced, a delight to fly, it was one of the most specialized designs ever to go into large-scale production. There was a window

Junkers Ju 88 Dive Bombers

Figure 17

An advertisement produced by the Junkers aircraft company.

in the floor so that the pilot could spot the target, and there were lines inscribed on the canopy to gauge the angle of dive. An automatic trim change was connected to the dive-brakes. These air-brakes made the dive – vertical if the pilot was experienced – very slow, so that his aiming could be done with great care. But the Junkers Ju 87B – the type used in 1940 – could carry only a 1,100-lb bomb or one 550-lb and four 110-lb bombs, while the Do 17 carried 2,200 lbs and the He 111 4,400 lbs, in any configuration of types and sizes. The Ju 87B's range limited it to targets well within 200 miles of its base, which meant the English coastal region. And the very poor aerodynamic shape of the aircraft meant there was little chance of improving the bomb-load or of adding armour. Even during the fighting in Poland, the 'Bertha' had suffered severe casualties in the face of small-arms and anti-aircraft guns. So at the time of the Battle of Britain the far better Ju

87D was on the drawing board. Meanwhile the Stuka crews had to manage with the Bertha, which with a top speed of 232 mph was the slowest operational aircraft used by either side.

The Ju 87R (*Reichweite:* range) was no better than the B version except in having long-range fuel tanks. These aircraft were flying in early 1940. The first deliveries went to the highly skilled I/StG 1.

The Stuka units were still getting a great deal of publicity from the propaganda machine. For a keen young pilot there was more prestige in a posting to a Stuka unit (or to a Messerschmitt Bf 110 unit) than in being chosen for single-engine fighters.

Messerschmitt Bf 109 and Bf 110

The Luftwaffe's fighter force consisted of two types of fighters. The only single-seat fighter in service was the Messerschmitt Bf 109. Its range was limited. From the most northerly of France's airfields it could get only as far as London and back.

However, the Luftwaffe had faced up to the problem of fighter protection for bomber fleets in a way that no other air force had done. It had provided long-range fighters for the escort role. These twin-engined Messerschmitt Bf 110s had been given the excellent DB 601A engines, and the pick of the Luftwaffe's fighter pilots had been taken from Bf 109 units. It was part of a plan to establish Göring's *Zerstörer* (destroyer wings) as elite units.

The Bf 110 was a much maligned aircraft and has often been written off by historians as a negligible factor in the 1940 battles. It was worth giving it respectful attention. Built into the nose of the Bf 110 there was a battery of four 7.92-mm MG 17 machine guns and two 20-mm MG FF cannons. There was also a rear-facing machine gun for the second crewman.

It is easy, with the advantage of hindsight, to scorn the Luftwaffe's *Zerstörer* theories. But the Luftwaffe kept the

Bf 110 in production until the last days of the war, providing it all that time with the same high-performance engines that were needed by the single-seat fighters. And the role of any fighter is two-fold: the Bf 110 was not able to tackle enemy fighters on equal terms but it was effective, later in the war, used against bombers. On the eastern front and against the USAAF Fortresses in daylight, and with airborne radar – in the night-fighter role – the 'Ironside' earned its keep. It was about the cheapest twin-engined operational machine used by the Germans.

Even for the exacting, sometimes impossible, task of escorting the 1940 bomber fleets, the Bf 110 was not a complete failure. The 110's turning circle was very wide, and its acceleration poor, but its speed of 336 mph was very nearly as fast as a Spitfire, and much faster than any Hurricane.[1]

The Bf 110 was a heavy machine, well suited to the classic fighter pilot's tactic of diving upon an enemy, delivering a long burst from the forward-facing armament (which from the Bf 110 was usually fatal), and then breaking contact to run for it. As high escort, confined to this tactic, it was formidable.

Comparisons – the Men

The Germans had no shortage of pilots and air crews. For years pilots had been coming from the training schools at the rate of 800 per month, and a high proportion of German crews had flown under combat conditions in Spain, Poland, and France. Their tactics were tried and tested and their flying skills incomparably better than those of the RAF squadrons.

Göring had ensured that his Luftwaffe would attract a very high standard of recruit. To this purpose he arranged that the pay, uniforms, and conditions were excellent.

[1]Dowding himself wrote that the top speed of six Hurricanes tested in speed trials averaged 305 mph. At 16,400 feet, this was the speed at which the Bf 110 could cruise!

C. G. Grey, an English visitor to the pre-war Luftwaffe unit at Gatow-Kadow, 'was taken into a big Mess with an attractive bar, a reading room and a silence room for writing and I remarked that their officers were lucky to have such comfort.' But this was the Mess for the transport drivers. Taken to the Officers' Mess, he found it 'more like a luxury hotel than any kind of military establishment. It was comfortable as though intended for the use of civilized people, whereas, as I wrote at the time, every [Royal] Air Force Mess that I had been in looked as if it had been designed and equipped by the Sanitary Section of the Prisons Board.' The sleeping accommodation was not big barracks and huge dormitories but small bedrooms for three, four, or five airmen. Each was decorated with soft furnishings, framed pictures, and cut flowers in vases.

And Göring arranged that when an airman's service expired there were jobs open in civil aviation, which Göring also controlled. Government loans were available. While the relationship between officers and men in the RAF was excellent, C. G. Grey – who had been so impressed with the standards of the German accommodation – made a special point of the 'comradeship' that existed between all ranks of German airmen. There was a clear-cut line between officers and men but 'the line was not a barrier.' Grey's opinions are worth recording for three reasons: he was an expert observer, with no sympathy for Nazism, and was writing while the war was still being fought!

As might be expected, German flying training was very thorough. Pilots posted to bomber squadrons usually arrived having had about 250 hours' flying experience, including lots of night flying and another 50 hours of simulated blind-flying in the Link trainer. And at the specialist school, the pilots would have been flying the type of aircraft that they would have at the squadrons, and with the same crews.

The emphasis was on the bomber force, and it was not the pilot who captained the aircraft, it was the observer. Such captains were trained to do the job of every member

Figure 18

The Luftwaffe Chain of Command – from Hitler to Bomber Crew

Hitler combined supreme civil power (including the control of police and SS units) with the role of supreme commander of the armed forces (Wehrmacht).

The *OKW* was no more than the 'office' through which Hitler controlled the Wehrmacht.

OKH. High Command of the army. Until Hitler used the OKW to undermine its authority, all army operational orders originated here.

OKM. Naval High Command. As OKH.

Only Göring and Milch combined the civil authority of the Air Ministry with command of the air force. Göring was Commander in Chief of the Luftwaffe (*OB.d.L.*) and his command was not called OKL until 1944.

The *Air Fleets* were self-contained organizations, from signals to weather forecasting, and each had defined territories in which to operate.

Originally the *Fliegerkorps* was intended as a 'general' HQ of mixed units but by now they were specialized. This one was a long-range bomber and reconnaissance command.

The *Geschwader* had been intended as the largest formation with one type of aircraft, but because old Dorniers were being replaced by newer Heinkels this could not be kept to. A *Geschwader* theoretically had 120 aircraft (3 × 39 plus a Staff Flight) but during the Battle of Britain some had no more than 80. A *Geschwader* commander was called a *Kommodore* irrespective of his rank.

A *Gruppe* was normally kept together on one airfield.

A *Staffel* consisted of 10–12 aircraft, almost invariably of the same type. It was led by a *Staffelkapitän* (irrespective of rank). The *Staffeln* are always numbered

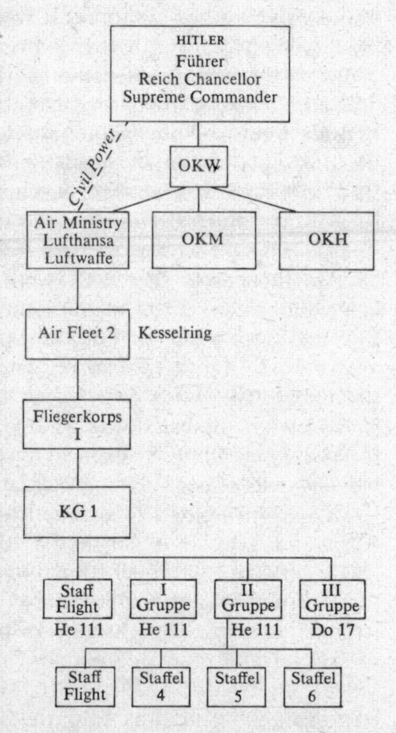

1, 2, 3, etc., while the *Gruppen* are shown as I, II, III.

Notice the way in which the *Staffeln* are numbered through the whole *Geschwader*, so that 9/KG 1 is obviously a *Staffel* of *III Gruppe*.

of the crew, including the pilot's. The captain had usually done about 150 flying hours as a pilot, as well as being skilled in navigation, radio, gunnery, and bomb-aiming.

When war began, all training was shortened and simplified. During 1940 more and more captains were put into the pilot's seat. Such men were given a special 'double badge' – and provided a cadre of skilled men quite beyond those of any other air force. It was these exceptional flyers that became casualties and prisoners during 1940. No wonder then that so many of the Luftwaffe's survivors looked back to 1940 as the turning point in its fortunes. All the air forces of the belligerents changed as they brought in conscripts to dilute the professionals, but for the USAAF and the RAF the training became more realistic and in some ways much better than it had been in peacetime. For the Germans it would only get worse.

As war began the RAF were getting only 200 pilots each month from the training schools, and the quality of training was low. As late as December 1939, one fully operational fighter squadron had to borrow a Harvard training plane when four pilots arrived from the training school having never flown a monoplane. Soon afterwards a new Commanding Officer arrived and admitted he had never flown a monoplane either.

In the spring of 1940, Squadron Leader Johnny Kent, a Canadian regular officer and RAF test pilot, managed to get a posting to an operational squadron. He described his brief course at the Operational Training Unit in stark terms. He fired the eight guns of his Hurricane at a ground target set up in the Dee Estuary. After a half-second burst, all his eight guns failed to fire. When he returned cursing jammed guns, he was told that he had used up all the bullets they could spare. Kent said 'many of the new boys never fired their guns at all until they went into action for the first time.' There was virtually no instruction or practice in air-firing at all. Hardly any of Kent's instructors had been on operations and one had not served on a squadron for over three years.

The peacetime RAF concentrated upon the sort of tight formation flying that was a feature of the air displays. Gunnery was the most neglected aspect of the fighter squadrons' work. To say that RAF fighter pilots were inferior in marksmanship to the Luftwaffe crews is misleading. Few RAF fighter pilots had had sufficient gunnery experience to know what their skills might be.

By the spring of 1940 the weaknesses of the Auxiliary Air Force scheme were becoming evident. Not only were the AAF pilots considerably older than the average, but these men had grown up in the same neighbourhoods and these squadrons had the special intimacy of a happy club. (Inevitably one compares the 'Pals Battalions' of the First

ILLUSTRATIONS

35 Two Hawker Hurricanes of 501 (County of Gloucester) Squadron These aircraft are taking off from the satellite airfield at Hawkinge on 15 August 1940. The machine on the left is flown by Flying Officer K.N.T. Lee, remembered by his friend, Billy Drake, as one of the few flyers to be totally without fear. He scored six victories before being killed.

On the day this photograph was taken the air fighting was dramatic and extensive; this Auxiliary Air Force squadron shot down two Junkers Ju 87B dive-bombers of 10/LG 1 near Folkestone.

The short life of fighter aircraft at this time is exemplified by P 3208 SD–T, seen on the right. It came out of the factory on 6 July and lasted 28 flying hours. Both these Hurricanes were written off three days after this photograph was taken when on 18 August, 501 Squadron flying out of Hawkinge lost no less than seven aircraft.

36 A propaganda exercise Unteroffizier Horst Perez, pilot of this Bf 109E of II/JG 26, could never have guessed, as he took off from his airfield at Marquise-Ost in the Pas de Calais, that his aircraft was on its way to the New York docks, where this photograph was taken. This Messerschmitt, from Galland's *Schlageter Geschwader*, was shot down at East Dean, near Eastbourne. The British realized that winning the Battle was only marginally more important than convincing the USA that they were winning. Only then would they get the supplies, the financial credit and the political and moral support that was needed so desperately. It was shipped to America and Canada as part of the 'Bundles for Britain' campaign.

35

36

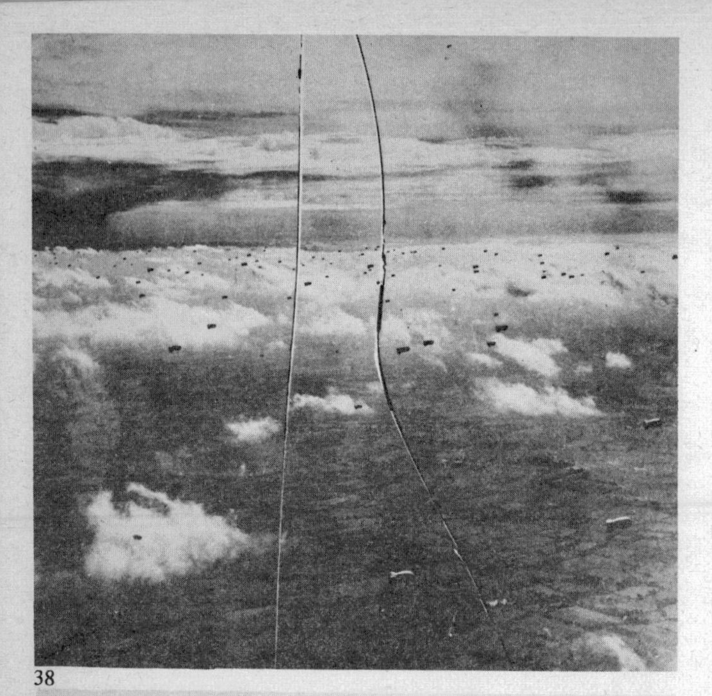
38

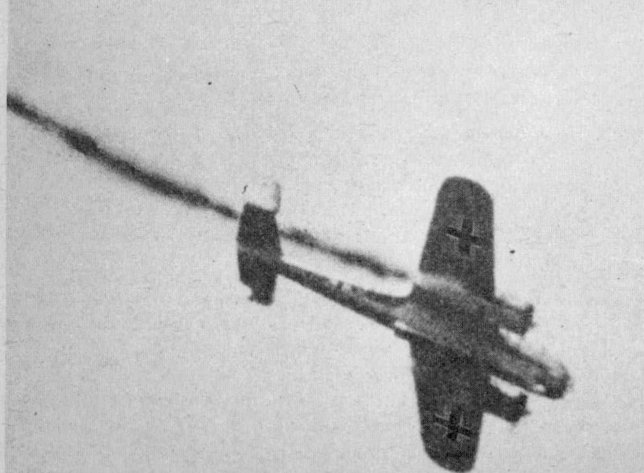
39

World War in which men who joined the army together remained together.)

To such communities death comes as a terrible blow. The icy reserve that the veteran uses to protect himself against grief was not available to the men of the AAF. By the end of July – before the Battle of Britain really began – 609 Squadron had lost seven of its original twelve pilots (plus two of its replacements). Even highly professional military formations cannot endure those kind of losses.

And it was becoming evident that only very exceptional men could continue to function as fighter pilots after the age of thirty. This eliminated more AAF flyers, although

37 Dorniers over England The Dornier originated as the 'Flying Pencil' and was intended as a high-speed civil aircraft that would earn money from air mail. From this notion came the idea of the '*Schnellbomber*' that would be able to fly faster than the fighters that chased it. But the improvement in fighter design meant that the Dorniers were vulnerable. To minimize casualties the Germans evolved a technique of bombing from a shallow dive that increased the bomber's speed. After bombing, the lightened Dorniers could escape by very low-level flying so that the ground Observers did not see them until they were almost overhead. In this German photograph a formation of Dorniers is seen flying low over the English countryside, possibly in the approach run to such an attack. Notice the variation in German markings: the crosses on the second machine's wings are almost twice the size of the others.

38 The balloon barrage (steel cables suspended to protect vital places against low-flying attacks) seen from the air This remarkable photograph provides an idea of how frightening a balloon barrage could be to a flyer, even if the whole idea was treated with derision by most people on the ground. The two vertical lines are damage to the negative; the photographer has used a glass negative.

39 A Dornier in flames Sunday 18 August was a day of extensive air fighting. *Kampfgeschwader 76* was sent to attack airfields near London, and its Dornier 17s bombed Biggin Hill, Kenley, and Croydon. This photograph was taken by a news agency on that day. Although the wartime censor has deleted the location of the crash, it is reasonably certain to be one of the two Dorniers downed near to the airfields. The discreet retouching of the German markings – perhaps to reassure newspaper readers at the time – does nothing to detract from this remarkable photo.

they were valuable additions to Training Command. Aware of the lowering of morale, Fighter Command began assigning tough Regulars to the squadrons. Soon all that remained of the Auxiliary Air Force were squadron badges and memories.

Comparisons – the Commanders

The Luftwaffe, hitherto a tactical supplement to the blitzkrieg, a force that had taken orders from the army, was about to take upon itself a strategic role. Moreover, it was asked to create a strategy, and then to translate that strategy into day-to-day tactical objectives for its bombers and fighters. The experience of its staff officers was not equal to this task.

As Keith Park left his job as Dowding's Chief of Staff to become Commander of 11 Group, so Albert Kesselring moved into his office in occupied Brussels and deployed Air Fleet 2 for the coming battle. So far there had been no conferences, no staff studies, and no close co-operation with Sperrle, commanding neighbouring Air Fleet 3. When, on 30 June, Göring issued his general directive, it talked of cutting Britain off from its supplies, and of destroying the RAF, but in fact it was little more than a legal authorization for the money that Kesselring and Sperrle were now spending on the captured air bases.

One of the great successes of the Luftwaffe's operations in May and June had been the way the Junkers Ju 52 transport planes had moved personnel and equipment forward to the newly occupied airfields. The Luftwaffe Signals Service used the Junkers aircraft as flying radio stations and direction-finding units. This had been a vital, but little publicized, part of the victories but now the confusion of that leap-frogging of bases had to be sorted out. Phone and Telex networks were being laid, hangars built, runways lengthened; spare parts, ammunition, bombs, and all the complexities of the air war required suitable buildings, as did the men.

A great deal of money was spent on the anti-aircraft defences for nearly a hundred newly acquired airfields, although the Germans were not to know that Dowding had already decided he had no fighters to spare for attacks against the Luftwaffe bases. Later, some experts criticized this decision but there is little doubt that such 'intruder' flights by the RAF would have confused the already complex radar picture to a state of chaos.

'Smiling Albert' Kesselring, 55 years old, was one of the most skilful and popular German commanders. Later in the war he was to make a new reputation as a commander of land forces in Italy.

He had been moved from the army to the air force against his will but once there he dedicated himself to the job. At the advanced age of 48 he learned to fly and usually piloted himself on his visits to units. In the 1930s he had become the Luftwaffe Chief of Staff. As a spokesman for the professionals, Kesselring had often found himself in conflict with Göring and Milch.

It was after one such terrible row with Milch that Kesselring asked to be retired. Alarmed by the idea of losing one of the Luftwaffe's very best men, Göring talked him into staying, and offered him command of an Air Fleet as a way of distancing himself from Milch.

When war began the shrewd and ambitious Milch realized that, as the emphasis changed from civil aviation to military force, the experience that had given him his initial start in the Air Ministry was being eroded by the knowledge and training of the long-time professional soldiers around him. Milch decided that a field command would consolidate his strong position.[1]

Milch's allegiance to Hitler was unequivocal. Whether this was due to his monarchist inclinations or his instinct for survival, it certainly proved valuable when on bad terms with Göring, as now he was. Often it was rumoured, in the

[1]As war began, with the German invasion of Poland, Göring and Milch had already arranged the withdrawal of their own close relatives from front-line units to safer jobs in the rear.

corridors of the vast Air Ministry building, that Milch was about to take over Göring's job, to which Göring countered with rumours that Udet was about to take over from Milch.

Hitler had taken a personal interest in the Luftwaffe's bomb shortage (refusing until 12 October 1939 to allow the manufacture of more of them, on the grounds that Britain and France would soon make peace with him). When bomb manufacture was resumed, Milch managed to get control of it instead of relying upon Udet's Air Armament Department. And as part of his plan to become a field commander Milch had taken a Dornier Do 17 for himself and flown over the Polish battlefronts, including a flight to watch the Stukas bombing Warsaw into rubble.

When a Bf 108 courier aircraft forced-landed in Belgium in January 1940, carrying plans pertaining to the imminent invasion of that neutral country and its neighbours, the commander of Air Fleet 2 was fired. It was exactly the job that Milch wanted. But Göring told Milch that, although he agreed to such an appointment, there was an objection from the Luftwaffe Chief of Staff. The objection is easy to understand but the idea that Göring would have heeded it, less so.

By this time Göring had realized that whatever shortcomings Udet had – and they were many and varied – he presented no danger to Göring's power. Outsiders were always tempted to guess (wrongly) that Göring and Udet had been close friends since the First World War but now a real friendship had grown between the two of them. Göring's door was always open to Udet, who sometimes went to him with departmental problems that he did not want Milch to know about. And Udet no longer referred to Göring as 'the Fat One,' using instead the more respectful nickname 'Iron Man.' And Udet trusted *Der Eiserner* in a way that no adroit politician could possibly deserve.

Göring was well aware of his right-hand man's limitless ambition and when Milch's attempt to get command of Air Fleet 2 was blocked, Göring was happy to see this key post

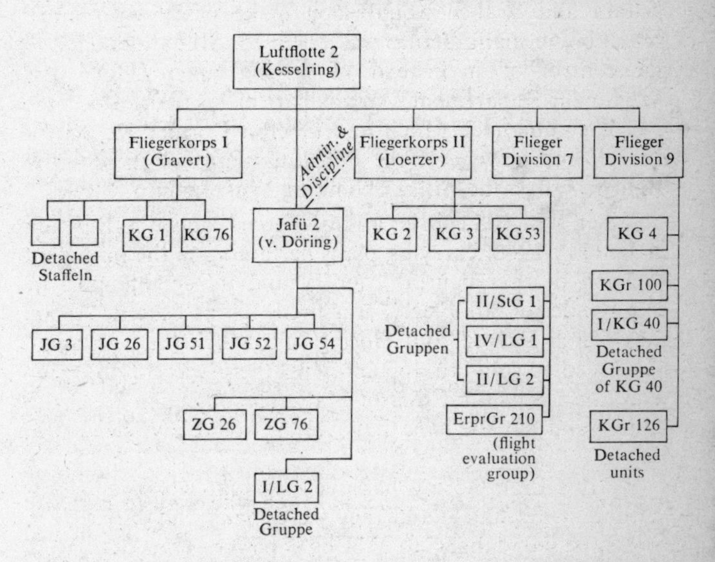

Figure 19

LG=*Lehrgeschwader*, or teaching or experiment wings (now doing combat flying)
StG=*Stukageschwader*, or dive-bombing wing
KG=*Kampfgeschwader*, or bomber wing
JG=*Jagdgeschwader*, or fighter wing
ZG=*Zerstörergeschwader*, or destroyer wing (twin-engined Bf 110 fighters)
II/LG 2=The second *Gruppe* of LG 2
4/LG 2=The fourth *Staffel* of LG 2

Note: I/LG 2 was flying Bf 109Es and under command of *Jafü*, while II/LG 2 was in *Fliegerkorps II* flying fighter-bombers.

given to Kesselring (no friend of Milch, as his previous offer to resign indicated).

But for a man keen to get to a battlefront, Berlin was the place to be in 1940. Milch now turned his eyes to the coming invasion of Scandinavia. This campaign was planned and conducted under the personal direction of Hitler. For the transport of soldiers to Norway, a special unit was created from Lufthansa air crews, under the supervision of that company's traffic manager. This was the sort of operation that Milch could handle expertly. After the initial assault had been successful, Milch was permitted to reorganize the Luftwaffe's units in Scandinavia so that they became Air Fleet 5. During the days before the newly appointed commander of the Air Fleet arrived, Milch achieved his ambition of commanding an air force in battle. As a result, Milch was given the coveted Knight's Cross. The 'tin tie' was the highest award for valour in Hitler's Germany and more usually awarded to Luftwaffe aces who had shot down twenty enemy aircraft.

Now Milch found it difficult to reconcile himself to the desk in Berlin. He took his personal aeroplanes to the west front and followed the fighting across France. He regularly visited the operational units and liked to watch bombing operations from the air. It was Milch who went to Dunkirk and afterwards told Göring that the air bombardment had not destroyed the British Expeditionary Force nor prevented its evacuation. This did nothing to sober Göring's over-confidence about the coming assault against Britain. And for that, too, Milch had an idea that was no less than Napoleonic. He urged an immediate paratroop landing on selected airfields in southern England (paratroops were a part of the Luftwaffe). Fighter and dive-bomber squadrons would then fly into the captured airfields to use them, while transport aircraft would ferry troops in. Luckily for the Stuka units and the Junkers transports – which had suffered no less than 40 per cent casualties in the Dutch fighting – Göring shrugged off this lunatic idea with the excuse that he had only one paratroop division, and he knew the army would never agree to lend him men for such an operation. Milch listed this as Germany's first big mistake.

Hugo Sperrle, commander of Air Fleet 3, was a year older than Kesselring and eight years older than Milch. He was a huge bear-like man whose slow movements and style made some condemn him as lazy. Milch thought this, just as Sperrle regarded his boss as no more than an airline official dressed up in soldier's uniform, and yet the two men got along well together.

Sperrle was far more experienced in air force matters than any other senior officer. He had been a military flyer in the First World War, had commanded the Condor Legion in Spain, and had spent a long period in his present job of Air Fleet commander. But he was a forbidding man, with no taste for the techniques of the propaganda units with their writers, cameramen, and film crews. Sperrle, a large man with heavy jowls, is invariably pictured with a scowl that was perhaps necessary to hold his monocle in place. Not only was Sperrle's physical girth comparable with that of Göring but so was his life-style. Sperrle took as his HQ the fabulous Palais du Luxembourg, one-time palace of Marie de Médicis. Of him Albert Speer said,

Udet's Caricature of Milch

Figure 20

Keen for a combat command, Erhard Milch used his position as Inspector General to hurry from battlefront to battlefront – he watched the bombing of Warsaw from the air – and he was never short of advice or criticism.

Figure 21 Sperrle and Kesselring

The great bear-like Hugo Sperrle commanded Air Fleet 3 from Paris, while 'Smiling Albert' Kesselring commanded neighbouring Air Fleet 2 from Brussels, or sometimes from the underground HQ in the Pas de Calais that his staff called the 'Holy Mountain.' Here the two men who fought the Battle of Britain from the German side of the Channel are seen as drawn by Udet.

'The Field Marshal's craving for luxury and public display ran a close second to that of his superior, Göring.'

When, in July 1940, the Luftwaffe's one Field Marshal (Göring) was increased to three (with Göring raised to a newly created rank even higher), it was these men – Milch, Kesselring, and Sperrle – who were so honoured. Kesselring later said that these promotions took place only because Hitler believed that the war in the west was virtually ended. In fact it was about to begin, and it was a daunting prospect by any standard. Not only were the Luftwaffe chiefs attempting a form of conquest – victory by bombardment – that was unprecedented in the history of warfare but they had to work with a time limit. Mastery of the air must be German before the coming of the autumn storms that would make seaborne invasion virtually impossible. And in spite of the high morale that had been a product of the German victories, the Luftwaffe had suffered serious losses. If aircraft lost in flying accidents are included in the total, the months of May and June cost the Luftwaffe no less than 1,469 aircraft. Now the Air Fleets needed time to replenish and reorganize, but no time was to be granted.

The same could be said of RAF Fighter Command. The best had been given to 11 Group in south-east England but it was by no means ready for battle, while fighter squadrons elsewhere in Britain were, at this time, in chaos. At least one squadron was still flying old Hurricanes with fabric-covered wings. No. 73 Squadron had been the last to withdraw from France, where in a previous war its Sopwith Camels had flown. It had numbered 'Cobber' Kain, one of the RAF's first aces, in its ranks. But every one of its Hurricanes was undergoing repair, and there were only seven pilots fit to fly. No. 87 Squadron had only half its establishment of ground crews, and there were no armourers at all. Every squadron had shortages of some kind, and by the beginning of July, one third of the RAF's operational aircraft still had not been fitted with the IFF device that distinguished them, on the radar, from enemy blips.

Dowding – Fighter Command Commander in Chief – was deeply concerned with the task of bringing his squadrons to battle readiness, but he was keeping one eye on the calendar. His Air Ministry bosses had fixed 14 July as the day he must retire. Incredibly, the men of Whitehall had ignored all Dowding's enquiries about this forcible ending of his career, and it was not until 5 July that the Air Staff deigned to answer him. A smooth letter from the Chief of Air Staff said he would be very glad if Dowding could continue until the end of October.

Understandably irritated, Dowding replied: 'Apart from the question of discourtesy, which I do not wish to stress, I must point out the lack of consideration involved in delaying a proposal of this nature until ten days before the

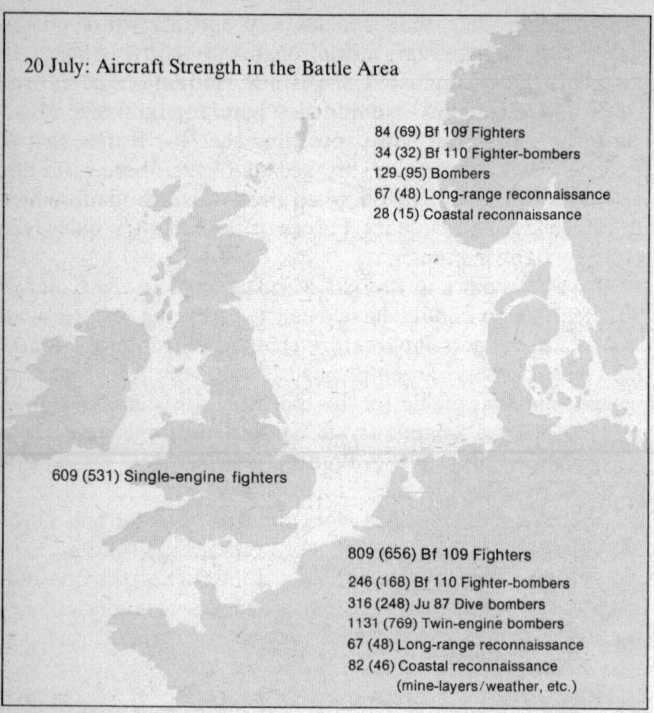

20 July: Aircraft Strength in the Battle Area

84 (69) Bf 109 Fighters
34 (32) Bf 110 Fighter-bombers
129 (95) Bombers
67 (48) Long-range reconnaissance
28 (15) Coastal reconnaissance

609 (531) Single-engine fighters

809 (656) Bf 109 Fighters
246 (168) Bf 110 Fighter-bombers
316 (248) Ju 87 Dive bombers
1131 (769) Twin-engine bombers
67 (48) Long-range reconnaissance
82 (46) Coastal reconnaissance
(mine-layers/weather, etc.)

Figure 22

The figure shows the aircraft on hand, followed in parentheses by the aircraft actually serviceable and ready to fly. The single-engine fighter strength of the opposing forces is shown in large figures. The single-seat fighters in Norway and Denmark were for local defence and did not have enough range to cross the North Sea.

RAF fighters include 27 Boulton Paul Defiant fighters which had proved, on 19 July, to be no match for the Bf 109, and were soon withdrawn from the fighting.

date of my retirement. I have had four retiring dates given to me and now you are proposing a fifth . . .'

Dowding suggested that the Air Ministry stick to the

first retiring date that had been proposed, which would retire him in two years' time, on his sixtieth birthday. In his reply Dowding listed the other retirement dates and short-notice changes. He added a petulant reminder about his brush with Churchill concerning the Hurricanes sent to France. 'I am anxious to stay because I feel there is no one else who will fight as I do when proposals are made which would reduce the Defence Forces of the Country below the extreme danger point.'

It was a rebuke to the Air Minister, and to the Chief of Air Staff, who should have been confronting the Cabinet with these dangers long before the personal intervention of Dowding himself. To emphasize the way he felt, Dowding sent a copy of the letter to the Air Minister as well as replying to the Chief of Air Staff. Dowding's reply was well justified but it did nothing to help his cause. His enemies were biding their time.

There were soft replies from the Air Minister and Chief of Air Staff, the latter smoothly remarking that he 'was glad to have your support at the Cabinet when the question of sending fighter squadrons to France was under consideration.' Having rewritten history to his own satisfaction, the Chief of Air Staff refused to give Dowding any assurance that he would be kept in the RAF beyond October. But Dowding felt reassured. At last he had given his grievance an airing, and compared with his previous treatment – rude letters, curt telephone calls, and ignored requests for information – smooth evasions were a decided improvement. For the time being, he seemed to have only the Luftwaffe fighting against him.

PART FOUR

Tactics

'The odds were great; our margins small; the stakes infinite.'

—WINSTON S. CHURCHILL

The supply of missiles – rock, spear, or arrow – had limited the duration of ancient battles, as had fatigue and darkness. Only when armies were supplied on the battlefield did the word 'battle' cease to mean a short clash of arms by daylight. By the twentieth century, the length of battle was unlimited. The Battle of Britain lasted not hours but months. I have divided the battle into four phases. Each is marked by a change in German tactics and targets but the four phases are not precise ones. The periods overlap, techniques were tried out side by side, and different types of target came under attack on the same day.

PHASE ONE Starting in July there was a month of attacks on British coastal convoys and air battles over the Channel: *Kanalkampf*.

PHASE TWO From 12 August – the eve of *Adlertag* (Eagle Day) – came the major assault. Göring and Nazi propaganda writers called it *Adlerangriff* (Eagle Attack). It continued for just over a week.

PHASE THREE What the RAF called 'the critical period', in which RAF fighter airfields in south-east England were priority objectives. This lasted from 24 August until 6 September.

PHASE FOUR From 7 September. The attacks centred on London, first by daylight and then by night.

Phase One: *Kanalkampf*, the Battles over the Channel

To begin, *Oberst* Johannes Fink, *Geschwaderkommodore* of the bomber unit KG 2, was created the *Kanalkampf-führer* (commander of the air fighting over the Channel).

His task was to close the Channel to British shipping. To do it he was given command of two *Stukagruppen* and a *Jagdgeschwader* of fighters to add to his own bombers. Fink set up a command post on Cap Blanc Nez, five miles west of Calais, in a bus parked very near the statue of Louis Blériot, first man to cross the Channel by air.

There was sound reasoning behind the German attacks against coastal shipping in July and early August. It had been decided that the Luftwaffe would launch its major offensive only after Hitler gave the order. It was presumed that the Supreme Commander was co-ordinating the plans of the army and navy: timing the air offensive so that the invading army would find the British defenders stunned into the sort of paralysis that the Luftwaffe had produced in France and Poland.

Meanwhile attacks against Channel convoys were a 'heads I win, tails you lose' proposition. If the RAF sent fighters to cover the shipping, they would be drawn into a battle of attrition and made tired before the Germans launched *Adlerangriff*. If RAF Fighter Command refused to be drawn, the bombers would sink the British ships.

Dowding had not calculated for shipping protection in his original plans, and now he warned the Air Staff, and the Admiralty too, that he could only protect shipping by committing a dangerously high proportion of his total force. So the convoys could have only minimal air support.

Britain's radar network was not very effective during this *Kanalkampf*, for the fighters and bombers of the Air Fleets could climb to operating heights and get into formation out of 'sight' of the British radar. To cross the Channel took only five minutes but a Spitfire needed fifteen minutes to climb high enough to fight them.

As more and more ships were sunk, the pressure on Dowding increased and it is typical of certain members of the Air Staff at this time that they felt able to offer Dowding advice. They told him to put his fighters onto the coastal airfields, so that they need only take off when the Germans were close. To a limited extent this was being done, but it was very dangerous to be so near to enemy formations before gaining equal – or better – height, for the German airmen were formidable.

Kanalkampfführer Fink was 50 years old and still flying operational bombing missions. The *Kommodore* of the fighter *Geschwader* assigned to him was also a veteran and an even more remarkable flyer.

Oberst Theo ('Onkel Theo') Osterkamp was a slim, fastidious man, with a large forehead and pointed features that made him 'gnome-like' to some. This impression was reinforced by anyone who had been on the receiving end of his quick mind, sharp tongue, or his machine guns. In the First World War Osterkamp had been an outstanding ace, credited with thirty-two kills and awarded the *Pour le Mêrite.* A close friend of von Richthofen, he had trained alongside Oswald Boelcke, had survived an air battle with Charles Guynemer, and been shot down by Albert Ball. He was one of the few such men to fly a fighter plane in the Second World War, and already the amazing 'Onkel Theo' was becoming an ace all over again.

Until the last week of July, Osterkamp's JG 51 was the only single-seat fighter unit in action across the Channel. And the strength of this unit had fallen until, on 12 July, the third *Gruppe* of JG 3 was assigned to them, to keep their serviceability up to the region of sixty or seventy aircraft.

Using their small force, the two colonels Fink and Osterkamp showed considerable skill as they probed the British defences, discovered the response times, and found and hit coastal convoys, which were numerous along the south-east coast. Usually the fighters remained close to the bombers, but now and again 'Onkel Theo' released them for fighter sweeps across Kent. These *'Freijagd'* (free-hunt) flights were of limited duration because of the Bf 109's short range.

Dowding's response was cagey. Park (Group commander for south-east England) sent only small formations against the raids and let the *Freijagd* fly unhindered. In the radar stations, the girl operatives began to realize that they succeeded only by working quickly – by making 'educated guesses' about enemy intentions while the bomber formations were still at the extreme edge of radar range.

9 July

Al Deere, from Wanganui, New Zealand, had travelled half-way across the world in order to join the RAF in 1937. By July 1940 he was flight commander with 54 Squadron, and after a month of intensive air fighting he had got his DFC from the hands of the King, at a ceremony held at Hornchurch airfield. By now he was as experienced as any fighter pilot that the British had.

On 9 July[1] he was leading a formation on his fourth flight of the day when they found a German rescue float-plane, painted white with eight large red crosses, flying at wave height. It was escorted by a dozen Bf 109s, flying close behind it.

While one section attacked the float-plane, Deere dived upon the Messerschmitts, which split into two formations, climbing steeply to right and left respectively, turning as they went. Deere remembered this tactic and later used it with some success. Now Deere's flyers broke and individual combats started. Deere noted with satisfaction the way the new De Wilde bullets made 'small dancing yellow flames' as they exploded against the enemy fighter. He found this a valuable way of judging the effect of his gunfire.

> I soon found another target. About 3,000 yards directly ahead of me, and at the same level, a Hun was just completing a turn preparatory to re-entering the fray. He saw me almost immediately and rolled out of his turn towards me so that a head-on attack became inevitable. Using both hands on the control column to steady the aircraft and thus keep my aim steady, I peered through the reflector sight at the rapidly

[1]Deere's autobiography, *Nine Lives* (Hodder & Stoughton, 1969), gives this date as 11 July, but the combat report and the account of a Heinkel He 59 (the float-plane) being towed into Deal from the Goodwin Sands are both dated 9 July.

> closing enemy aircraft. We opened fire together, and immediately a hail of lead thudded into my Spitfire. One moment the Messerschmitt was a clearly defined shape, its wingspan nicely enclosed within the circle of my reflector sight, and the next it was on top of me, a terrifying blur which blotted out the sky ahead. Then we hit.

The crash snatched the control column out of Deere's hands and the cockpit harness bit painfully deep into his shoulders. The engine was vibrating, and the control column was jumping backwards and forwards. As Deere watched, the engine gave forth smoke and flames, and before he could switch off the ignition the propeller stopped. Now Deere could see that its blades were bent double: the Bf 109 had scraped along the top of his Spitfire.

Unable to get his hood open, Deere coaxed the aircraft into a glide towards the distant coastline, while he struggled to get out. With skill to match his amazing good fortune he brought the wrecked aircraft down into a field, very near to Manston airfield. Still unable to open his hood, he smashed his way out of it, his 'bare hands wielding the strength of desperation,' he said. He got clear of the wreckage, which burned brightly as the bullets exploded. 'Won't you come in and have a cup of tea?' said a woman coming out of a nearby farmhouse.

'Thank you I will,' said Deere, 'but I would prefer something stronger if you've got it.'

Modestly Deere got back to his squadron expecting nothing more than a couple of days off. But they were so short of pilots that his commander asked him to fly again immediately. The squadron had lost two pilots to the Messerschmitts and when Deere got to dispersal there were only four Spitfires serviceable. 'You needn't expect to fly this morning,' he was told.

'I'm in no hurry,' said Deere.

10 July

The Luftwaffe needed regular weather reports and more photo coverage of its targets. Not realizing what a sitting duck lone aircraft were for radar, the Germans came one at a time, flying out over the North Sea to what they hoped was an undefended landfall. Often it proved fatal for the German crew, but sometimes there were surprises. On 10 July, a Do 17 looking for a convoy off the North Foreland had no less than an entire *Gruppe* of JG 51 flying escort on it. The other actions of the day were no more than skirmishes but by the end of it Fighter Command had flown over 600 sorties.[1]

11 July

On this day there was an endless stream of lone German aircraft. The RAF responded by sending lone aircraft to meet them. Often the squadron commanders reserved that job for themselves. Not long after dawn, for instance, Peter Townsend – the commander of 85 Squadron at Martlesham – was at the controls of his Hurricane VY-K, climbing out of ground mist into low grey cloud and heavy rain. The Controller's voice took him up to 8,000 feet where, in cloud, he made a perfect interception.

This Dornier Do 17M was Y5+GM from *Kanalkampfführer* Fink's own *Geschwader*, II/KG 2, the '*Holzhammer*'. It came to England in a wide sweep out over the North Sea, reaching the coast near Lowestoft. Forbidden to bomb the mainland in daytime, after what one of the crew described as a little 'sight-seeing' they dropped their ten tiny (50-kg) bombs over some shipping in the harbour.

The crew had mixed feelings about the cloud and rain; it made the pilot's job more difficult, and reduced visibility for the bomb-aimer and gunner, but it was reassuring to think that any RAF fighters would be having the same sort of problems in locating them. The Germans were content, and as the nose of the Dornier turned for home the crew began singing 'Goodbye, Johnny . . . ' The melody was

[1]A sortie is a unit by which air activity is measured. A sortie equals one aircraft making one operational flight. Therefore ten sorties can mean ten aircraft flew one mission or one aircraft flew ten missions.

interrupted by the sudden shout of a gunner, Werner Borner, '*Achtung, Jäger!*'

The *Jäger* was Peter Townsend, who could hardly see through his rainswept windscreen, and so slid open the cockpit cover to put his head out into the rainstorm. He had not had to rely on visibility until the last few moments, for the single Dornier had provided the radar plotters with a blip on the cathode-ray tube no more difficult to interpret than the ones set up as pre-war exercises.

And Townsend was a peacetime pilot, a flyer of great skill and experience. His eight Browning machine guns raked the bomber. Inside the bomber there were 'bits and pieces everywhere: blood-covered faces, the smell of cordite, all the windows shot up'. Of the crew, the starboard rear gunner was hit in the head and fell to the floor. A second later another member of the crew – hit in head and throat – fell on top of him. There was blood everywhere. But 'our good old Gustav Marie was still flying,' remembered one of the crew. Townsend had put 220 bullets into the Dornier but it got home to Arras, and all the crew lived to count the bullet holes.

The German bombers were robust enough to endure terrible amounts of gunfire, especially small-calibre gunfire. Their strength did not depend upon bracing wires and wooden spars: these metal bombers had armour protection, with some of the vital mechanical parts duplicated. Even more valuable were the self-sealing fuel tanks. Of a very simple layered construction, they had a crude rubber middle layer. As a puncture allowed fuel to spill, the crude rubber dissolved, swelled, and sealed the hole. The events of the day were to prove how effective these devices were in getting damaged bombers home.

Not only did Townsend's machine-gun bullets fail to shoot down his Dornier but a lucky shot from one of its machine guns hit his Hurricane's coolant system. The engine stopped when still twenty miles from the English coast. Townsend took to his parachute and was fished out of the ocean by a trawler that sailed into a minefield to reach him.

A little later, another squadron commander found another Dornier. This time the commander was the remarkable Douglas Bader. This peacetime fighter pilot had had both legs amputated after a flying accident but when war began he had been allowed to rejoin the RAF and fly once more as a fighter pilot. Already he had caught up with his contemporaries, and at the end of June he'd been made a Squadron Leader and assigned to command 242 (Canadian) Fighter Squadron. This squadron was flying old Mark I Hurricanes with two-blade fixed-pitch propellers. It consisted of Canadians who were serving in the RAF (it was not an RCAF unit) and had seen some air fighting in France. The squadron was deficient in equipment and morale when Bader arrived. He was now in the process of remedying those defects.

On the morning of 11 July at about seven o'clock Bader answered the phone in the dispersal hut near the aircraft. There was a single 'bandit' flying up the coastline near Cromer and the Controller wanted a flight of Hurricanes to intercept it. Bader looked at the low cloud and decided that the Hurricanes would not be able to form up, so he would go alone. It was a significant decision from the man who later became the most enthusiastic proponent of 'big wings,' in which the fighters went to battle in large formations. It is interesting, too, to record that Bader (who was later to urge that the Controllers should advise rather than order the fighter pilots about the enemy) this day found his victim without the assistance of the radar plotters.

His victim was a Dornier Do 17 of *Wetterkundungsstaffel* (weather reconnaissance unit) 261. It had already fought off two Spitfires. One of them – flown by the commander of 66 squadron – had been damaged in the oil tank.

When Bader found his Dornier it was just under the cloud base at about 1,000 feet. Methodically Bader closed without being spotted until he was about 250 yards behind; then the German rear gunner opened fire. Bader fired two bursts as the Dornier turned to face back the way it had come and made a shallow climb until disappearing into the cloud. Cursing, Bader flew back to Coltishall and reported that his Dornier had escaped, but a few minutes later the telephone told him that the plane had crashed into the sea just a short time after his action. Modestly Bader described this as 'a lucky start for the new C.O. of 242 Squadron,' but there was no doubt that his success had come from skill and experience. There could be no such successes stemming from luck alone.

The fighting over the sea was an added worry for Dowding, for, unlike the Luftwaffe, his pilots had no dinghies, no sea dye, and no air-sea rescue organization. Landing fighters on the water was unwise: the radiators hit the water and tipped the aircraft upside down, in which position they sank. Yet landing in the sea by parachute gave small chance of being found. But so far there were no complaints or even hesitation. This day's fighting showed the way in which his squadron commanders were determined to lead the action. To forbid them to do so would be a blow to morale, but how many such men could he afford to lose?

The RAF fighter pilots – like the Regular officers that so many of them were – had tried to adapt the tight vee formations of peacetime to the needs of war. But tight formations require all a man's concentration and leave no spare moments for looking round. The modern high-speed monoplanes were more complex than the biplanes and, apart from watching the sky for enemy aircraft, pilots needed to attend to their instruments. And in tight formations, each aircraft blocks a large sector of his neighbour's sky. Adding a 'tail-end Charlie' to weave from side to side at the rear of the formation, and thus protect the tail, had resulted in the loss of too many tail-end Charlies. By the middle of July, weavers were seldom seen.

Before the war, the RAF had practised 'Fighting Area

Attacks': carefully choreographed flight movements that, typically, provided a line of fighters with a burst of fire, as each took a turn at the victim. But the Germans would not readily play victim, and what had worked well enough at air displays was no tactic for modern war. Squadrons engaged in the Channel fighting soon saw the advantages of the loose *Schwarme* the Germans flew, and depleted squadrons gave the RAF an excuse for trying new formations.

The *Schwarm*

D

A

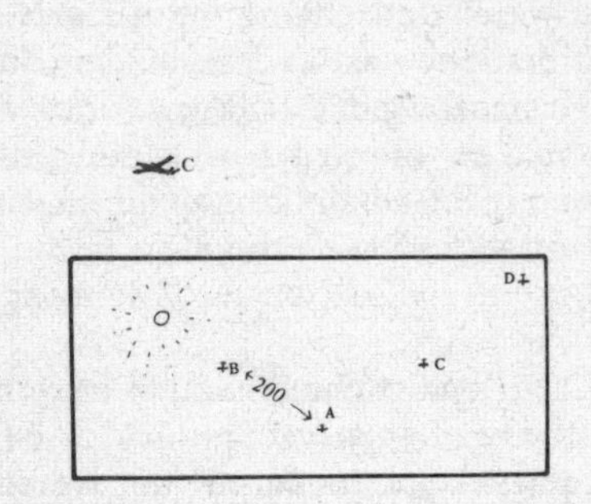

B

Figure 23

The *Schwarm* – called 'finger four' by Allied pilots – was evolved by Luftwaffe pilots during the Spanish Civil War and codified by Werner Mölders, the German fighter ace.

A is the leader; *B* is the leader's wingman, who never leaves his side. He flies on the sun side of the leader and low so that the others do not have to look into the glare of the sun to see him.

C is the leader of the second pair (*Rotte*); *D* is his wingman. His job in this formation is to watch the sky around the sun. A skilful enemy will attack from there.

The box shows the same formation in plan view. Note that all aircraft are at different altitudes.

The *Rotte*, or pair, was the basis of the formation that Werner Mölders, the German fighter ace, had started to evolve in the skies of Spain. The vee, a human triangle, is not psychologically stable, as any reader of romantic fiction knows. The *Rotte* consisted of a leader and his wingman. The leader was the senior flyer and best marksman; his wingman stayed glued to him and was responsible for guarding the tail. When two *Rotten* joined to make a *Schwarm*, the senior pilot took charge but the pairs remained effective. Wingmen were usually told that even if the leader flew into the ground the wingman must follow. There were other subtle advantages to the German formations: for instance, the slightly different altitude of each aircraft was another way in which collision risk was reduced.

The RAF tried such formations unofficially. But, dogged by peacetime flying regulations, no Fighter Command formation was as loosely spread as were those of the Germans. And tight formations were easier to see in the sky. The sad truth was that no RAF unit could learn overnight the stalking skills that several years of combat had taught the Germans.

17 July

This fact was demonstrated on a miserable day of rain and cloud when twelve Spitfires of 64 Squadron flying out of Kenley were 'bounced' off Beachy Head. The Germans came out of nowhere, knocked a Spitfire down, and disappeared so fast that no member of the RAF formation even got a glimpse of the enemy aircraft.

Still lacking any proper tactical directives – except a vague new order about attacking the British Home Fleet – the Luftwaffe brought more and more units into the fighting. As well as Air Fleets 2 and 3 in France and the Low Countries, Air Fleet 5 in Scandinavia was sending missions across the North Sea. *Küstenfliegergruppen* (coastal aircraft units) continued the exacting task of dropping mines into the Firth of Forth and the estuaries of the Thames and Humber, and were at it almost every night. There were surprise attacks on factories as far apart as Glasgow and Yeovil, and after-dark experimental night-bombing units were flying over Britain testing their radio-guidance system.

18 July

Just as the Air Fleets lacked a common strategy, so they lacked a sound appreciation of Britain's defences, upon which their tactical policy might have been based. And yet, on 18 July, a ruse devised by Air Fleet 2 suggested that someone on the staff realized how British radar worked. Shortly after eight o'clock in the morning, RAF radar operators saw a *Staffel* or so of aircraft circling for height and getting into formation for an attack on a coastal convoy that was moving through the Straits of Dover.

No. 610 (County of Chester) Squadron, from Biggin Hill, flew out to find the convoy. They kept just under the low cloud until they found it. As these Auxiliary flyers got there, they were bounced by Bf 109s. One Spitfire was shot down. The Germans, who had formed up in the manner of a bombing *Staffel*, were entirely fighters. They escaped without a scratch.

19 July

By now RAF loss rates were rising fast enough to draw on a graph and prove that Fighter Command would cease to exist within six weeks. And this was before the promised *Adlerangriff* had even started. That no one at Fighter Command drew such a graph – as far as we know – must have been partly due to the exaggerated RAF claims. These persuaded even some senior RAF officers that the German Air Fleets were taking severe punishment. But on 19 July those RAF optimists might have had second thoughts. Although the size of the air battle was very small, the casualty types were significant. Of five German aircraft lost, only one was a fighter. The others were, in effect, stragglers, including one old He 115 float-plane. The

RAF loss, on the other hand, was ten fighters. In fighter-to-fighter combat, the RAF were proving markedly inferior to the Germans.

This was the day when the RAF sent into battle the Boulton Paul Defiant two-seater. The Defiant was an updated version of the Bristol Fighter that had proved so successful in the First World War, but in 1940 it was a disaster.

Oberleutnant Hannes Trautloft, a veteran of Spain and an outstanding pilot, was leading the third *Gruppe* of JG 51. There were now only fifteen fighters left of his original forty. Trautloft saw nine strange-looking aircraft and noticed the gun turret behind the cockpits. He designed his attack accordingly. The Boulton Paul Defiant had no forward-facing armament. As one pilot put it, 'The Defiant could only attack another plane after it had passed it.' But with a power-operated turret that weighed three-quarters of a ton, and an extra man, the Defiants didn't pass many other aircraft. Of the formation of nine, only three got back to Hawkinge and one of those was so badly damaged that its gunner baled out.

None of 141 Squadron's Defiants would have survived had 111 Squadron not arrived. This Hurricane Squadron was making a name for itself by using a new tactic. The German fighter pilots favoured nose-to-nose, fighter-versus-fighter attacks. Now the Hurricanes were flying line-abreast, head-on through German bomber formations. Although this tactic usually succeeded in forcing the bombers to break formation, 111 Squadron was losing enough Hurricanes in head-on collisions with the enemy to make the pilots doubt its value.

24 July

Ever since 'Dolfo' Galland had submitted his excellent reports about the employment of aircraft in the army-support role, he had been assigned to this specialization. Much to his disgust he had been given a job in the Berlin Air Ministry. He returned to operational flying only in close-support units (*Schlachtgeschwader*). This meant flying antiquated biplanes, such as the Heinkel He 45 and Heinkel He 51. Even when Germany invaded Poland, Galland could not get an aeroplane any better than a Henschel Hs 123, a close-attack biplane with radial engine. Eventually, by conspiring with a friendly physician, he was able to get his medical records endorsed with a note to say that he should not fly in open-cockpit aircraft. What might have sentenced him to a short life with the Stukas got him a job with fighters. But as Operations Officer with JG 27, paperwork left him little time for combat flying until, on 12 May, he flew as part of the great German thrust westwards into France and the Low Countries. He shot down three Hurricanes in one day.

Galland was very conscious of the way in which Mölders – the subordinate who had taken over from him in Spain – was now recognized as Germany's ace fighter pilot. Galland was not too proud to ask Mölders for advice and now says, 'Werner Mölders taught me how to shoot and bring down aircraft.' In June, as the Luftwaffe lined up for the air war against England, Galland was assigned to command III/JG 26. He shot down two enemy fighters on the first day with his new command. During July, says Galland sardonically, Hitler's creation of a dozen new Field Marshals in the Kroll Opera House, Berlin, filtered down as far as him. Galland was made *Major*. This had no effect upon Galland's command of his *Gruppe* (about thirty fighters). In the German armed forces, a new appointment gave no entitlement to new rank.[1]

By now Galland was a well-known face among the fighter pilots. His jet-black hair, combed straight back from a high forehead, and the large Groucho Marx moustache and easy grin reassured the fighter pilots that

[1]A notable example of this was Wolfgang Falck, who not only was given command of a night-fighting *Geschwader* (NJG 1) while remaining a Captain but eventually commanded eight *Gruppen* (in effect three *Geschwader*) without ever being promoted beyond Colonel.

their *Gruppenkommandeur*[1] was still 'one of the boys.' And so did the big black cigars, to which he was so addicted that he had an ashtray installed in the cockpit, enabling him to smoke right up until the moment he went on to oxygen. But only a fool would fail to see that behind the grin there was a cold, calm, and calculating fighter who, at this date, was determined to beat the score of Mölders.

His rival had claimed his twenty-fifth victim about seven weeks previously, over France, but afterwards he was shot down and made a POW until the French armistice. Galland was determined to make the best of Mölders's set-back. At midday on 24 July, Galland led his Messerschmitts into battle again, but the Luftwaffe were beginning to find the Spitfire a tough one to down. This morning, as we shall see, the Spitfires handed out rather more punishment than they took.

July was a month of experiments. Kesselring discovered that attacking two coastal convoys at the same time forced the defence to divide. This worked well about 8 a.m. on 24 July, when two co-ordinated attacks were made: one on a convoy off Dover and the other on one that was entering the Thames Estuary. The defence – 54 Squadron from Rochford – sent after one raid, saw both, and had to split up to attack them. The raiders escaped without casualties but the bombing failed to hit any of the ships. About 11 a.m. two *Staffeln* of Do 17s returned to the Thames Estuary to attack a convoy. 'Dolfo' Galland's Bf 109s were assigned as escort. Park sent 54 Squadron to attack them, and then, knowing that Galland's fighter escort would soon run short of fuel, he ordered 610 Squadron (Biggin Hill) to patrol Dover, and so cut off their escape route. In fact, 610 ran into JG 52, who were coming north to help the returning Messerschmitts. There was a fight. The raid's

[1]The flyer leading a *Staffel* was called a *Staffelkapitän*, the one leading a *Gruppe* was a *Gruppenkommandeur* (as Galland now was), and leading a *Geschwader* was a *Geschwaderkommodore* (as Mölders was to become at the end of July).

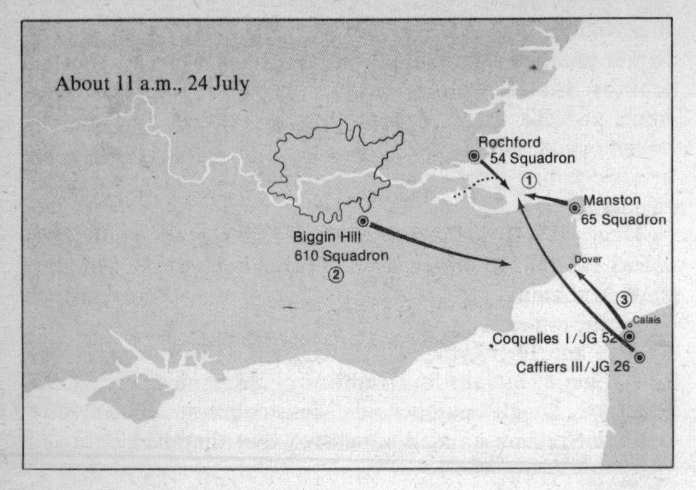

Figure 24

A convoy (dotted line) left the river Medway and entered the Thames Estuary. It attracted a bombing raid consisting of Dornier Do 17s escorted by Messerschmitt Bf 109s of the third *Gruppe* of JG 26, *Schlageter*, led by Galland.

(1) No. 54 Squadron was sent to intercept and a battle developed. While this was happening, 65 Squadron from Manston went to attack the now unescorted Dorniers. Tight formations and disciplined gunfire from the bombers prevented close attacks and they escaped without loss. Two of the forty Messerschmitts were shot down, and as they were all running short of fuel they dived out of combat and went home very low across Kent.

(2) Meanwhile 610 Squadron from Biggin Hill were sent to patrol Dover in the hope of cutting off the escape of Galland's fighters.

(3) But another German fighter unit was coming to take over the escort duty. A fight developed between these Messerschmitts and the Spitfires from Biggin Hill.

escort – Galland's III/JG 26 – and JG 52 each lost three fighters. The two RAF squadrons lost three Spitfires.

As the engagement ended, the elated Spitfire pilots dived upon another formation, and shot down one of them. The victorious pilot reported that there had been no return fire and identified his victim as a Chance Vought V.156. RAF intelligence thought the Germans were so short of aircraft that they were now using captured French ones, until the Royal Navy reported the loss of a Blackburn Skua of 806 Squadron, Fleet Air Arm.

The fighter pilots were learning about their adversaries. The Bf 109, with its fuel-injection engine, not only dived without missing a beat or two (unlike the carburettor-fed Merlins) but could outdive the RAF fighters. Galland's Messerschmitts had dived out of combat and escaped that morning when their fuel ran low.

But the Luftwaffe had never before faced a fighter as good as the Spitfire. This was acknowledged by the disproportionate number of Messerschmitt fighter pilots who, on becoming POWs, insisted that they had been shot

Figure 25 Galland and Mölders

Udet drew the two famous fighter aces as rival huntsmen. Galland, on the left, with Groucho Marx cigar and moustache, and the solemn 'Daddy' Mölders, on the right, are counting the bag.

down by Spitfires. The Hurricane pilots, who sometimes had their claims disallowed because of it, called it 'Spitfire snobbery.'

RAF regulations said that the eight Brownings should be adjusted so that the bullets converged at a point some 650 yards ahead of the aircraft. As one pilot of 54 Squadron said at the time, 'All this guarantees is a few hits by the indifferent shot; the good shot on the other hand is penalized.' The pilots who were prepared to get close were scattering gunfire all over the place.

Already the regulations were being ignored. Armament Officers were having the guns adjusted the way the pilots wanted them (and eventually this was officially approved).

The courage to fly very close distinguished just about all the men who became aces, but without the skill of deflection-shooting such a pilot could not make a kill. This aiming-off is not to be equated with the hunter shooting at a bird in flight. The fighter pilots were moving at three or four hundred miles an hour in three dimensions. And so was the target. To hit it required an instant assessment of enemy speed, enemy size, angle between the two aircraft, and the distance. (Later in the war there were gun-sights that did some of this calculation, but in 1940 pilots on both sides had only a ring sight reflected on the windscreen.) The split-second judgment required for this kind of fighting was something that many superb pilots were never able to acquire.

In the First World War, some ace fighter pilots had become obsessional about the types of bullet they used, arranging them in the belts in certain set sequences according to personal taste. The provision of eight separate identical guns made varying the ammunition very simple. A common mix was four guns with normal bullets, two with armour-piercing, and two with the new De Wilde incendiaries. This later ammunition was very popular with the fighter pilots. Dowding said that they valued it far beyond its true worth but he was not taking into account the way that, although it had no tracer or smoke trail as previous incendiary bullets had, it made a bright yellow flash on impact. This proved a valuable aiming device. Believing that his pilots should have what they wanted, Dowding made special efforts to increase supplies of the De Wilde bullets. 'Sailor' Malan and Al Deere believed that the 250-yard harmonization and De Wilde bullets made the difference between damaging enemy aircraft and destroying them.

During July the fighter pilots rediscovered that aerial victory went to the formation that caught an enemy unaware. The old hands attacked out of the sun, and visibility was the paramount factor in the fighter pilot's war. German pilots who had found their Emils good enough for Spain, Poland, and France, now demanded a better clearview cockpit cover. RAF pilots were constrained by their Irving flying suits, gloves, and the seat's Sutton harness which, one inspector said, 'seemed specially designed to foul oxygen and wireless leads.' The RAF flying helmets had earphones that tangled into the collar part of the 'Mae West' life jackets. To relieve themselves of this tangle many pilots adjusted the cockpit heaters and flew in uniform jackets or shirt-sleeves.

But for the ground staff there were few days suitable for shirt-sleeves. July was a month of dull, wet weather: haze, drizzle, low cloud, electrical storms, and even fog. Often it was the appalling visibility that enabled a convoy to get through the Channel intact. There was so much rain that some airfields on both sides were made unusable by flooding.

And then 25 July provided one of the rare breaks in the bad weather: the morning sky was blue.

25 July

Kesselring was playing cat and mouse with a convoy through the Dover Straits. CW8 (west-bound coal convoy number eight) consisted of 21 colliers and coasters. Only 11 passed Dungeness, and only 2 got to their destination undamaged. Just after noon, a force of Bf 109s headed for

Dover, flying almost at sea level. They were a device to bring the RAF fighters down to sea level and so give a clear run to the Stukas. No. 65 Squadron went down to fight. All the aircraft were so low that when one Bf 109 – of JG 52 – misjudged an attack, he hit the water and disintegrated.

Hurricanes of 32 Squadron from Biggin Hill and 615 Squadron from Kenley joined the fighting against forty Bf 109s. There is an old fighter pilot's maxim, 'Never throttle back in combat,' and maximum boost caused both sides to run low on fuel after only a few minutes. As the fighters disengaged, three *Stukageschwader* came in at medium altitude and dive-bombed the now-unprotected convoy.

The convoy's naval escort put up anti-aircraft fire and called urgently for fighter cover. Nine Spitfires of 54 Squadron hurried to their aid. When they arrived they found Kesselring had sent an overwhelming force of Bf 109s there to wait for them. Among 54 Squadron's losses was a flight commander. None of the German fighters was shot down.

The Sector Controller realized that if he answered the German attacks plane for plane, he would be bled dry. So at 2:30 that afternoon, when thirty Ju 88s came to bomb the convoy, he sent only eight Spitfires of 64 Squadron. They met a fighter escort of fifty Bf 109s. Undismayed, the newly appointed squadron commander called 'Tally-Ho!' and attacked. The Controller sent the rest of 64 Squadron – three Spitfires – and 111 Squadron, to the battle. The latter formed up line-abreast and did a head-on attack on the Junkers bombers, which broke formation and turned away. On seeing this, the Messerschmitts of the fighter escort also withdrew.

But it was still only afternoon: the men of the convoy had not yet earned their day's pay. As they passed Folkestone, the Bf 109s repeatedly strafed them at sea level, gaining the naval gunners' attention so that about sixty Stukas could dive-bomb them out of the afternoon sun. The attack had been nicely timed between RAF patrols, and with unhurried precision they sank five ships and damaged four. At this moment, a force of German motor torpedo boats attacked the convoy too. By nightfall two damaged destroyers moved into Dover harbour; one of them was under tow. The Admiralty concluded that coastal convoys should no longer try to get through the Straits of Dover except under cover of darkness.

Although Fighter Command had lost only seven aircraft – against sixteen German raiders shot down – it had nothing to celebrate. No. 54 Squadron was retired north for a rest. In its three weeks in action the Squadron had lost five pilots killed – including a very experienced flight commander – and three pilots wounded. It had flown 800 hours, completed 504 combat sorties, and lost twelve aircraft.[1] It was a warning of what could happen to the whole of Fighter Command if it was drawn into ever larger battles. Instead of cancelling the coastal convoys – the cargoes were coal, which could have been moved by rail and later was – the Admiralty and Air Ministry pressed Dowding to commit more of his fighter force to protecting the shipping. Dowding resisted.

The US ambassador in London – Joseph Kennedy, the father of the man who became President – had little faith in Britain's ability to survive, and he didn't mind who knew it. As early as 1 July the British Prime Minister had written in his diary, 'Saw Joe Kennedy who says everyone in USA thinks we shall be beaten before the end of the month.' Now there was only a week of it left. The British Foreign Office heard that Kennedy had summoned neutral journalists to a press conference in order to tell them that Hitler would be in London by 15 August. Such behaviour infuriated Foreign Office officials – one wrote, 'He is the biggest Fifth Columnist in the country' – but there was little they could do about him. Joseph Kennedy wielded great political influence in the USA (and had got the

[1]A typical Fighter Command squadron at this time had twenty-two pilots and sixteen operational aircraft, plus two more aircraft as Command reserve.

London Embassy in recognition of past help). Now it was election year in the USA. President Roosevelt was running against Wendell Willkie for an unprecedented third term. He needed Kennedy's support to win the election, and the British wanted Roosevelt to win. It was a dilemma for all concerned, not least for the Americans, who didn't want to send expensive war supplies to a nation just about to collapse.

To get a second opinion, Roosevelt sent another Irish-American to Britain. 'Wild Bill' Donovan was ostensibly in England to study the extent of German espionage and the nature of British counter-measures. In fact, he was to report to Roosevelt Britain's chances of survival. Sending a man on an intelligence mission that was really a cover for a diplomatic function was a curious reversal of the usual way of doing such things.

ILLUSTRATIONS

40 RAF fighter pilots sitting in their dispersal hut To make them less vulnerable to air attack, fighter aircraft were dispersed round the airfields. For the pilots, there was accommodation of the sort shown here. The pilots are sitting round a small coal stove, for the huts were icy cold at dawn when their day began. Often their food was brought out to them and at many airfields the dispersal huts had no washing facilities or toilets. These publicity photographs taken in the spring of 1940 depict the fighter pilot's life at its most comfortable.

41 Scramble This photograph was taken shortly after the previous one. A phone call from the Sector Controller sends the pilots out to their aircraft. The flyers are dressed in the flying suits and sheepskin jackets that regulations specified (partly to protect the men in the event of fire) but as the weather became warmer the men flew with minimum equipment and sometimes in shirt sleeves. On the wall of the hut a blackboard shows the names of the pilots against the code letter of the aircraft. The top three are at 'readiness' and the second three 'available'.

42 A Hawker Hurricane goes down in flames The white worm-like line, at the right wing-root in the first photograph, is tracer striking the target. The German fighters seldom had cameras fitted to their fighters and so cine-camera photographs of RAF aircraft under attack are rare.

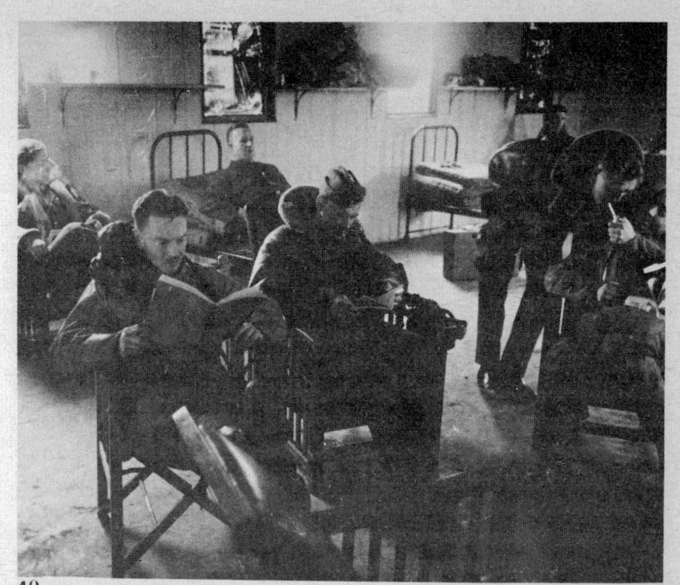

40

41

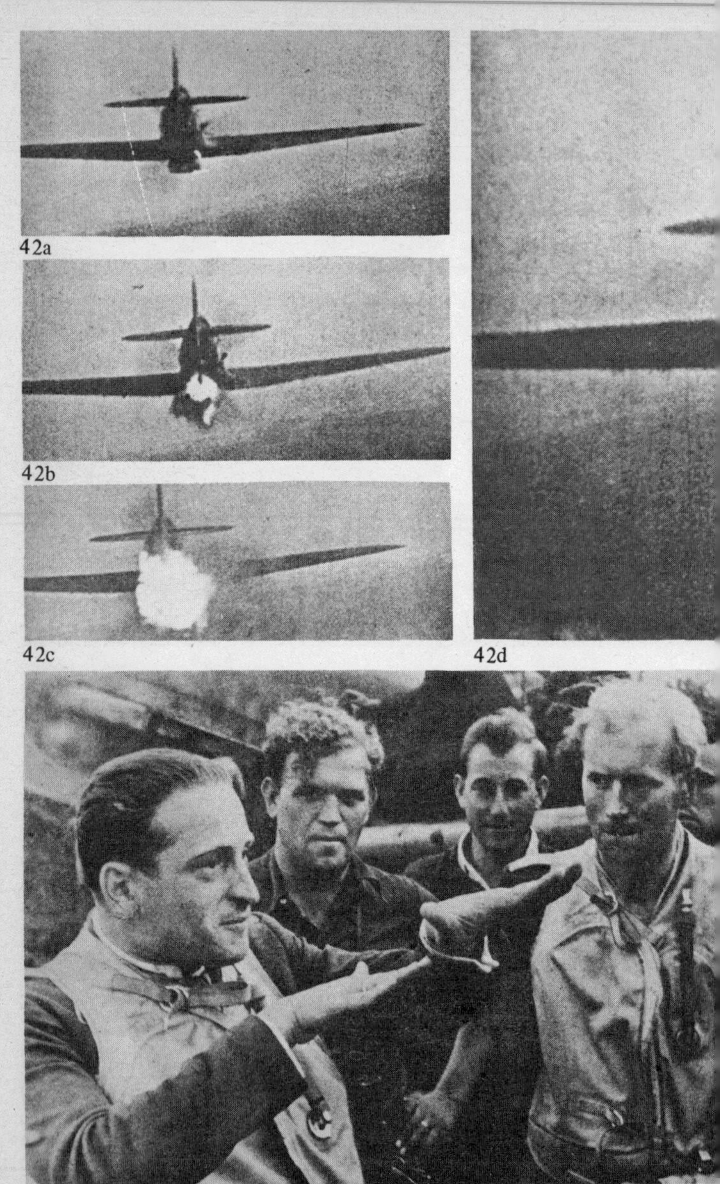
42a
42b
42c
42d
43

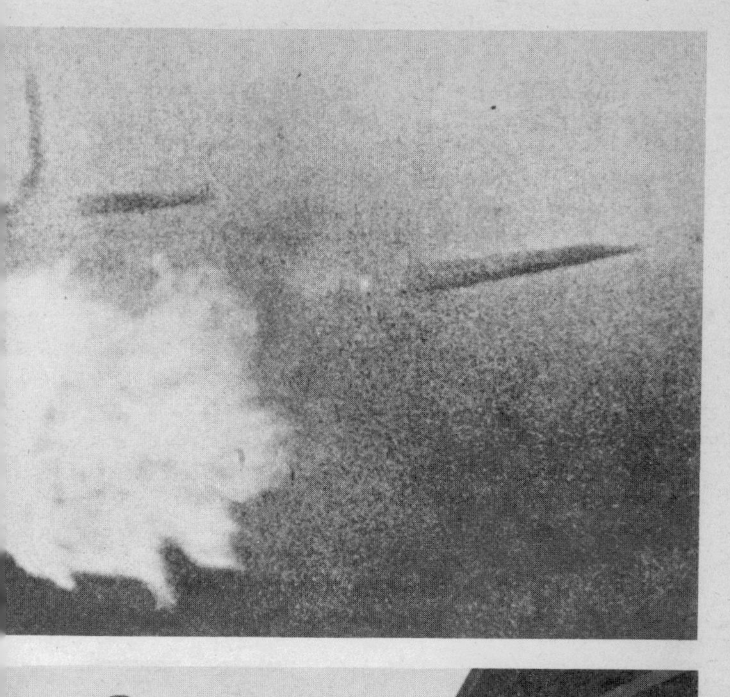

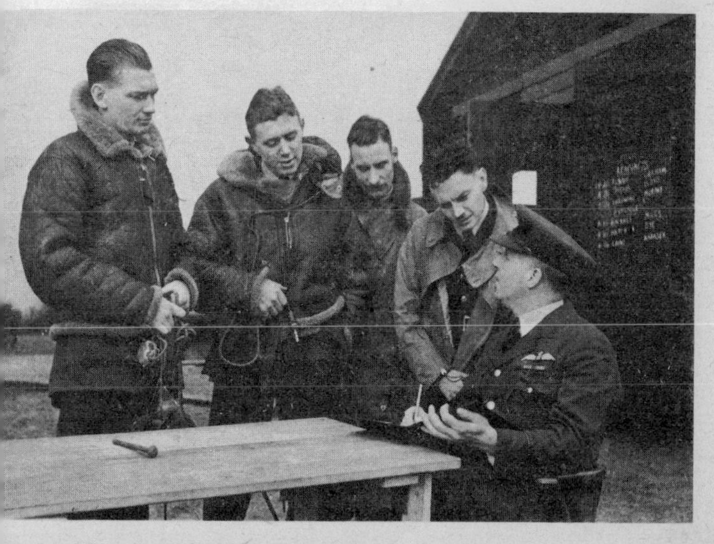

45

28 July

A few days later, the storm clouds again gave way to a clear blue sky. At about 2 p.m., when most of England was sitting down to the ritual of Sunday lunch, something happened that was so unusual in the air war that this might have been unique: two ace pilots clashed in combat.

The South African 'Sailor' Malan ended the war as one of the top-scoring aces on the Allied side. He was important, too, for the influence he had upon RAF tactics and formations.

Born in Wellington, South Africa, Adolphus Malan was a man of burly build with an amiable smile that made the men who met him unready for the deep and clinical hatred that he had for his German opponents. He told one of his fellow officers that to badly damage enemy bombers – so that they arrived home with dead and dying aboard – was better than shooting them down: it had more effect on Luftwaffe morale. So that is what he tried to do.

Malan had been a merchant navy officer before volun-

43 A German fighter pilot describes his victory His wingman (at right) watches closely, biting his lip and wide-eyed with the tension of combat. Behind them stand the ground crew, called 'black men' by the Germans because of their black overalls.

44 RAF fighter pilots report to their Intelligence Officer after a sortie The Intelligence Officer is a First World War pilot but many such men were civilians until the outbreak of war (many were ex-school teachers) and had no previous service experience. Such men found it difficult to interrogate the professional service pilots who fought the Battle and for this reason many victory claims were allowed without proper evidence. Total RAF claims were wildly inaccurate.

45 Air activity over Folkestone seldom slackened during the summer of 1940 Press photographers went there confident of their chances of action pictures. Here a *Daily Mirror* cameraman took an amazing photograph. The unmistakable shape of a Spitfire is seen turning, so that its pilot can see the Messerschmitt Bf 109 which has just cleared the Mole at Folkestone harbour, its undercarriage dangling. Sometimes the lowering of the wheels was used as a sign of surrender, and willingness to land in enemy territory. Sometimes it just meant that the hydraulics were shot to pieces.

teering for the RAF in 1935. He proved to be an exceptional pilot, according to his flying instructors. He was a flight commander by the time he saw action in May 1940. On the receiving end of his bullets this day was an even more revered master of the fighter pilot's trade: the legendary Mölders. Both men have been mentioned by their peers as possibly the greatest fighter pilots of the war.

Werner Mölders was a handsome young man whose drawn face, deepset eyes, bony nose, and thin mouth were seldom captured on film in the act of smiling. He was an introverted man, and this serious demeanour earned him the nickname 'Vati' ('Daddy'). So determined was he to be a fighter pilot that (like many others before and since) he endured the agonies and humiliation of constant air sickness.

Mölders took over Galland's command in Spain just as the new Bf 109 fighters replaced the old biplanes. This changed the odds and he returned to Germany with fourteen destroyed enemy aircraft in his log book. He was a skilled administrator and a dedicated teacher, as well as Germany's top fighter ace. Many Nazis took exception to the way that 'Vati' Mölders made no secret of his Catholic religion, but Göring made quite sure that no harm came to him on that account. In 1940 it was decided that the coveted Knight's Cross of the Iron Cross would be given to a pilot who shot down twenty enemy planes. Mölders was the first fighter pilot to get it. He was to become the Luftwaffe's General of Fighters before his twenty-ninth birthday.

Sunday 28 July was an auspicious day for Mölders. This was his first day as *Kommodore* of the entire JG 51. (The previous day 'Onkel Theo' Osterkamp had gone to become *Jafü* 2, the commander of all the fighter planes in Air Fleet 2.) Concerned as he might be by his seven weeks out of action, and the victories of Galland and *Hauptmann* Helmut Wick (the other two top German aces), Werner Mölders could this day reflect with satisfaction that he was the youngest *Kommodore* in the Luftwaffe.

With Mölders there were four *Staffeln* of Messerschmitts, and in keeping with Fighter Command policy, Spitfires were sent against them, while Hurricanes were vectored on to the German bomber formation. 'Sailor' Malan was leading twelve Spitfires of 74 Squadron from Manston. As they closed, Malan chose a victim in the leading flight, fired, and watched him go down. Mölders was leading that formation; he turned and shot down a Spitfire. For Mölders this was his 129th combat mission of the war and his twenty-sixth victory (not including the fourteen aircraft shot down in Spain). He came round again, looking for his twenty-seventh.

Both Mölders and Malan were fast, but Mölders was split-seconds faster. Even as Malan was scoring his victory, Mölders was already on his tail. Malan turned in towards the attack – the classic reaction of the fighter pilot – and kept turning tightly enough to bring Mölders into his sights. His machine-gun bullets raked the Messerschmitt. Had Spitfires been armed with cannon, Mölders would not have been able to nurse his badly damaged machine back to his base at Wissant. When he landed, his leg wounds were bad enough to put him into hospital. It was to be another month before Mölders could claim victim number twenty-seven.

Enough Messerschmitt pilots failed to make it back across the Channel for German rescue float-planes to be sent out to search for them. These large twin-engined rescue aicraft were painted white, with eight large red crosses in evidence. The Air Ministry had decided that any seen near Allied shipping or the English coast should be shot down. This instruction had been passed to all squadrons on 14 July, and in keeping with it, Hurricanes of 111 Squadron shot one down into mid-Channel and did considerable damage to another that was on the water ten miles west of Boulogne.

The resulting controversy was not confirmed to the rival propaganda industries. Some RAF pilots vowed that they would not obey such an instruction. Others wanted to see it in writing. Publication of this Air Ministry Order, on 29 July, with its legalistic phrasing and vague talk of confining such attacks upon unarmed aircraft to 'areas in which operations are in progress,' did nothing to improve matters or even clarify them. For it was only where operations were in progress that drowning aviators would be found.

Mölders's badly damaged fighter plane provides an example of another problem. On this day alone, two Junkers Ju 88 bombers of 9/KG 4, the *General Wever Geschwader* based at Amsterdam-Schipol, were damaged by anti-aircraft gunfire over the Thames Estuary. One did not get back as far as its base. Both crashed on landing and were completely written off. Almost all the survivors were wounded. Another Ju 88 – of the *Edelweiss Geschwader* – had engine failure, and forced-landed heavily enough to be severely damaged. Neither was Mölders's Bf 109 the only fighter that would not be ready to fly next day, or for many days after that. Official Luftwaffe records show a Bf 109 of II/JG 27 crash-landed away from its base, with its pilot wounded. It was badly damaged, and two more Bf 109s were written off in crash landings, one of which killed the pilot. Two more fighters of JG 51 were damaged in forced landings that afternoon, and there was the Heinkel float-plane damaged near Boulogne, and a Do 17Z of KG 2 that was written off in an accident that had nothing to do with enemy action.

It was like this almost every day: collisions during taxiing, take-off, or landing, as well as curious entries that show aircraft that simply disappear, as a Ju 88 of II/KG 51, the *Edelweiss Geschwader*, had done on the night of 25 July. There is no record of its being encountered anywhere, by army, navy, or air forces on either side of the Channel. These marginal losses sometimes account for the arguments that arise about the battles of 1940.

Britain's Civilian Repair Organization

In Britain there was a highly efficient organization that

salvaged every scrap of airframe that could be collected. Airframes were melted down, and much of the German alloy took to the air again, as part of RAF machines.

For damaged RAF aircraft there was an amazing record. Of all the fighters struck off squadron strength because they could not be repaired locally, no less than 61 per cent flew again. This was due to the efforts of the Civilian Repair Organization – the CRO.

Peacetime military flying provides only a fraction of the immense amount of aircraft repairs that can be expected in combat. The Munich crisis caused the RAF to prepare for war. Most urgently needed was a vehicle that could transport a fighter plane by road (wings removed and stowed alongside). A specification was issued for a suitable low-loading trailer, and a prototype 'Queen Mary' was tested within ten days. Manufacturing started immediately. Such vehicles contributed greatly to the repair figures.

Also as a result of the Munich crisis of 1938, Lord Nuffield – the millionaire motor manufacturer and philanthropist – organized the Civilian Repair Organization. In May 1940 the CRO became responsible to the newly created Minister of Aircraft Production: an asthmatic newspaper tycoon who had in the First World War been given a peerage by Lloyd George for political services.

The controversial Lord Beaverbrook ran his Ministry as he ran his newspapers. Over his desk there was displayed the notice 'Organization is the enemy of improvisation.' He dismissed the suggestion that his role was to manufacture the aircraft that the Air Ministry wanted. Says his biographer, A. J. P. Taylor, 'Beaverbrook decided what types of aircraft were produced and in what numbers. The Air Ministry had been pushed aside. It merely appointed the commanders and operated such strategy as Beaverbrook permitted.'

Luckily for Fighter Command – and for Britain – Beaverbrook took an instant liking to the taciturn Dowding. Both men had sons who were fighter pilots in the Battle. The views expressed by Dowding's enemies at the Air

Ministry only confirmed Beaverbrook's opinion of the Air Ministry.

Beaverbrook claimed that all aircraft in RAF Storage Units should be under the control of his Ministry. While the Air Ministry argued bitterly that they were theirs, the 'Beaver' sent his men to padlock the hangars. Delighted with the shock he caused by this, he spread the story that he was going to store fighter aircraft in Winchester Cathedral.

Each evening, during the Battle of Britain, Beaverbrook received a call from his son – Squadron Leader the Honourable Maxwell Aitken – to be sure he was safe after the day's fighting. He also phoned Park, at 11 Group, to ask how many Spitfires and Hurricanes he needed. The next day the replacements were sent. The Air Ministry were given no chance to interfere: they were not consulted or even informed.

The rare quality that the British showed for merging civilian and military authority was nowhere more evident than in the CRO. Defying all precedents, the 'Beaver' cannibalized damaged aircraft to make one complete fighter out of two or three damaged ones. His men were sent to raid the RAF squadrons for spare parts and engines, which were delivered to the production lines. 'Better a stringency in spares and a bountiful supply of aircraft than a surplus of spares and a shortage of aircraft,' explained Beaverbrook.

He used businessmen – most of them specially commissioned and few of them paid – to sort out production problems and bottlenecks. Not many of them came from the aircraft industry, for as Beaverbrook reasoned, 'industry is like theology. If you know the rudiments of one faith you can grasp the meaning of another.'

Spitfire production lagged far behind that of Hurricanes. In 1938, Kingsley Wood – the Air Minister who had been so reluctant to bomb Krupps in Essen – had decided that it was better to give the new Spitfire contract to the Nuffield Organization rather than to Supermarine, the company that had created the Spitfire and was already manufacturing it.

The second Spitfire factory – or 'shadow factory,' as it was called in the jargon of the time – was built at Castle Bromwich, Birmingham. It should have been well started on its contract for 1,500 Spitfires by January 1940, but by the time Beaverbrook took over on 14 May not one had been completed.

One of Beaverbrook's first actions was to phone Supermarine and tell them to take over the second factory. He told them to forget about plans to make Wellington and Halifax bombers there too. He wanted Spitfires. There were bitter protests, including some from Lord Nuffield, whose firm had been running the unsuccessful factory. He went to Churchill and tried to get Beaverbrook sacked. He failed, and by 6 June the first Spitfire was assembled and in the air. By the end of the month there were another nine. The numbers were small but this factory was farther away from the danger zone and from here came the slightly improved Spitfire II, with built-in armour, cartridge starters, and the higher-boost Merlin XII engine.

Some of Beaverbrook's decisions were more long-reaching than this. Henry Ford refused to support Britain's war effort and so would not build Rolls-Royce Merlin engines under licence in the USA. It was Beaverbrook who asked Packard to do so, and personally promised them enough money to enlarge their factory for that purpose. It was an audacious gesture, if not to say reckless, but Churchill backed Beaverbrook, and this decision not only guaranteed the supply of the finest (piston) aero-engine of the war but paved the way for building Merlin-powered Mustang fighters.

Another of Beaverbrook's enthusiasms was ferrying aircraft across the Atlantic. He did it without War Cabinet approval and despite the Air Ministry's contention that it was impractical. It proved very practical indeed. During the winter of 1940–41, 160 aircraft flew across the Atlantic.

Only one was lost. Characteristically, the Air Ministry discontinued the ferrying when Beaverbrook left office.

In the short term, it was through the Civilian Repair Organization that Beaverbrook contributed most to the Battle of Britain. No less than one third of all 'new' aircraft supplied to the fighter squadrons came from repair units. In addition, July saw the first use of his 'out-patients departments' to which fighter pilots, fresh from battle, flew their damaged machines for a while-you-wait service. Later Dowding said, 'The country owes as much to Beaverbrook for the Battle of Britain as it does to me.'

Neither the Air Fleet commanders nor Fighter Command had a clear picture of the damage that was being done to their respective enemies. The fighter pilots' claims were wildly exaggerated and the German propaganda service announced as losses only about half of the true German casualties. The RAF announced their own true losses but believed too readily their fighter pilots' claims. The fact that so much air fighting had taken place over the sea made it impossible for either side to verify claims. All Dowding could be sure about was that his July fighter aircraft losses totalled 145, and take comfort from the fact that this was only about a week's output from the factories.

Aircraft supply had enabled Dowding to get his squadrons back to the normal establishment of 20 fighters plus 2 reserves (Dunkirk air fighting had forced Fighter Command to lower the squadrons to only 16 aircraft plus 2). And because Fighter Command had very nearly the 1,454 pilots that was its full establishment, Dowding raised the establishment to 1,588. This gave him an immediate deficiency – on paper – of 174 pilots. It also set a dangerous trap for historians assessing Fighter Command's losses during this period.

Loss in quality was far more difficult to assess. This was only a period of preliminary skirmishing, and already eighty flight commanders and squadron commanders had been knocked out of the Battle. As August began, only about half of Dowding's pilots had ever seen a German, let alone had combat experience. Even if the Training Units promptly replaced every casualty suffered, Fighter Command would continue to be diluted in quality. And the Luftwaffe's nuisance raiding by lone bombers was seriously restricting RAF flying training. So was the bad weather.

Quality of effort was the basis of Dowding's worst fears. Not simply pilot training, or even experience, but also the loss of quality that fatigue would bring. There was a formal demand from the Admiralty (via the Air Ministry) that Dowding must fly standing patrols over the convoys; and this was the very thing that radar was designed to obviate. Dowding compromised. But even so, there were many July days when Fighter Command put up as many as 600 sorties. The strain on the pilots and the maintenance crews was terrific but there could be no question of a general rotation of squadrons yet, even if those in the quieter sectors had been up to operational standards. And they weren't.

Dowding's pilots, maintenance crews, and support organizations could not keep up this pace for a prolonged period and then fight a major battle. The Luftwaffe, on the other hand, could afford this loss ratio, if at the end of it Fighter Command ceased to exist. Meanwhile, the Air Fleets were able to arrange their flying schedules as they chose but Fighter Command was forced to put its standing patrols up every day.

8 August

By now, eighteen ships and four RN destroyers had been sunk. In daylight, the Straits had become so dangerous that destroyers had been withdrawn from Dover. Instead of transferring the coal to the railways, the Admiralty decided it would be enough to schedule the coastal convoys so that they reached the Dover Straits as darkness fell. The first such convoy, CW9, was assembled at Southend. The masters of some two dozen colliers were gathered in the dance-hall on Southend pier and addressed by an RNR

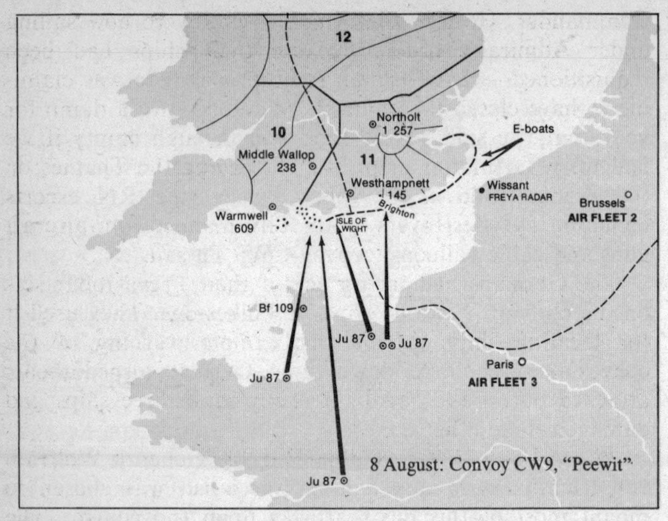

8 August: Convoy CW9, "Peewit"

Figure 26

The British sailors who died this day were the victims of two aspects of official stupidity. Firstly, the coastal convoys, carrying domestic cargoes, were still being sent through the dangerous waters of the Channel (instead of the goods going by railway, as they did later). Secondly, the Admiralty, refused to allow for the fact that the Germans might have excellent radar.

Sailing in darkness, convoy CW9 (code-named 'Peewit' by the RAF) was easily detected by the big Freya radar at Wissant. German torpedo boats attacked at dawn. Three ships were sunk and three damaged.

The Ju 87 dive bombers of *Fliegerkorps VIII* attacked the convoy south of Brighton but were frustrated by the RAF fighter defence and balloon cables flown from the ships to inhibit this kind of attack.

A further attack was mounted about midday, when Stukas from the élite *Lehrgeschwader 1* as well as *Stukageschwader* from Malo, Caen, and Angers, escorted by Bf 109s, flew to bomb the convoy near the Isle of Wight. The *Lehrgeschwader* were exceptionally skilled units originally assigned to evaluate tactics and equipment. RAF squadrons, sent to defend the convoy, are circled.

German results could have been more destructive had the two Air Fleets not had separate weather forecasting, planning staffs, and communications networks. As it was, Kesselring's Air Fleet 2 took no part in the action.

On the other hand, Fighter Command's 10 and 11 Groups had worked well together. The same could not be said for later occasions that called for equal co-operation from Leigh-Mallory in 12 Group.

Commander. He told these men – who were now sailing under Admiralty orders because their ships had been requisitioned – that German radio propaganda was claiming to have closed the channel. 'We don't give a damn for your coal,' he said. 'We'd send you through empty if we had to. It's a matter of prestige.' Leaving the Thames on the evening tide of 7 August, with nine RN escorts including two destroyers, with fully manned anti-aircraft guns and cable balloons, convoy CW9 set sail.

The Germans had set up one of their Freya radar sets on the cliffs at Wissant, opposite Folkestone. They used it for locating shipping, and had ample warning of the convoy's approach. As dawn came, German torpedo boats attacked out of the half-light. They sank three ships and damaged three others.

Fliegerkorps VIII, commanded by General Wolfram von Richthofen, a dive-bomber specialist, was chosen to mount most of this day's attacks upon the convoy. The cloudbase that morning was a little over 2,000 feet: there was not much head room for dive-bombing, especially since there were cable balloons on the ships. Park committed about five squadrons. In spite of their fighter escort, the Ju 87s, arriving in small relays, found it almost impossible to get a clear bombing dive at the target.

At midday the Luftwaffe tried a different tactic. About thirty Bf 109s of JG 27, and some Bf 110s, flew escort for three *Geschwader* of Ju 87s.

The Ventnor, Isle of Wight, radar found an unusually clear blip on the cathode-ray tube. The clarity was due to the size of this formation of aircraft. The Sector Controller fed over thirty Hurricanes and Spitfires into the air above the convoy. The battle began, and JG 27 skilfully engaged the British fighters, leaving the Stukas free to bomb. The accuracy of the dive bomber was forcibly demonstrated in the next ten minutes, as four merchant ships were sunk and seven were badly damaged. As the attack continued, the ships scattered, so dispersing the protection of the balloon barrage.

Determined to destroy every ship in the convoy, von Richthofen's *Fliegerkorps VIII* mounted another attack that afternoon as the convoy was trying to reassemble off the Isle of Wight. Eighty-two Ju 87s, and almost as many fighters, took part in the attack. Again they ran into RAF fighters vectored by very accurate plots from the radar chain.

By the end of the day the convoy was shattered: loose cargo, such as coal, produces progressive list in rough water and can easily capsize such vessels. Six ships limped into their nearest port. Of the twenty merchant ships that had originally set out for Swanage, Dorset, only four got there.

And for the men who survived cannon shell, burning fuel, or disintegrating aeroplanes, there was no succour in the sea. At Bembridge, Isle of Wight, the lifeboat *Jesse Lumb* was launched at 5:45 p.m. into what was recorded as 'a strong south-west wind and very rough sea.' They reached a place around which a plane was circling, to find, not airmen, but an RAF power boat that had been machine-gunned and was now flying a distress signal.

Fighter Command, a force designed specifically to defend Britain's coastline, had no proper air-sea rescue organization. Now there were a mere eighteen motor boats trying to provide a rescue service along the entire south coast. Or were they only providing some kind of bogus reassurance to the flyers?

The German air force provided their crews with a proper air-sea rescue organization. The key to this was the float-planes, that were able both to search *and* rescue. And the Luftwaffe gave their flyers flares and sea dye, yellow skull-caps, and one-man dinghies that enabled a fighter pilot to get out of the sea. Even in summer, British waters are cold. Immersed in them, with only a 'Mae West' life jacket that had to be inflated from the lungs of exhausted or injured men, many RAF flyers died in sight of England's beaches. Even in summer temperatures, few men remained conscious after two hours in the sea.

During this month there were no more such 'prestige'

coal convoys through the Channel. Those same men in the Admiralty, supported by their Air Ministry counterparts, who had pressured Dowding to fly standing patrols over the domestic shipping now discovered that these cargoes could be moved by rail. Had this discovery come a few weeks earlier, many RAF pilots – including a high proportion of flight commanders and experienced Regular officers – would have still been alive. In just three weeks of July, no less than 220 RAF flyers had been lost in the sea. Also, there were the injured and dead sailors.

But in Britain this day was one of rejoicing. The Air Ministry mathematicians kept to their usual routine of giving the true figures of RAF losses while accepting without question the wild claims of the RAF pilots. They announced that sixty German aircraft had been destroyed. People who knew that the pilots were being too optimistic kept the opinion to themselves. In any case, the true figures (thirty-one German aircraft shot down, for the loss of nineteen RAF fighters) were praiseworthy. The Nazi propaganda service announced that forty-nine RAF fighters had been shot down: and the Germans also celebrated. They had done great destruction to the ships and the *Kanalkampfführer*'s task was fulfilled, even if the original battle-group he had been given had proved inadequate.

The extremely poor intelligence estimates upon which the Luftwaffe High Command depended had overestimated the fighter strength of the RAF but it had badly underestimated the rate of manufacture. The restraint that Dowding showed, as he committed only small numbers of aircraft, the lack of RAF fighter pilots for interrogation, and the sort of reports that Luftwaffe air crews brought back from the Battle, all these factors encouraged the Luftwaffe High Command to believe that Fighter Command had very small resources left. In this context, the comparatively large air battles of 8 August (in which a couple of hundred aircraft fought) were interpreted by German intelligence as Fighter Command's last desperate fling.

If the Luftwaffe's view of the RAF was sanguine, the

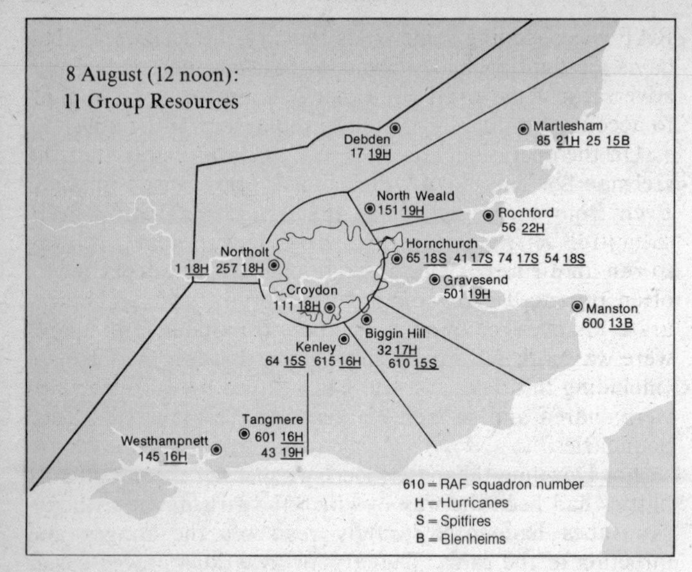

Figure 27

If we freeze one moment of the battle – noon on 8 August – it is possible to examine in detail the fighting down to the last pilot and plane. Here are shown all the fighter squadrons available to Park in 11 Group. Squadron numbers are shown, and the aircraft 'serviceable' that morning – Hurricane or Spitfire – are underlined. The twin-engine Bristol Blenheim squadrons are shown but were not used for night fighting.

Although Park preferred to fly his squadrons in pairs (one Hurricane and one Spitfire squadron), this was not always possible. And, although Kenley and Biggin Hill had paired squadrons, this meant that stores and workshops had to have spares and facilities for two entirely different aircraft types.

At this moment shown, some squadrons were occupying satellite airfields. Martlesham was a satellite of Debden. It was also a satellite of North Weald, and so was Rochford. Gravesend and Manston were satellites mostly used by Biggin Hill squadrons, just as Kenley used the old London airport at Croydon, and Tangmere used Westhampnett. Some of the satellite airfields were very primitive.

Notice the very small scale of the battles. Seldom has such a tiny number of men decided the course of history. Notice too the small proportion of Spitfires compared to Hurricanes, and this was in the Group that was given priority of quantity and quality. For the difference between aircraft 'serviceable' and 'available,' see text.

RAF was shedding some of its fears of the Luftwaffe. The day's air fighting had shown the Ju 87 a most vulnerable adversary, while the Hurricanes had proved good enough to account for nine out of ten of the destroyed Bf 109s.

On the operational level, it was becoming clear that the German system of Air Fleets had grave disadvantages. Even from early July, when the Air Fleets' staff officers submitted separate plans to Göring, it was clearly no way to run an air force. The separate meteorology departments often produced contradictory weather forecasts. The separate channels of manpower, fuel, armament, and spares were wasteful. And many ships going through the Channel (including this day's convoy) had escaped because the ships were shared and scattered across the German Air Fleets' boundaries.

For Dowding the most cheering aspect of these 8 August battles had been the way in which the girls at the cathode-ray tubes had so accurately read off the ranges and direction of the raids. The larger formations proved easier to read off and the operators had proved remarkably good at translating the blurred fidget of light into an assessment of the raid's strength. The height of the attackers had proved more difficult to judge. This was to be expected from the equipment and so it was to remain throughout the battle, not only for the radar operators but also for the Observer Corps. And yet the height estimation affected the reported position (calculated by simple trigonometry), which is why the tracks zig-zagged across the plotting tables, seldom running in the straight lines that the aircraft actually flew. But it was good enough.

Nationally, the morale of the British public was at an all-time high, and the RAF fighter pilots had created a tradition of engaging the big formations irrespective of odds, and in spite of knowing that there were hundreds of Hurricanes and Spitfires standing idle on British airfields. It was an act of faith in Dowding, although not an unquestioning one. 'The utter futility of sending very small sections of fighters to cope with the intense enemy activity in the Portland area is bitterly resented by the pilots,' some fighter pilot wrote into 609 Squadron's Operation Record Book, but they continued to attack.

The 'Tally-Ho!' tradition was inaugurated by peacetime pilots, leading flights and squadrons. As the Battle continued, and their places were taken by Auxiliaries and Volunteer Reservists, that aggressive spirit was something that no one cared to, or dared to, discontinue. In this respect, it was Fighter Command's career officers who won the Battle.

11 August

'Sailor' Malan, who had damaged Mölders's Messerschmitt on 28 July, was this day commanding 74 (Tiger) Squadron for the first time in the air. By the end of July he had won the DFC and bar, and on 11 August he flew three times and claimed two Bf 109s and two Bf 109s severely damaged.

But Malan was 30 years old, officially too old to be a squadron commander. Flying in line-astern formation with Malan that day there was the remarkable Warrant Officer Ernie Mayne. Near the French coast 'Sailor' Malan made a tight turn, and Mayne, at the rear, had to turn tightest of all. He blacked out as the blood rushed out of his brain, and his Spitfire fell through the air from 24,000 feet to about 4,000 feet. Mayne recovered in time to save himself from crashing into the sea. Still dazed, he headed towards a nearby formation in the hope that they would lead him home. 'Well of course they were Huns. I think that woke me up a bit. When I saw the crosses I had a shot at one, but then I thought this is no place for you, you'd better b— off. So I did, and got home, but the falling hadn't done my ears any good.'

That was an understatement. WO Mayne went into hospital as a result of falling almost four miles through the sky. He was 40 years old, probably the only RFC veteran to fly a Spitfire in the Battle. But this was this NCO's last operational sortie.

Later in the war, with the expansion of Bomber Command, sergeant air crew were recruited directly from civilian life. But in the Battle of Britain period NCO pilots were either members of the RAF Volunteer Reserve or Regular airmen who had been through the RAF Apprentice School for technical trades. These 'brats' began training when aged between 15½ and 17, having committed themselves to remain in the RAF until aged 30.

Sergeant pilot Frank Carey was an ex-brat. Born in Brixton, London, in 1912, he had joined the RAF only a few days after his fifteenth birthday. After three years as an apprentice, he went to 43 Squadron as a mechanic, and then spent a year on an engineering course. Selected for pilot training, Carey arrived back at 43 Squadron as a Sergeant pilot in September 1935. In January 1940, Carey damaged a Heinkel 111. It was the Squadron's first success. He got the DFM (the other-ranks' equivalent of the DFC that was awarded to officers), and then was made an officer. He went to 3 Squadron in France and within hours of arriving was credited with his new Squadron's first success too. By the summer of 1940 Frank Carey was back in his old 43 Squadron but now he was a flight commander and their top ace. By the time he was wounded in August he was credited with eighteen victories. By the end of the war he was a Group Captain.

Sammy Allard was another outstanding Sergeant pilot. With characteristic generosity and modesty, Peter Townsend, commanding 85 Squadron (once the home of First World War aces Mick Mannock and Billy Bishop), acknowledged Allard as the best pilot in the Squadron. Allard won the DFM and bar, getting a commission in time to win the DFC too. By October he had destroyed nine enemy aircraft and was a Flight Lieutenant.

But not all the Sergeant pilots got promoted to officer rank. Sergeant Alan Feary was the only NCO pilot with 609 Squadron all through the summer months. 'He must at times have felt dreadfully lonely . . . ,' said the Squadron history. Excluded from the social life of their fellow pilots, these NCOs were often treated with reserve by the old-timers who controlled the Sergeants' Mess, some of whom regarded flying as a quick and easy way to get three stripes.

In other squadrons NCO pilots sometimes outnumbered the officers. For instance at 501 Squadron in September, with three officer pilots in hospital, there were twelve pilots in the Sergeants' Mess, with only the Commanding Officer, two flight commanders, and four pilots in the Officers' Mess.

These ex-tradesmen, who had spent so many years

ILLUSTRATIONS

46 A Messerschmitt Bf 110 flying over the white cliffs of Dover How could the German propaganda service resist it? They didn't and this photograph was given top priority for distribution throughout the world, including a huge double-page-spread in colour in the international propaganda magazine *Signal*. Less publicized was the terrible casualty rate that these 'destroyer' aircraft suffered. From *Adlertag* (13 August) until the end of that month, the Bf 110 units suffered no less than 40 per cent casualties. This particular aircraft can be traced to a unit (II/ZG 2) that was entirely disbanded because of the number of planes lost.

47 A captured German rescue float-plane On 9 July 1940 this Heinkel He 59 from *Seenotflugkommando* (air-sea rescue unit) 1 at Boulogne was shot down by Squadron Leader J. F. Allan of 54 Squadron during a battle in which Al Deere collided head-on with a Bf 109 of JG 51. The rescue float-plane crash-landed on Goodwin sands and was towed to Deal by the Walmer lifeboat. The crew were made prisoner. A few days after this the British Air Ministry ordered the fighter squadrons to attack all such red cross rescue planes. The Luftwaffe then camouflaged them and gave them machine guns to defend themselves.

48 Rescue from the sea This amazing sequence of photographs shows a Messerschmitt Bf 110 ditching in the sea near to the French coastline. By now the Germans had painted their rescue float-planes in camouflage colours, and one of them arrives very quickly at the scene of the crash. The crew decide not to inflate the dinghy and they swim across to the Heinkel. However, the waterlogged flying clothes make them so heavy that the rescue crew have great difficulty heaving the flyers out of the water. Notice the way that the Heinkel pilot stops the engines so that the slipstream doesn't make the rescue more difficult. The Heinkel is very low in the water because the floats are used as fuel tanks. In this case the tanks seem to be rather full.

46

47

48a 48b 48d 48e 48g 48h

48c

48f

48i

49

working on the airframes and engines, had a close affinity with the machines they flew. Some of them found it difficult to subject their carefully tuned fighters to the sort of rough abuse that was a necessary part of normal combat (for similar reasons top racing and rally drivers are seldom recruited from the men who tune the cars). When Sergeant Feary of 609 (West Riding) Squadron was shot up in a dog-fight with some Bf 109s and Bf 110s, he tried to nurse his Spitfire home. The 609 Squadron diary recorded, 'He seemed to regard his Spitfire with the kind of jealous care and affection that some others bestow upon animals, and the notion has been advanced by those who knew him well that this trait in his character may have contributed to the loss of his life, causing reluctance to bail out from a spin which he was unable to control.'

Sergeant 'Ginger' Lacey, with 501 (County of Gloucester) Squadron, an Auxiliary Air Force unit, had never been a brat. Lacey had learned to fly as a member of the RAFVR on weekends and at summer camps. He had only become a full-time fighter pilot at the outbreak of war. Of

49 War photography A German army propaganda company (notice the operator's cuff band) was sent to take photographs across the Channel, using a 35-mm camera and this extraordinary lens. The giant optic was aimed with a pair of waist-level 'handlebars' and sighted with a separate telescope mounted on the side of the lens. The trailer provided a housing for the photographic apparatus and became a mount, complete with staircase and handrail, when the camera was in use. As well as the ditching sequence, this camera team took the photograph of the Dover radar towers (Plate 10).

50 A ground crew at work fitting the cowlings over the Jumo engines of a Heinkel He 111H before an air test The shortage of really good aero-engines restricted the efficiency of the Luftwaffe throughout the war. Earlier He 111 bombers had been fitted with the superb Daimler Benz DB 601 engines but now these were diverted to fighter production and the Heinkels had to make do with Jumo engines of the sort that these men are working on. This meant that the Heinkels were the slowest of the German bombers. As a stop-gap measure they were fitted with up to 600 lbs of armour plate and extra machine guns, but these aircraft were already being relegated to the role of transport and communication.

all the men flying Spitfires and Hurricanes in the Battle of Britain, about a quarter were non-commissioned ranks (nearly all of them Sergeants). Of these NCO pilots, about two-fifths were VR men.

But there was another type of NCO pilot; these were experienced flyers from foreign air forces, mostly Poles and Czechs. Such men were usually given ranks below those they had held abroad.

Of all the Sergeants engaged in the air battles, none was more remarkable than Josef Frantisek, a Czech Regular airman who had taken an aeroplane and left his country after the German occupation. He joined the Polish air force and fought against the Luftwaffe for three weeks until escaping to Rumania. He escaped from an internment camp and travelled through the Balkans. When he got to the Middle East he persuaded the French to send him to France. He flew with the French air force until June 1940, scoring several victories and winning the *Croix de Guerre*. Again he escaped the advancing Germans, and this time he joined the RAF. After a conversion course he was posted to 303 (Polish) Squadron.

Sergeant Frantisek had flying and air-fighting skills in abundance but he lacked any kind of air discipline. Once in the air, he simply chased Germans. More than once this conduct endangered the men who flew with him. He was repeatedly reprimanded until finally the Poles decided to let him be a 'guest of the Squadron.' This gave him the unique privilege of fighting his own war, in his own way, and his own time. It proved a wise decision. Modern research suggests that he was the most successful fighter pilot serving with the RAF.[1]

The Luftwaffe also had NCO pilots making reputations as air fighters. One of the most famous was Siegfried Schnell of II/JG 2, the *Richthofen Geschwader* (where his name was being mentioned even in comparison with

[1]Ministry of Defence (Historical Branch) records show Lock and McKellar as the highest scorers with twenty victories each. Sergeant Frantisek is placed third.

Hauptmann Helmut Wick, a fast rising star of the fighter force and soon to lead the *Geschwader*). Both the *Hauptmann* and the young NCO were on their way to getting the twenty confirmed kills that almost automatically brought the Knight's Cross. And that decoration, conspicuously worn at the collar, granted the holder the sort of respect and adulation that pop stars and footballers win. It meant the best seat in restaurants, a place at the head of the line, deference from even the most senior officers, pictures in the newspapers, and hugs from the girls.

Kurt Bühligen was also in the *Richthofen Geschwader*. A young NCO who was eventually to get the very highest awards for valour and become one of the few aces to shoot down over 100 machines while fighting on the western front. There was another such NCO flying alongside the famous Mölders in JG 51 (a unit that was in later years to bear the name Mölders, just as JG 2 was named Richthofen); this was Heinz 'Pritzl' Bär.

Born near Leipzig in 1913, the son of a farmer, Bär had flown gliders, and then powered gliders, to get his pilot's licence in 1930. But no matter how he tried, he could not get a job flying for Lufthansa. In 1937 he joined the Luftwaffe. He scored his first aerial victory in France within a month of the start of the war. During the Battle of Britain period, Bär was credited with seventeen victories and was soon commissioned. By the end of the war Bär was to become one of the top German aces, having fought on every front, won the Knight's Cross with oak leaves, swords, and diamonds, flown the Me 262 jets, and been credited with 220 victories. He was the highest scoring ace of the fighting in the west, and the most successful ace with jets (sixteen victories).

At this stage of the war it was hard to predict which of the fighter pilots would become top aces. Some pilots such as Georg-Peter Eder (who ended the war with seventy-eight victories) went through the summer of 1940 without scoring even one victory.

There were other examples in which outstanding pilots

of 1940 were afterwards assigned to jobs that gave them few chances of combat flying. At the end of July, 48-year-old 'Onkel Theo' Osterkamp was officially ordered to cease combat flying. Since forming JG 51 in 1939, he had flown constantly and had now added six victims to his First World War total. In August he was awarded the Knight's Cross and appointed to take over *Jafü 2* (commanding all Kesselring's fighters). But Mölders's fight with Malan, and the injuries he had suffered, meant that Osterkamp was now trying to do both jobs. Luckily for him, the staff of both *Jafü 2* and of JG 51 were at Wissant airfield at the extreme tip of the Pas de Calais.

And 'Onkel Theo' was by no means the only First World War veteran to fly in the Battle of Britain on the German side. JG 2's *Kommodore*, Harry von Bülow-Bothkamp, was credited with no less than eighteen victories, to add to the six he had earned in the First World War. He was 45 years old. Commanding his *III Gruppe* there was 41-year-old Erich Mix. He had shot down three Allied planes in the First World War and was now on his way to the thirteen more that he downed in the Second World War.

Added to these must be several veterans who flew in the bomber units. The amazing *Oberstleutnant* Joachim Huth had lost a leg in the First World War but now led the Bf 110s of ZG 76. Oldest of all was Eduard Ritter von Schleich, who'd won thirty-five victories in the previous war when his all-black Albatros DV 2 earned him the nickname 'Black Knight.' He'd flown in Spain and had only recently been ordered off combat flying with JG 26, at the age of 51.

Remarkable in another way were the Americans who'd decided to make the war their own. The trio serving with 609 Squadron were particularly colourful. Andy Mamedoff, from Miami, had spent the pre-war years barnstorming his own plane round the USA. 'Shorty' Keough, a Brooklyn-born professional parachutist, was under five feet tall and needed two air-cushions under his parachute pack in order to see out of the cockpit. The third member of the trio was 'Red' Tobin, the son of a Los Angeles real-estate man. Obsessed with aircraft, he'd flown 200 hours on light planes while working as a studio messenger with MGM. Tobin signed up to fly in Finland, against the invading Russians, but the war ended and he went to France instead. The Americans escaped on the last boat to leave, on the day that the armistice was signed. After four weeks at an RAF Operational Training Unit they were posted to a Spitfire squadron. All saw combat; Tobin scored a victory during the Battle and Keough was credited with a half-share in a shot-down Dornier. In October 1940 they went to help form the first Eagle Squadron of American flyers. All three pilots were killed over Britain in 1941.

Phase Two: *Adlerangriff* (Eagle Attack)

During July, the Luftwaffe monitoring service and the German Post Office established listening units along the Channel coast. The operators found a maze of radio activity on the 12-metre band. Some experts guessed these signals were connected with the mysterious 350-foot-tall masts along the English coast.

As the *Kanalkampf* developed, the German monitors found other things to puzzle over. Replying to the excited slang of the fighter pilots came other calmer voices on the high-frequency radio-telephones. Of unvarying volume, and fixed position, the god-like voices steered the RAF formations and informed them of the German strengths, tracks, and altitudes.

German intelligence studied all the reports of these voices, and on 7 August issued this secret report to the operational commands.

> As the British fighters are controlled from the ground by radio-telephone, their forces are tied to their respective ground stations and are thereby restricted in mobility, even taking into consideration the probability that the ground stations are partly mobile. Consequently the assembly of strong fighter forces at determined points and at short notice is not to be expected.

It was a disastrous error of judgment. German intelligence's failure to understand those strange voices on the air was even worse than not knowing about them. Believing that the RAF had this primitive sort of radio control, with squadrons tied to their local station, led the Luftwaffe to think that mass attacks would encounter only the local fighters.[1] And it did not even take radar into account.

It must be remembered that the secret of radar was still shared by only a small number of men and women. *Generalmajor* Wolfgang Martini – of Luftwaffe Signals Service – was certainly informed of all the technical advances, and it was he who insisted that attacks must be made upon these *Funkstationen mit Sonderanlagen* (radio stations with special installations), as they were marked on Luftwaffe target maps. So it was decided to devote the day before *Adlertag* to attacks upon these stations and upon RAF fighter airfields near the coast. This combination of raids would thus confirm, or deny, that the RAF fighters were depending upon the stations.

The four-engined FW 200s, under *Marine Gruppe West* at Lorient, had ranged far into the Atlantic, watching the region of high pressure over the Azores. As it began moving, the Air Fleet's orders were dated and put onto the teleprinters. *Adlertag* was fixed for 13 August, with preparatory attacks the day before.

The RAF also had access to the reports from men eavesdropping on German frequencies. The German weather-reconnaissance units were not asked simply for general information but for weather conditions at the intended targets. As an added risk to security such aircraft sent radio reports while still over Britain. This, and any other Luftwaffe radio traffic, was correlated by a secret unit known as the Y service. And as each German aeroplane was prepared for an operational flight, its radio

[1]It is ironic to record that when the Luftwaffe set up its own radar and reporting network, it made exactly this mistake. It tied fighters to each local radar set, and so was totally swamped by RAF night bombers which arrived in dense streams.

was tested. Monitoring of these test signals provided intelligence with a fairly accurate guess at the number of aircraft to be used in the following 24-hour period. As Eagle Day approached, the listening service was able to tell Dowding that he was about to be attacked on a scale far exceeding all previous attacks.

12 August

Erprobungsgruppe 210 (flight evaluation group) was a recently formed unit. Its primary task – of evaluating the new Messerschmitt Me 210A-O under battle conditions – had been temporarily put aside. This was fortunate for them, since the Me 210A-O was one of the most notorious aircraft design failures of the war. As far as is recorded, no example of it participated in the Battle.

ErprGr 210's present task was that of evaluating the *Jabos*, which were Bf 109 and Bf 110 aircraft in the role of a light, low-level bomber that could revert to the fighter role after the bombs had been dropped.

This highly skilled unit had shown enough success to be briefed for the most vital of *Adlerangriff*'s preparatory attacks. At 8:40 a.m., sixteen aircraft took off from the airfield at Calais. Their task was a pinpoint bombing attack upon four radar stations.

Already Bf 109s of II/JG 52 had passed over Dover and chased across Kent. Spitfires of No. 610 (County of Chester), an Auxiliary Air Force squadron, were sent after them. In the dog-fight that followed, the Germans deliberately moved the battle eastwards. This would leave the air clear for *ErprGr 210*.

Hauptmann Walter Rubensdörffer – a 30-year-old Swiss – brought his formation of Bf 110s along the Channel at 18,000 feet. They approached Dover at right angles, to make the radar operator's task more difficult. It was the Rye radar that picked them up. It was noticed that the track was heading straight at them. The 19-year-old girl operator was slightly irritated by the way in which the Filter Room, at Fighter Command, gave the plot an X

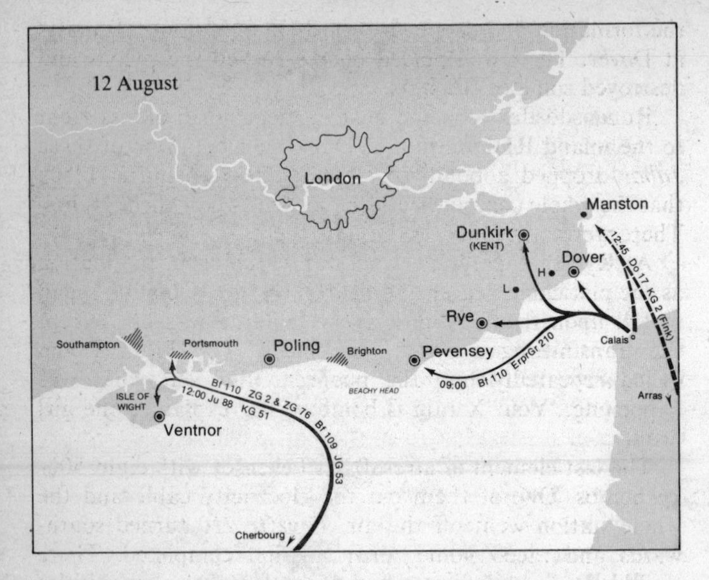

Figure 28

The most important assignment for the day before *Adlertag* was that of *ErprGr 210*, which used Bf 110s equipped with bombs to make precision attacks on the radar stations.

About noon another large formation approached Brighton and then flew along the coast trying to get behind the long-range radar at Ventnor, Isle of Wight. However, they were seen by the Poling radar, which had not been attacked that morning, and also by Observer Corps personnel at the coast.

This raid divided: one part went to bomb Portsmouth and the other attacked the Ventnor radar from the north. At nearby Southampton, the Supermarine factory was – up to about this time – the only place where Spitfires were manufactured. It was not included in the targets.

Lympne and Hawkinge airfields, attacked this day, are shown as L and H on the map.

code. That meant a report of doubtful origin: possibly friendly aircraft, or a mistake.

The first element of four Messerschmitts peeled off from

the formation and dropped towards the 350-foot-tall masts at Dover. Their well-placed bombs rocked the pylons and destroyed some of the huts.

Rubensdörffer took the next element north across Kent to the inland RDF station at Dunkirk, Kent. One of these *Jabos* dropped a bomb so close to the transmitter block that the whole concrete building moved two or three inches. There were other hits on the huts there.

At Rye the operators were still watching in fascination as the plot came nearer and nearer. Suddenly bombs began to fall upon them. Almost every building was hit, except the transmitting and receiving block. The Filter Room called repeatedly into the phone to find out what was happening. 'Your X raid is bombing us,' explained the girl primly.

The last element of aircraft hit Pevensey with eight 500-kg bombs. One of them cut the electricity cable and the whole station went off the air. *ErprGr 210* turned southwards and raced home, their mission completed. There could have been no better demonstration of the capabilities of the Bf 110 in the fighter-bomber role. Of the four radar stations attacked, only Dunkirk, Kent, remained on the air.

With a 100-mile-wide gap torn out of the radar chain, no fighters could be sent to intercept the formations that now attacked the fighter airfields at Lympne and Hawkinge. The former was only used as an emergency satellite, so the serious damage done to it was not vital to Fighter Command. Hawkinge, however, was important. The damage there included the destruction of two hangars, and station workshops, and four fighters damaged on the ground.

The *Stukagruppen* also benefited from the radar gap, and ships were attacked as they moved along the Kent coast. In the absence of radar, the fighters arrived late. The Ju 87s all returned safely.

It was nearly noon when the radar station at Poling – which had not suffered an attack – read a very large formation approaching Brighton from due south. This was the whole of KG 51 – nearly 100 Ju 88s – plus ZG 2 and ZG 76: 120 Bf 110s. As high-flying escort came twenty-five Bf 109s from JG 53, The *Pik As Geschwader*, named after the ace of spades emblem that was painted on their fighters.

Before it reached Brighton the whole formation turned west, following the coast towards the Isle of Wight. As they came to Spithead, all of the aircraft except fifteen Ju 88s turned north to Portsmouth. Going through a gap in the balloon barrage – caused by the harbour – they made a fierce attack upon the docks and the town.

The Hurricanes of 213 Squadron steered clear of Portsmouth, where they could see intense anti-aircraft fire colouring the sky along the line of the Germans' bombing run. The big battleship HMS *Queen Elizabeth* was in the harbour, and the Ju 88s followed their *Kommodore* in a steep dive-bombing attack. However, all the ships escaped and a brewery suffered. At least one *Staffel* had virtually no experience of dive-bombing, and the dive-brakes of one machine jammed in the down position. Two of the Ju 88s fell victim to the anti-aircraft guns. Then the *Kommodore* of the *Edelweiss Geschwader* turned to lead his formation out of the target area. The Hurricanes dived upon them. The *Kommodore*'s Ju 88 flew back the way it had come until it was shot down into the sea south of the Poling radar station. None of its crew survived.

Meanwhile, the fifteen Ju 88s that had detached from the main formation turned south across the middle of the Isle of Wight to attack Ventnor radar station from the landward side. The aerials, as tall as cathedral spires and sited on the hills above the town, provided the specially designed radar with very-long-range detection but they were a conspicuous target. The bombers put fifteen 500-kg bombs into the compound, and destroyed every building there. The aerials were also damaged: the radar flickered and died.

Coastal posts of the Observer Corps had been reporting the German formation ever since it approached Brighton.

By the time that the bombs were dropping on the Ventnor radar, Spitfires of 152 and 609 Squadrons were closing on them.

Artfully, Park had put his fighters into the battle piecemeal. Ten thousand feet above the bombers, the high-flying escort of Bf 109s circled, waiting for the main body of RAF fighters to arrive. Only when the bombers had lost ten of their number did the *Pik As* formation leader dive into the battle.

In previous attacks the Luftwaffe had sent fresh Bf 109s to escort their bombers home. Park was prepared for this too. When more Bf 109s were seen heading west over Beachy Head, he placed a dozen Hurricanes – of 615 Squadron – between them and the battles over the Isle of Wight.

It was a measure of the skill and importance of Rubensdörffer's *Gruppe* that they were put back into the Battle so soon after returning from the morning's attacks on the radar stations. Again they crossed the narrow Straits of Dover. It was still not one o'clock as the Messerschmitts bombed and machine-gunned the coastal airfield at Manston. They arrived just as Spitfires of 65 Squadron were taking off for a patrol.

Behind the fighter-bombers – *Jabos* – there were eighteen Dornier Do 17s of KG 2. Like the Junkers Ju 88s of the Portsmouth attack, these bombers were led by their *Geschwaderkommodore*. In the case of the *Holzhammer* this was the *Kanalkampfführer* himself: *Oberst* Fink.

Manston airfield disappeared under a great cloud of smoke and flame as 150 bombs hit workshops, hangars, and a Blenheim twin-engined night fighter. Perched on cliffs overlooking the sea, Manston provided a chance for Fink to turn out to sea and disappear before any fighters could be scrambled to the airfield's defence. For many of the RAF men at Manston, this attack was more than they could take. 'Hundreds' of airmen went down into the bomb shelters and stayed there for days in spite of threats, orders, and entreaties by their officers.

Even the bravest patriots at Manston found it difficult to understand why the airfield was not evacuated. The installations were damaged so badly that flying operations were difficult and no pilot attempting either landing or take-off did it without apprehensively searching the sky for German prowlers.

And yet Fighter Command refused to withdraw from Manston, believing probably that such a move would be made into a propaganda victory by the Germans. But even this can hardly account for the way in which 600 (City of London) Squadron was kept at Manston during the long, grim, summer days of August.

This Auxiliary squadron flew Bristol Blenheims, twin-engined bombers ordered by the RAF at a time when their performance was superior to the current fighters. But when monoplane fighters replaced the biplanes, the Blenheims became obsolete. Far too vulnerable for daylight operations as bombers, or to be adapted to fighter configuration, the Blenheims were, in 1940, all too often mistaken for Junkers Ju 88s, with fatal results.

Now the Blenheims had been fitted with an amazing new device: the world's first radar set small enough to be carried inside an aircraft. At night the Blenheims chased lone German bombers around the home counties, but the slow Blenheim needed too large a measure of luck to prove effective in the night-fighter role either.

Of all the people at Manston, the air crew of 600 Squadron had more reason to complain than any. And yet their resilience and cheerfulness were a notable contrast to the breakdown of morale that was evident all round them. And when the ground staff went into the shelters and refused to come out, it was the air crews of 600 Squadron who could be seen day after day in August helping to refuel and rearm the Spitfires. As Al Deere of 54 Squadron pointed out, 'More often than not this was done under fire from the enemy and despite the fact that the 600 Squadron pilots should have been resting from the previous night's operations.'

But in the sky, too, men were discovering that mental and physical exhaustion prepares the way for fear. One of the Spitfires which landed at Manston that afternoon was piloted by a young Sergeant pilot who had been flying on operations continuously since Dunkirk was evacuated. Now he simply avoided combat and had been doing so for several days. He left the formation at the first sight of the enemy, fired his guns, and turned for home. 'He's not just tired, he's yellow,' complained one of the 54 Squadron officers. Sadly, the others agreed with him. Afraid that the Sergeant's fears would communicate themselves to the new pilots, he was left off the next day's flying orders, and sent immediately on leave, pending posting.

It was a day of remarkable triumphs for the German Air Fleets: a perfect preparation for a major offensive. And yet, when Kesselring sent his Dornier bombers to attack the Kent coast that evening, they found that the RDF stations had already been patched up to continue operation. Only Ventnor had been damaged badly enough to make a hole in the chain, and to disguise that deficiency its signals were being transmitted by another station.

The German radio-intercept service regretfully reported that none of the British stations had ceased its signals. None of the returning crews had been able to report a demolished mast. The 350-foot-high lattice construction masts were difficult to hit from straight and level flight and difficult to damage by blast, while their very height inhibited the dive attack. The Germans took it for granted that any control rooms and electronic gear would be deep underground and invulnerable to bombing.

Göring's *Adlerangriff* was launched without any cogent strategy, as *Der Eiserner* gave his bombing fleets long lists of objectives. Ships and installations were to be destroyed, as were commercial ports and harbours, coastal shipping, and a long schedule of 'blockade targets.' RAF units of all kinds must be bombed, as well as factories producing aircraft, aircraft components, or aircraft armament. The Royal Navy was also to be attacked from Dover to Scapa

Flow. This was particularly difficult as the Luftwaffe had no armour-piercing bombs, which were necessary to sink big warships.

Göring assigned no priorities to this plethora of targets, and no one was quite sure whether it was intended to destroy Fighter Command by bombing or by bringing its fighters to battle in the air. *Oberst* Paul Diechmann, *Fliegerkorps II* Chief of Staff, said that if the 'special radio stations' were bringing the RAF fighters into battle, wouldn't it be better to let them do so, and destroy them in the air? There was no official answer.

If the strategy was indecisive, the tactics were equally so, for the Luftwaffe intelligence service had only the vaguest understanding of the RAF's defensive system. For instance, the Portsmouth/Ventnor raid had been planned so that the attackers came in parallel with the English coast. This would be a good way to avoid radar surveillance during the approach (for it was the flatness of the sea that provided a clear picture). But this route overlooked the way in which the radar station at Poling would see approaching planes beautifully, and it ignored countless Observer Corps posts which were sited along the coast, as well as inland, and were all connected by telephone to the fighter control system.

It was due to poor intelligence that the Luftwaffe's operational maps did not correctly distinguish between airfields used by Fighter Command, those used by other air force units, and those unused. After the war, some Luftwaffe commanders explained that this was thought unimportant, because they believed the RAF Squadrons to be as mobile as the Air Fleets. As an error, it reveals a profound misunderstanding of the fighter control organization, which depended upon an elaborate network of Operations Rooms, sector airfields, Observer Corps posts, and D/F rooms: all of them linked by telephone cables and depending upon electricity.

The Luftwaffe's intelligence specialists showed no better understanding of Britain's aircraft industry. Most British schoolboys knew that the Spitfires and Hurricanes were powered by Rolls-Royce Merlins. There were only two factories making them and one of these was the world-famous home of Rolls-Royce at Derby. The Spitfire was even more vulnerable, for there was only one factory in full-scale airframe production, and that was the well-known Supermarine factory at Southampton, dangerously close to the Luftwaffe's bomber bases. With astounding ineptitude the Luftwaffe's intelligence experts had this site marked as belonging to A. V. Roe, a company making bombers.

Those three targets would have been worth almost any sacrifice to destroy before *Adlertag*. But in the event, none of the attacks selected for Eagle Day could possibly have resulted in a mortal blow to Fighter Command.

13 August

Adlerangriff began with an unbelievable series of staff blunders. First the 'weather-frogs' got their forecast wrong, and there was mixed weather that included cloud, mist, and drizzle. Göring personally issued a postponement order. But this order failed to reach *Oberst* Fink's KG 2 headquarters at Arras.

The 50-year-old Fink had been in the forefront of the battle ever since being made *Kanalkampfführer* in July. He was the oldest *Kommodore* flying on operations. Just after five o'clock that morning he climbed up into his bomber and again led the *Holzhammer Geschwader* on its mission.

During July the tired old Dornier Do 17s had suffered losses out of proportion to their sortie rate. Many had been destroyed while flying solitary photo-reconnaissance missions over Britain. (For this reason some of the reconnaissance units were now receiving the faster Messerschmitt Bf 110, a twin-engine fighter modified for cameras.)

Even for *Adlertag*, the entire *Holzhammer Geschwader* could put only seventy-four Do 17s into the air. And so the crews, in their obsolescent bombers, took heart as they crossed the cloudy coastline of France and saw fighter escorts climbing to join formation with them. They too failed to get the postponement order. The fighters were Bf 110s of ZG 26 – the *Horst Wessel Geschwader* – led by their one-legged *Kommodore* who, like Fink, was a veteran of the First World War. This man – *Oberstleutnant* Huth – now flew his Bf 110 in a series of jinking turns across the path of Fink's Dornier. Fink, who had previously been the chief accident investigator of the Luftwaffe, no doubt disapproved of what he later described as 'high spirits' but soon the clouds hid the fighter escort from view.

In fact, the Luftwaffe Signals Service had failed to provide the Dorniers with the correct crystals for their radio wavelengths. The Bf 110s had received their recall while in the air. Huth's jinking 'high spirits' was his attempt to tell Fink to turn round and take his bombers home again. But Huth was no more successful in communicating the recall to the bombers than were the radio operators on the ground. Unaware that the rest of the Air Fleets were grounded, Fink flew on. The clouds that had caused the postponement now made it difficult for the RAF fighters to find them. By luck or by judgment, or a combination of both, Fink emerged from the clouds very close to his target.

Fink's *III Gruppe* were over the Isle of Sheppey, in the Thames Estuary, before they were found by 74 Squadron, led by 'Sailor' Malan. There was a running fight. They bombed from 1,500 feet. In the distance they saw the London balloon barrage. As they turned away, Fink's Staff Flight, leading the formation, ran into 111 Squadron. This had been the first RAF unit to get monoplane fighters, and their accumulated experience stood them in good stead throughout the battle. Of the five Do 17s that KG 2 lost that morning, four were destroyed by 111 Squadron. The other Dornier had the bad luck to run into one of the very few cannon-armed RAF fighters in service: a Hurricane flown by Pilot Officer I. S. Smith of 151 Squadron.

Of the rest of Fink's *Holzhammer Geschwader*, another five Dorniers returned to their airfields too badly shot up to fly. Fink climbed out of his pilot seat in a terrible fury. He phoned Kesselring at Blanc Nez and made an angry complaint about the confusion. At Kesselring's underground HQ – unofficially called *Heiliger Berg* (Holy Mountain) – it had been a busy morning. Not only was 'Robinson,' the railway train of the Luftwaffe's Chief of Staff, in France, but 'Asia' the private train of Göring, meant that the Commander in Chief was heading his way too. In spite of these other claims for his time and attention, Kesselring made a journey to Fink at Arras to apologize in person. Fink's losses confirmed the High Command's fears; whatever sort of radio control the RAF were using, it had not been put out of action by the previous day's pinpoint attacks.

The muddles continued. A free sweep by I/JG 2 (the *Richthofen Geschwader*) – to provide protection for the Ju 88s of KG 54 – went wrong when the bombers found the weather so bad that they turned back soon after crossing the coast. At least this *Totenkopf Geschwader* had only one casualty: an engineer who bailed out from an aircraft (marked B3 + TP of the sixth *Staffel*) when it was attacked by fighters near the Isle of Wight. This airman landed safely in Britain by parachute but his Junkers 88 recovered and got home safely. He was found on a country road in flying suit and uniform but since no aircraft had crashed nearby his presence was a mystery at the time. He was on his first operational trip.

Another *Gruppe* of KG 54 was briefed for a feint attack at Portland, to draw the fighters. They were grounded by the postponement order but their Bf 110 fighter escort – the whole first *Gruppe* of ZG 2 – had not received the order, even though it was, by now, midday. They flew off without the bombers. Over Portland they found Hurricanes of 238 Squadron waiting for them. For although the radar at Ventnor was still out of action, the rest of the chain was working. The homeless airmen and airwomen were coaxing signals from damaged aerials and mobile generators.

By mid-afternoon, the weather had improved. The Air

Fleet teleprinter clattered with new orders, and the aircraft took off for the official *Adlerangriff*. The plan was for heavy bombing raids on military targets over the whole of southern England, concentrating upon Fighter Command airfields. The major flaw in the plan was the fact that the Luftwaffe had no idea which airfields *were* Fighter Command airfields. Fink's unescorted Dorniers had, that morning, delivered an accurate blow at Eastchurch airfield, where air reconnaissance photos had shown Spitfires. But it was a Coastal Command airfield and the Spitfires were there only temporarily. Other airfields attacked were similarly irrelevant to the Battle: the RAF research centre at Farnborough and Odiham near to it.

Long-range Stuka units were in the forefront of the assault. A *Gruppe* of the elite LG 1, commanded by *Hauptmann* Berndt von Brauchitsch – the son of the army's Commander in Chief – made a dive-bombing attack upon Detling airfield, near Maidstone.

The way had already been cleared for IV (Stuka)/LG 1 by the crack fighter unit JG 26. This was the *Schlageter Geschwader* of Galland and Priller, led this day by *Major* Gotthardt Handrick, the 1936 Olympic Pentathlon champion. They engaged Spitfires of 65 Squadron, and lured them into the upper air, while von Brauchitsch's Ju 87s dived upon Detling. It was a few minutes after five o'clock in the afternoon, just as the mess halls were filling with airmen. Sixty-seven of them were killed. The Operations Block was devastated, and twenty-two RAF aircraft were destroyed on the ground. All of IV (Stuka)/LG 1 got back safely. It was a well-planned operation, completed with textbook-like perfection. Twenty-two aircraft destroyed on the ground in one attack represents a telling blow to any air force, and so does the loss of so many trained men. But RAF Detling was not a part of Fighter Command and its fate could have no effect upon the outcome of the air battles.

The RAF Sector Controllers were learning the tricks, too, and when a fighter sweep by JG 53 – the *Pik As*

Geschwader – tried to draw the fighters away west of the Isle of Wight, they did not go. In fact, the tactic worsened matters for the bombers that followed. The RAF, drawn into the air by the fighter sweep, now had altitude enough to attack the bombers. Nine Ju 87Rs – a *Staffel* of II/StG 2 – were spotted over Lyme Regis by Spitfires of 609 Squadron. Only three Stukas escaped destruction, and one of those was damaged.

As evening came, the Press Officers and propaganda pundits of both sides began their exaggerated claims. In fact, the Germans had lost forty-six aircraft and had shot down thirteen RAF fighters. Additionally one fighter had been destroyed on the airfield at Eastchurch.

It was clearly a British victory – or was it? No less than forty-seven RAF aircraft had been destroyed on the ground, and to add to that loss, there came from RAF Bomber Command the news that eleven Vickers Wellington bombers had been shot down over Germany.

And in an attack that had more effect upon morale than upon the Fiat and Caproni aircraft factories, thirty-six bombers of the RAF flew all the way to Milan and Turin and back.

The German night bombers were also active against the major cities of England, Scotland, and Wales. Of all these attacks, two scored unusually accurate hits on aircraft factories: Shorts in Belfast and, far more important, the factory at Castle Bromwich, Birmingham, which had just begun producing the Spitfire Mk II. Both of these attacks were made by Heinkels of the specially trained *Kampfgruppe 100*, a unit that was to play an important part in future attacks.

The Air Fleets had mounted their greatest effort so far: 1,485 sorties. Fighter Command had responded with 700 sorties. Compared with July, when the Controllers had been using 600 sorties a day just to protect the convoys, this was nicely anticipated.

Like two men who have exchanged blows, both sides reeled back: surprised, pained, and apprehensive. The next day's air fighting was much reduced in scale. But now both air forces were locked in battle, and as the summer days shortened, the Luftwaffe had to force a quick, violent conclusion.

Both sides continued to overestimate the damage they were inflicting. This did not affect the British very much, because their strategy was simply to keep Fighter Command intact as a fighting force until the weather became too bad for an invasion attempt. They could never hope to *destroy* the German Air Fleets.

The Germans, on the other hand, had to destroy Fighter Command before moving on from RAF targets to invasion targets. So it was vital for Luftwaffe strategy that they maintained an up-to-date picture of the state of their enemy. But they did not do so. They gave too much credence to the air-combat reports, and they did not distinguish between targets that were essential to Fighter Command and those that were not. Even when the targets were the right ones, there was a tendency to – both figuratively and literally – tick off the targets attacked, as if they no longer existed.

German intelligence had formed a very accurate assessment of the number of fighter aircraft available in July. But they went wrong in calculating the rate of manufacture. And even more wrong in guessing what Beaverbrook's repair units were doing.

Neither did the Germans accurately estimate the supply of pilots. The situation was grave but not so grave as the German planners hoped. They calculated that, by now, the RAF squadrons in 10 Group, 12 Group, and 13 Group had been stripped to reinforce those in 11 Group – the front line.

So it was decided to test Fighter Command's overall strength by launching simultaneous attacks from all sides. *Luftflotte 5*, in Norway and Denmark, had gained considerable experience from isolated attacks and reconnaissance flights against Scotland and the north of England. Now it was to contribute a major part of the day's carefully planned offensive.

15 August

The day began with another example of Luftwaffe staff muddle. The weather experts forecast heavy cloud. On the strength of that forecast, Göring decided that the great assault could not take place. Instead he would hold an inquest on *Adlertag*. It was typical of him that he should want to play host at Karinhall, his great house and hunting estate. So the Air Fleet's senior staff journeyed all the way to Schorfheide, 40 miles outside Berlin.

By mid-morning the cloud had reduced to scattered patches in a clear blue sky, and the wind was a negligible 2 mph. German air reconnaissance reported that the same fine weather extended from central France across most of England.

The detailed orders for this massive air attack had long since been distributed to the Air Fleets. The spearhead of the attack was to come from *Fliegerkorps II*. Originally such units had been intended as mixed commands but gradually they had become more specialized. This one comprised two Dornier Do 17 bombing *Geschwader* – one of them Fink's – and the *Condor Legion Geschwader* with Heinkel He 111s, plus three separate and self-contained Ju 87 *Gruppen* and the outstanding *Jabos of ErprGr 210*. All of this was under the command of General Bruno Loerzer, the First World War friend of Göring who had plucked him from the obscurity of an arthritic ward of a military hospital to a front-line flying unit. Needless to say, Loerzer was invited to this day's great social event, Göring's luncheon followed by a military discussion. It was a sort of day which Göring much enjoyed, from the lavish hospitality – champagne, excellent food, brandy, and cigars – to the lecture, or tirade, that inevitably ended such occasions. And all that was taking place in distant Karinhall.

Bruno Loerzer was often to be seen at Göring's elbow, enjoying his jokes, holding his maps, and listening attentively. Some said he spent far too much time away from *Fliegerkorps II* HQ in Ghent, Belgium, and certainly his Chief of Staff, *Oberst* Paul Diechmann, was well able to handle the command in Loerzer's absence. On this fateful day, Diechmann looked at the clear blue sky and decided to launch the whole assault on his initiative.

So at the HQ of IV (Stuka)/LG 1 the teleprinters came to life. Two *Staffeln* of von Brauchitsch's Ju 87s were assigned to dive-bomb the RAF airfield at Hawkinge. More Ju 87s (from II/StG 1 in the Pas de Calais) were to attack Lympne. A *Gruppe* of Dornier Do 17s of KG 3 – the *Blitz-Geschwader* – were sent to Rochester airfield and another *Gruppe* headed for RAF Eastchurch. As the bombers finished forming up near the coast, a great umbrella of fighters – husbanding their fuel by last-minute take-offs – rose to escort them.

Having committed his units to one of the great air assaults in history, Diechmann went over to Kesselring's 'Holy Mountain' to see how it developed. Kesselring was of course away at Karinhall but his Operations Officer, *Major* Hans-Jürgen Rieckhoff, was there. He had heard the aircraft, and wondered what was afoot. He was appalled to hear what *Oberst* Diechmann had done, in spite of Göring's instructions.

Diechmann pointed out that Göring had not forbidden that the attack should start this day; he had simply called a conference based upon a weather forecast which had proved entirely wrong.

Rieckhoff reached for the phone to countermand the orders but Diechmann said it was too late, the bombers were on their way to England. Rieckhoff decided to phone Kesselring immediately. He placed a call with all possible priority but when he got through to Karinhall he was told that it was Göring's instruction that the conference was not to be disturbed under any circumstances.

Fliegerkorps II's decision to launch the attack committed to action units from Lannion in Brittany all the way to

Stavanger in Norway. It was to be the most intensive day's fighting of the entire battle.

Artfully, Air Fleet 5 began by sending a formation of Heinkel He 115C reconnaissance float-planes – from *Kustenfliegergruppe 506* – for a feint attack upon the Scottish coast. This was to draw 13 Group's fighters far to the north of the real attacks.

The main force consisted of seventy-two Heinkel He 111 bombers of KG 26, *Löwen-Geschwader*, a unit famous as torpedo and anti-shipping specialists. Escorting them were

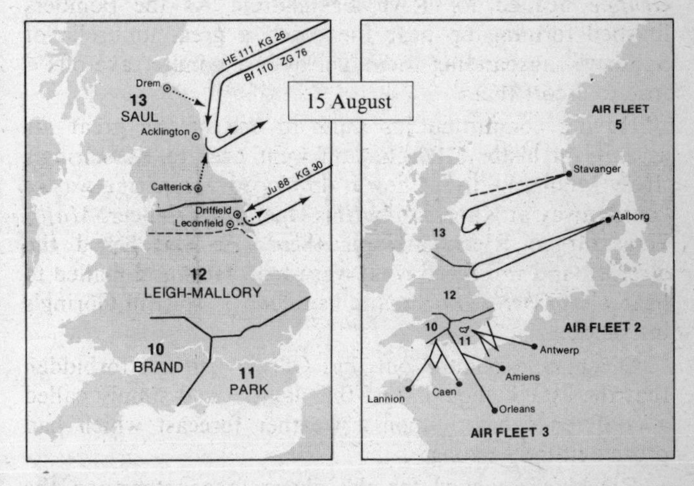

Figure 29

The gigantic air assault was launched by the action of a comparatively junior officer (see text). For the first time, Air Fleet 5 joined in the attacks against Britain, using feints (broken line, of right hand diagram) by Heinkel float-planes.

The northern two Groups were not taken by surprise. Air Vice-Marshal Saul's Controller was particularly bold in his use of fighters (dotted line). Leigh-Mallory (who was criticizing Park for not deploying fighters boldly enough in countering attacks against the south coast) now reacted timidly, using only fighters from the sector that was attacked.

twenty-one Messerschmitt Bf 110 twin-engined fighters: the second and third *Staffeln* of ZG 76. There was every reason to believe that they would provide adequate protection, for they had decimated an unescorted force of RAF Wellington bombers over Heligoland in December 1939. So confident were the commanders that to accommodate the weight of the extra fuel carried in the 1,000-litre 'Dachshund bellies' slung under them these special Bf 110D-1/R1 aircraft had left their gunners behind.

The day began badly for these long-range raiders. An error in navigation made their track so near to the feint attack that they were picked up on the British radar as one large formation. The defences were alerted.

The radar operators of this northern part of England's chain, lacking the experience of their 11 Group colleagues, estimated the raid at about thirty aircraft. At 12:15 p.m. the Controller scrambled 72 Squadron at Acklington in Northumberland. Its leader was at 18,000 feet, far out over the sea, looking for thirty German raiders, when he made contact. As well as two *Gruppen* of KG 26 Heinkel He 111s, there was a whole *Gruppe* of Bf 110s: about a hundred 'bandits' in all.

The twelve RAF fighters were 3,000 feet higher than the raid, and the RAF formation leader continued out to sea, in order to turn and attack out of the sun. Over the radio-telephone one of his pilots asked him, 'Haven't you seen them?'

In a reply that was to become famous throughout the whole of Fighter Command, the leader said, 'Of course I've seen the b-b-b-b-bastards. I'm trying to w-w-w-work out what to do.'

No. 72 Squadron split: one half to take the Bf 110 fighters and the other to attack the Heinkels. The *Gruppenkommandeur* of the Bf 110s was leading the fighter escort. He tried to jettison his long-range tank. These clumsy tanks were notoriously unreliable and this one did not fall away before a bullet touched off the vapour. His Bf 110 exploded like a bomb. Some of the Bf 110s formed a defensive circle, in which the tremendous forward-facing firepower could protect a neighbour's defenceless tail. For this trip – made without gunners – the circle was the only expedient.

Some Heinkels jettisoned their bombs and changed course towards patches of cloud. But with dogged determination most of the bomber crews stuck to their briefing, closing on the coastal towns despite repeated fighter attacks.

Courage of another sort was shown by the 13 Group Controller, who judged (rightly) that this was the entire Luftwaffe effort against his Group. With unprecedented boldness – for the air war in the south had predictable lines of thrust – squadrons from as far north as Drem in Scotland and as far south as Catterick in Yorkshire were vectored on to the German raid. These daring tactics decimated *Löwen-Geschwader* and their escort. Fifteen German aircraft were shot down, for a loss of only one RAF fighter.

The southern prong of the attack across the North Sea was made by Junkers Ju 88 bombers of KG 30, the *Adler-Geschwader*. These were among the newest of the Luftwaffe's aircraft. Their performance had persuaded Stumpff – commander of Air Fleet 5 – to let them go unescorted (and so give his Bf 110s to the Heinkels). To provide protection, a few of the Ju 88s had been specially modified with cannons on the nose.

This attack, from Aalborg, Denmark, made landfall in 12 Group, whose commander, Air Vice-Marshal Trafford Leigh-Mallory, the plump, neatly dressed protégé of Dowding, had spent most of his career in army-cooperation flying. He had been criticizing the way Park, commander of 11 Group, was handling the Battle, arguing that larger RAF fighter formations would be far more effective against the German raids. More and more he blamed Dowding, too, for not ordering Park to adopt these 'big-wing' tactics.

So it is interesting to note that while Air Vice-Marshal Richard Saul, of 13 Group, had boldly flown squadrons from as far north as Drem, Air Vice-Marshal Leigh-Mallory was nothing less than timid in his reaction. There were no 'big wings' deployed here. The attacked sector used only its own squadrons. Twelve Spitfires of 616 Squadron and six Hurricanes of 73 Squadron intercepted the Ju 88s. The *Adler-Geschwader* pressed on bravely to bomb the RAF station at Driffield, Yorkshire. They destroyed ten Whitley bombers on the ground. However seven of the Junkers Ju 88s were shot down and three more made crash landings in Denmark, Germany, and Holland.

Even considering the RAF bombers destroyed at Driffield, the Germans paid a heavy price. Of Air Fleet 5's raiding force, nearly 20 per cent had been lost. It was a disappointment to the Luftwaffe strategists. Clearly the northern Fighter Groups had not been depleted to reinforce 11 Group. It also proved that German bomber formations could not operate without (single-seat) fighter escort.

The single-seat fighter achieved paramount importance after this day's fighting. Gone were the theories of the *Schnellbomber* that outpaced its pursuit. From this day it was evident that any raid must be accompanied by aircraft as good as those that the defence used.

Now the Luftwaffe could go in strength only where their Bf 109s could go: and that meant a small segment of south-east England. This in turn provided Dowding with a possible last-ditch strategy of putting all his fighters on airfields beyond Bf 109 range. From there, if need be, they would still be able to fight the raiders from unbombed airfields.

And yet another tribute to the single-seat fighter was emerging from the statistics. The Luftwaffe bombing formations could only escape morale-shattering losses by providing two fighters for every bomber in its formations. On this day, for instance, the Germans flew 1,786 sorties, of which only 520 were bombing sorties. So nearly half the Air Fleet's available bombers had remained unused because of the lack of fighter escort.

In the south, Air Fleets 2 and 3 used the Bf 109 as

usual, but they could not prevent serious casualties among the more vulnerable aircraft types, for instance the Ju 87 and Bf 110. The raiders did considerable damage at the airfields, upon which their attacks concentrated. However, they were still attacking many airfields unconnected with Fighter Command, and tactically the most damage was done by some wild misses that severed power lines and thus put radar stations out of action.

In fighting that ranged from Scotland to Devon the RAF lost thirty-four fighters in the air, with another sixteen RAF aircraft lost on the airfields attacked. The Luftwaffe lost about seventy-five aircraft (although this is still disputed, and Hans Ring of the German Fighter Pilots' Association says fifty-five would be more accurate). Whatever the true losses, soon the Luftwaffe began to refer to this day as *der schwarze Donnerstag*: black Thursday.

Meanwhile the propaganda services performed with gusto. The Germans claimed 101 victories and the RAF an epic 182.

It was at Göring's top-level conference of Air Fleet and *Fliegerkorps* commanders that the most far-reaching events took place. Göring decreed that Luftwaffe officer air-crew casualties were now so severe that not more than one officer must fly in each aircraft, and the Stukas must have no less than three fighters each for protection. He added, 'It is doubtful whether there is any point in continuing the attacks on radar sites, in view of the fact that not one of those attacked has so far been put out of action.'

It was one of the greatest errors of the war.

16 August

The pressure continued. After the 1,786 sorties the Air Fleets flew on 'black Thursday,' they flew another 1,700 the next day and night.

In spite of Göring's order, the radar station at Ventnor was attacked again. It was only just back in operation after the damage done to it by the 12 August bombing. This time the Ju 87s did enough damage to put the installation off the air for seven days. A mobile unit was brought up to Bembridge but its performance was so poor that its only value was in persuading the Luftwaffe that no gap existed.

A demonstration of the Luftwaffe's tactical abilities was given that evening when two Junkers Ju 88s penetrated as far as Brize Norton airfield near Oxford. The route had been chosen and timed so that previous air fighting caused the RAF fighters to be back on the ground rearming and refuelling. Choosing their moment nicely, the Germans came into the circuit as if preparing to land. They even lowered their wheels, in the hope of being mistaken for Blenheims.

The bombs dropped by the two Ju 88s hit hangars containing fuelled-up aircraft. The resulting fires and explosions destroyed forty-six aircraft and damaged seven others. As well as these lost aircraft, which were mostly trainers, eleven Hurricanes were damaged when bombs hit the Maintenance Unit that shared the airfield. The Germans escaped without interception.

This attack pointed up the ever-present dilemma of the defences. Aircraft left on the airfields during these heavy attacks were lost by bombing and strafing. Yet if all the aircraft were sent into the air, they would all need rearming and refuelling at the same time. This would mean undefended sky, and more fighters on the ground vulnerable to follow-up attacks.

Returning from the air fighting on this day the pilots filed combat reports that showed a change in German formations. German fighter escorts were no longer flying higher than the bombers but keeping to the same level, usually ahead and alongside. In response to this, Fighter Command Controllers modified the practice of sending a Spitfire squadron after the high-flying fighters while a Hurricane squadron went after the bombers. Now all RAF fighters were ordered to seek out the bombers. Most of this fighting took place between 12,000 and 20,000 feet. It was a height where the RAF fighters were at their best. This was another reason why the German fighter pilots did not like flying as close escort.

The Bf 109E was superior to the British fighters at the higher altitudes. The previous November, during the 'phoney war,' or what the Germans called '*Sitzkrieg*,' a Messerschmitt Bf 109E-3 of II/JG 54 had landed on the French side of the Rhine. Not until May had this machine gone for evaluation at the RAF Experimental Establishment. The RAF were so sure that the air war would take place at low altitude that no oxygen was provided for any of the test flights. This was soon to be paid for. The Bf 109 with its excellent super-charger was able to cross the coast at 34,000 feet, having discovered that the Spitfires – despite their textbook ceiling of 37,400 feet – could not get above 30,000 without leaving a trail of straggling aircraft unable to keep formation. Height was everything to the fighters. And the Messerschmitts could open fire from a superior height (for their cannons far out-ranged the Spitfire's machine guns) and remain above the RAF formations.

Speed was often the difference between life and death. The unit workshops were spending a lot of their time adding extra machine guns to the German bombers; the Dornier Do 17s now had as many as eight of them.

And the Dorniers had evolved a technique of approaching their target in a long shallow dive. This enabled them to add 100 mph to their top speed, and at 370 mph they were difficult to catch, even in a Spitfire.

18 August

Speed was the primary limitation of the Hurricane, too. Adequate when vectored directly to the enemy formation, it was not much good for chasing a distant enemy. Against enemy fighters it was positively dangerous. This was the situation that the Hurricanes of 615 Squadron faced about lunchtime on Sunday 18 August. They were scrambled from Hawkinge to meet an estimated 150 bandits approaching from the south-east. They were still climbing when the Controller changed his orders. He told them that they would have to go after the German fighters at 25,000 feet. It was a job for which the Spitfire – with better speed and rate of climb – was far more suited.

Pilot Officer D. J. Looker in KW-Z was at an even greater disadvantage than the rest of 615 Squadron, for his usual aircraft was damaged, forcing him to fly in a Hurricane I, from reserve. It had fabric-covered wings and its fuel tanks were not self-sealing. Worse, from a handling point of view, it had a de Havilland variable-pitch (two-pitch) airscrew instead of a Rotol constant-speed propeller. This meant inferior performance and more work for the pilot.

No. 615 Squadron were still using the old formation (four vees) and were flying tightly together in the pre-war style. Undoubtedly this made them easier to spot. They were bounced out of the sun by the Bf 109s they were looking for, and the tail of KW-Z was hit by cannon shells. The Hurricane went into a spin, but Looker was experienced enough to regain control of it. He was reluctant to bail out, having just spent a month in hospital with leg injuries after a dog-fight during the battles in France. He dodged through the balloon barrage cables that were there expressly to inhibit such flying, and then put the Hurricane down at the first landing field he saw. It was the pre-war London airport at Croydon. As he came in, he ran the gauntlet of the anti-aircraft guns who thought he was a German bomber.

Pilot Officer Looker survived, but incredibly one of the airport officials at Croydon made a written complaint about his airport being used as an emergency landing field. Looker's Hurricane also survived, to become an exhibit at London's Science Museum.

The obsolete vee formation used by 615 Squadron this day – called by the Luftwaffe the 'bunch of bananas' – had proved dangerous, but this was not the only cause of Fighter Command's rumbles of complaint. The fact that the fighting formations and tactics were so obviously wrong encouraged the pilots to question the whole concept of radar-linked ground control. The fighter pilots could not see the overall picture, nor could they calculate the strain that standing patrols would have caused Fighter Command. In fact, it would have been impossible to patrol the south-east coast with the resources available.

And although the fighter pilots saw only their own, very small formations being sent against large numbers of Germans, there were often other RAF fighters being fed into the Battle before and after them. These Fabian tactics were a necessary way to preserve Fighter Command and ensure that the fighter force was not all on the ground to refuel and rearm at the same time.

But many of the complaints were a symptom of fatigue. For a fighter pilot, survival can depend upon peak physical condition, but alerts at first-light meant being on call at 3 a.m. At Biggin Hill, 32 Squadron slept under their Hurricanes, using their parachute packs as pillows. At Rochford, 151 Squadron's pilots simply slept in the cock-pits. Any pilot who got a full night's sleep three nights in a row was lucky.

The fighter squadrons were moved from airfield to airfield as Dowding's strategy, and squadron casualties and fatigue, demanded. Some of the airfields were pre-war RAF establishments with brickbuilt accommodation, hangars, workshops, and reasonable comfort. Others were more ramshackle. In each case a lot depended upon the man who ruled it; the Station Commander was senior in rank to the Squadron Commanders and decided everything except the operational flying.

Some 'station masters' devoted their whole energies to making the flyers comfortable. But at Warmwell, Dorset, the accommodation provided for the pilots of 609 Squadron was so bad that many of them preferred to sleep under filthy blankets in the dispersal tent, in spite of dirt, dust, a lack of toilets, washing facilities, or even running water.

The Station Commander showed no urgent desire to remedy this situation but he did complain to the fighter pilots that they were not getting to the Officers' Mess promptly for meals. As an incentive, he ordered that the dining room should be locked except at the prescribed meal times.

Squadron Leader George Darley later recalled, 'All our efforts to get the Luftwaffe to respect ... meal times having failed, deadlock occurred.' The fighter pilots went hungry.

The civilian cooks at Warmwell enthusiastically endorsed the Station Commander's decision, and announced that they were not going to get up to provide breakfast for the fighter pilots (who had to be with their aircraft very early). So Darley, commanding the fighter squadron, went himself to the Warmwell kitchen and prepared eggs, bacon, and tea for his men, but when the cooks complained of the dirty dishes he'd left, the Station Commander sent for Darley and told him never to use the kitchen again.

On the day that Darley was rebuked, 609 Squadron intercepted a formation of Ju 87s heading straight for Warmwell. They attacked them vigorously and only a couple of bombs hit the airfield. After landing, Darley says, 'I could not resist the temptation to ring up the Warmwell Station Commander and say that I did not expect any thanks for saving the hangars, personnel, and planes, not to mention the Officers' Mess and kitchen.'

But if Darley thought this would make this Station Commander change his unwelcoming attitude, he was wrong. From that day onwards, the men of 609 Squadron cooked their own meals, using camping equipment and pressure stoves, at the dispersal tent. Hearing of this, RAF men in the station cookhouse provided the fighter squadron with 'a mountain of eggs, tea, sugar, tins of Nestlé's milk, and packets of Kellogg's Corn Flakes,' with the message that they thought the fighter squadron was 'bloody marvellous.'

Many fighter pilots were withdrawing into a world of their own. Endless flying, some of it at high altitudes, lack of sleep, loss of friends, and the way in which so many of them had suffered physical hurts, if only from the process of bailing out, all ate away at morale. Men were affected in various ways; many pilots landed and had to tell the Intelligence Officer that they couldn't remember anything. One recalled his fellow pilots all being extremely polite to each other, lest one's last words to a friend were rude ones. At 54 Squadron tiredness provoked men into taking offence where none was intended. A pilot, sitting in front of a plate of eggs and bacon, swayed and nodded until his head came to rest in his food, and he was fast asleep. 'You're meant to eat the eggs, not put your face in them,' called another pilot to wake him up. 'George sat erect with a start,' remembered Al Deere, 'and looked around with hostility before departing in silence to his room. This action was most unlike George.'

At Manston 600 Squadron Blenheims had at last been ordered to withdraw. The airfield was still being used as a forward base for fighter squadrons but with so many of the ground staff resolutely refusing to leave the air-raid shelters, except after dark, it was not always easy to get the fighters back into the air.

19 August

Park chose Monday 19 August for a staff conference. He told his Sector Commanders and Controllers that their first priority must be defence of the sector airfields, from which the Controllers deployed their squadrons in battle. Secondly, they must continue to avoid fighter-to-fighter combat. Whatever the cost, they must prise the escorts away from their charges and concentrate upon shooting down bombers.

This simple – and as it turned out masterly – tactical plan ordained the sort of battle that the RAF would have to fight. To protect sector stations demanded that the German raids be intercepted as early as possible, so there would be no time to form up 'big wings' before going into battle. It also meant that some squadrons would be assigned to patrol the sector airfields instead of going to meet the raiders. Bitter disputes were to arise on both matters.

It could be argued that since the Luftwaffe had already reduced its bomber sorties because of a shortage of fighters, then the best tactics must be to shoot down enemy fighters. But Park knew that this was deceptively simple reasoning. To shoot down bombers meant that the German bomber crews would demand even bigger escorts, and would insist that the fighter escorts came down to the same altitude as the bombers. This would render German fighters vulnerable to his fighters.

Many RAF fighter pilots were unhappy about this. They clamoured for a chance to go after the German fighters. Young men, they had been nourished upon schoolboy fiction of another age. But like aviators of that previous generation, they had to come to terms with a grimmer reality: they were ordered to kill the men of the slower, more vulnerable bombers. They were to run away from enemy fighters unless instructed to pursue them.

The professional fighter pilot gained height as quickly as he was permitted, and treasured possession of that benefit. He hoped always to spot the enemy before they spotted him and hurried to the sun side of them to keep himself invisible. He needed superior speed, so he positioned himself for a diving attack, and he would choose a victim at the very rear of the enemy formation so that he did not have to fly through their gunfire. He would hope to kill on that first dive, and if he failed, the dedicated professional would flee rather than face an alerted enemy.

This was the classic fighter tactic, and even so it was dangerous. On 13 August, 56 Squadron had bounced a Stuka formation over Canterbury and been badly shot up by their rear-facing guns. 'We were taught a sharp lesson,' said one of the fighter pilots. But always it was height that the fighter pilots wanted. No wonder that the German fighter pilots would not stay with the dive bombers during their attacks. Luckily they were able to 'prove' it was impossible, due to the Stuka's dive-brakes.

Day after day of great air battles had not produced a decisive result for one side or the other. On this day, like Park, Göring called a meeting of his senior officers. Far from defining specific objectives, Göring said that the Air Fleets could decide their own targets (with the exception of London), and suggested that more attacks should be made on RAF bomber airfields, to hamper any counter-offensive.

The casualties suffered by the Ju 87 Stuka dive-bomber units, and their lack of success in the face of determined air defence, brought the decision to phase them out of the battle. Von Richthofen, commander of the Stukas, was at the conference. In his diary he noted caustically, 'The campaign against England is to proceed energetically but differently.'

Göring was beginning to admit that his twin-engined *Zerstörer* units were not having the kind of success he had so often predicted for them. He suggested that the Bf 110s should be provided with Bf 109 escorts: fighters to protect fighters!

From a planning point of view, to exclude Bf 110s from the fighter category was an instant depletion of hundreds of fighters. And yet it was only recognizing what was already self-evident; the specially selected crews were now decimated and demoralized. The great miscalculation had been to make no proper allowance for the Bf 110's poor acceleration. Once attacked it could not leap away from the stream of bullets. Even Kesselring admitted surprise at what he called the Bf 110's 'awkwardness.'

Göring had other ideas to help his Air Fleets. He appealed to the fighter pilots' sense of responsibility for their charges. He asked that fighter pilots and bomber crews get opportunities to meet each other, and that the same crews should always have the same escorts. The bombers must keep tightly together, he said, and threatened that any fighter pilots turning back because of bad weather would face a court-martial. It was the emotional pleading of a man who had no technical education, no real sympathy for what was actually happening to his crews, and no plan of action.

If Göring really wanted to do something about the relationship between fighter pilots and bomber crews, he would have given them radio communication. As it was, once airborne the fighter pilots were unable to talk to the bombers; they couldn't even speak to their ground control.

Whatever else was agreed at the conference, it had become clear that the single-engined fighter plane was the key to victory. Air Fleet 3's fighters were to be moved from the Cherbourg peninsula into the Pas de Calais, closer to England, and added to Osterkamp's command. To compensate Sperrle for his lost Bf 109 units, he was given the Bf 110s from Air Fleet 5 in Scandinavia. In future these northern units were only to be used for reconnaissance and night attacks against the British Isles.

ILLUSTRATIONS

51 Junkers Ju 88 bomber crews go to work Most of the photographs taken of the airmen, German and British, about this time are strikingly alike as the flyers pat their dogs, play chess or relax near their aircraft. But it would be difficult to imagine RAF crews, in the long rays of the early morning sun, marching to their aircraft singing as these men do.

52 Crewmen prepare to board their Dornier This was one of the 'Flying Pencils' prepared for export to Sweden and Yugoslavia and fitted with DB 601A engines. When the war began the Luftwaffe took over these Do 215A-1 aircraft. Because they were about 30 mph faster than the other Dorniers, they were assigned to special tasks such as reconnaissance.

The German censor has obliterated the unit badge on the nose, but this photograph was probably taken at Brest, France. The men are wearing full flying suits so that they can take their aircraft up to 30,000 feet and radio back weather reports about the proposed German objectives. The British radio-monitoring service intercepted such reports and were thus able to predict many of the raids a few hours before they began.

The man on the right is wearing a back-pack parachute and is probably a pilot. The other man's parachute-pack is between the pilot's feet. Solitary aircraft were usually picked up easily by the British radar and only by getting very high could the German crews increase their chances of survival.

52

53a

54

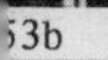

53b

53c

53d

55

56

Göring selected his two most outstanding fighter pilots – Mölders and Galland – for the award of a special gold pilot's badge, with jewels. And then he humiliated them with a lecture about the lack of aggression that their fighter pilots had shown. He demanded tighter and tighter escorts for the bomber formations. He wanted the bomber crews to see the protection they were getting, rather than just hope that it was a few thousand feet above them.

53 Inside a Dornier Do 17 It was a deliberate feature of German aircraft design (and tank design too) that crews were placed very close together in the structure. This was considered very good for morale; it also enabled men to change position or deal instantly with an emergency due to death or injury. Getting into this Dornier Do 17 was a carefully rehearsed procedure. The first picture shows the wireless operator climbing up through the floor to his position at the machine gun. The second picture shows the flight engineer following him; he also has a gun to man. The third man aboard was the pilot, and the fourth is the aircraft commander (unlike the RAF pilot the German was not always the captain of the aircraft he flew). This commander will sit upon the seat (folded at left-hand side of picture). He will also release the bombs.

54 A Fighter Command airfield under low-level attack as seen from a German bomber This photograph, taken during the summer of 1940, was probably made from one of the Dornier Do 17s which specialized in these low-level bombing attacks. Although when the Battle began many RAF aircraft were lined up on the airfields and so made sitting ducks for the Germans, soon they were dispersed and put into 'blast pens' of the sort shown protecting the Spitfire in the centre of this photo.

55 Returning from a raid A familiar sight on many of the Luftwaffe's airfields during the summer of 1940. This photograph, taken in August, shows a badly injured gunner being gently removed from his seat in a Junkers Ju 88. His flying overall has been partly undone and the doctor (stooping at centre) is opening his black bag. In the original print the pilot, still wearing all his flying gear including the helmet, can be seen waiting patiently. The position of the heads in the foreground suggests that the Junkers has made a wheels-up crash-landing.

56 The end of a Dornier Here one of the Dorniers from *Oberst* Fink's remarkable KG 2 (*Holzhammer*) has finally come to the scrapyard where the British heaped the wrecks until they could be melted down for alloy for the British aircraft industry. The precision bombing and low-level attacks of Fink's unit at Arras caused the Germans terrible casualties in the antiquated Do 17s they flew.

So that his new orders would be obeyed to the letter, Göring had selected his most outstanding fighter pilots, and given to each of them the command of a *Jagdgeschwader*.[1]

But no experienced fighter pilot was likely to show enthusiasm for flying close escort on bombers. The fighter pilots treasured altitude even more than speed (into which altitude could be transmuted at will). Now they were being asked to sacrifice both. Tying the fighters to the bombers would enable the British to choose their moment of attack and to break off combat at will. In any case, argued the Luftwaffe fighter pilots, they had already shown that they inflicted maximum damage on Fighter Command when left to their own tactics. And this was true.

Galland says, 'Constantly changing orders betraying lack of purpose and obvious misjudgment of the situation by the Command and unjustified accusations had a most demoralizing effect on us fighter pilots.

And by now the Bf 109 pilots were realizing that their fighters had certain disadvantages when in combat against Spitfires. When Göring asked the two fighter pilots if they had any requests, Mölders asked for a more powerful engine in the Bf 109, and Galland (in one of the most misquoted remarks of the war) asked for 'an outfit of Spitfires for my Group.'

The Messerschmitt's weak wings were providing its pilots with a new problem. The Spitfire pilots had discovered how to make use of the superior strength of the Spitfire wings. Faster in the dive, the Messerschmitts were being overtaken because they pulled out in a shallow curve,

[1]It has many times been written that on this day Göring kicked out the high-ranking *Kommodores* such as *Oberst* Osterkamp and replaced them with low-ranking fighter pilots like Mölders. But this is not so. Of the eight fighter *Geschwader* in the Battle, six had Majors in command already, and all the fighter pilots assigned to command *Geschwader* were already Majors. *Major* Mölders was not promoted at this conference; he had already been assigned (when Osterkamp became *Jafü* 2 on 27 July). However, a general rule was made about the maximum age of commanders: 32 years for *Geschwader*, 30 years for *Gruppe*, and 27 years for *Staffel*.

nervous that they might rip their wings off. The care with which the German pilots applied G force to their own machines prompted them to invent tactics such as Negative-G diving turns with bottom rudder. And it was this same caution, about the wing roots, that gave rise to the still widely held belief that the Bf 109 could not turn as tightly as a Spitfire. In theory its turn was tighter, but few pilots were prepared to test it to its limit.

The Luftwaffe intelligence report dated 16 August estimated RAF fighter losses at 574 since July, and added another couple of hundred fighters lost on the ground and by accidents, etc. Believing that the British factories had not supplied Dowding with more than 300 fighters, they now calculated that his total resources would be 430 fighters, of which 300 were probably serviceable. The airmen at Göring's conference were sceptical. These figures were difficult to reconcile with the mauling their missions were still getting at the hands of Fighter Command. They were right to be sceptical. In that same week when Göring thought the RAF had about 300 fighters serviceable, the true figure was over 700.

The Spitfire had proved itself an excellent all-round weapon, with faults but no inherent weaknesses. And the energies of Lord Beaverbrook were providing Hurricanes and Spitfires in ever-increasing numbers. By the end of August he would be able to report that 1,081 fighters were immediately available, and another 500 were undergoing repair.

It was the supply of pilots that was Dowding's headache. In the week since *Adlertag* he had lost nearly 80 per cent of his squadron commanders (dead, wounded, or withdrawn from battle). The men now leading the interceptions were often without any combat experience whatsoever. One squadron commander took over without ever having flown a Hurricane: he did three circuits and landings before leading his squadron into battle.

And if the commanders lacked experience of battle, the pilots following them had often logged no more than ten hours' flying in single-seat fighters. For such men, it was a brave feat to land a high-speed fighter, let alone to do battle in one. And on 10 August, Dowding agreed to cut the Operational Training period still further. Now the pilots would have only two weeks between learning to fly and coming into combat. Until July, this same course had lasted six months.

Dowding had already approved a secret plan for putting the OTUs into the fighting. A sequence of fighter squadron numbers – 551 onwards – had been set aside for this purpose. History records that the OTUs were never put into combat. But in fact, slashing the training period from six months to two weeks meant that the men who should have been students at the OTUs were already in combat.

In strategic terms such expedience was perhaps justified. By November the battle would be over, for better or for worse. The men arriving from OTUs after that would not affect the result. And yet, in human terms, it was a tragic decision. In wartime the OTU becomes a vital link between the theories of training and the hard facts of operations. The OTUs should have been telling their pupils about the new German tactics, and how to counter them. But the sad truth was that squadrons brought into the Battle for the first time seldom knew anything of modern air combat. Some had never fired their guns. And they were still flying the tight vee formations and were not even properly alerted to the dangers of 'the Hun in the sun.'

Neither were the squadrons in the north getting any practice or instruction about the fighting – some were not even flying. At Usworth in Durham, 607 Squadron had to pretend they were doing engine tests in order to fly their Hurricanes. The official excuse was a shortage of spare parts.

However exemplary the feeding of the fighter squadrons into battle, the preparation of the squadrons for battle was a scandal – for there was no preparation! In spite of the generous supply of aircraft, and the availability of battle-weary veterans withdrawn from the south, there was no attempt to combine these assets in such a way that the rotated squadrons went into battle with some idea of what they faced. Possibly the RAF had doubts about the morale of their battle-weary veterans, and feared the effect that the experienced pilots might have had upon the morale of the untried units.

Phase Three: the Attacks upon 11 Group Airfields, 24 August–6 September

The Air Fleets complied with Göring's demand for a round-the-clock offensive. They sent raiders – sometimes no more than a single bomber – to all parts of the United Kingdom by day and by night.

During daylight, Kesselring continued ceaseless air activity over his coastline, so that the British radar operators were unable to distinguish which aircraft were raiding formations forming up. This often enabled the real raids to attack coastal targets and get away intact. Hurriedly the fighters of Air Fleet 3 were moved to the Pas de Calais so that by 24 August they were all together. Now the German formations had large numbers of fighters flying tightly above them, and often there were more below them too. Neither side liked these tactics. Ten RAF fighters, climbing to meet ten German bombers escorted by ten fighters, saw it as a battle in which they were outnumbered two to one. The German fighter pilots saw it as a battle in which the odds were against them, for they faced an equal number of fighters, while trying at the same time to protect the bombers.

The fighter aircraft was designed with forward-facing armament, expressly for an attacking role. To be used, it had to fly towards an enemy. Keeping close to the bombers prevented the German fighter pilots from attacking in this way. No longer could the fighters dive out of the sun upon an unsuspecting enemy. The new tactics resulted in fewer losses in the bomber fleets, but German fighter casualties went up.

From the High Command's point of view, however, the new German tactics were effective. These tight formations forced their way through to the targets, and sometimes devastated them.

On 26 August the smouldering dispute between Park and his severest critic – Leigh-Mallory, commanding 12 Group – flared up. As was the usual practice, Park asked his northerly neighbours to patrol threatened airfields north of the Thames Estuary while he put his own fighters forward to intercept German raids. Park's airfield at Debden, Essex, was left undefended. The Germans bombed it. Park asked why Leigh-Mallory's fighters were not there, and the latter replied that he was asked too late.

The dispute was part of a long-standing disagreement between the two men. Unwittingly the bad feeling was fanned by the theories of the legless fighter pilot, Douglas Bader, who now commanded one of Leigh-Mallory's squadrons.

Bader, a 30-year-old Squadron Leader, was a graduate of the new RAF College, Cranwell. He had crashed very soon after graduation. Both legs had to be amputated. In spite of a demonstration that he could fly with tin legs better than most men could fly with real ones, the RAF refused to let him continue, so Bader's career seemed to be over before it had begun. Throughout his many years of civilian life Bader made continual applications to go back to flying, but not until November 1939 did the Air Ministry relent. The same courage and determination that had enabled him to conquer the double amputation made him a fabled fighter pilot. Within six months of his return he caught up with his Cranwell contemporaries.

Leigh-Mallory had much the same interest in Bader's career that Dowding had shown in Leigh-Mallory, Park, and Sholto-Douglas, who had been his subordinates a generation before. Squadron Leader Bader took command of 242 Squadron in June 1940, just in time for the Battle. Already his name was known throughout Fighter Command.

Bader argued that Park was wrong to put his fighters up in squadron-size units. Bader said that only very large formations of fighters, attacking together, could deal a lethal blow to the German formations.

These 'big wings' (they were sometimes called Balbos, after a famous Italian aviator) took a long time to form up in the air. For 12 Group, who usually had generous warning of a German attack, they were more practical than for the front-line needs of 11 Group. The big-wing advocates, however, were heard to say that it was better to decimate a German raid *after* it had bombed than to scratch at it *before* it had bombed. Such reasoning failed to take account of the importance of the sector airfields or of the whole control system. Yet, for that very reason, it appealed to men who felt constricted by the Controller's orders. For Leigh-Mallory, Bader provided an outspoken critic of two men he particularly disliked: Park and Dowding. And so it was a heaven-sent circumstance that had provided for Bader an adjutant who was a Member of Parliament of some fourteen years' experience.

It was a curious circumstance, and for Dowding it perhaps proved a fateful one. According to Bader's biographer, Paul Brickhill, this MP spoke directly to the Air Minister about the squadrons' problems. So it was arranged that he should spend an hour and a half with Churchill, who 'next day began sending for various Group commanders.' As we shall see, this astounding revelation shed light on later events that for many years remained a mystery.

Some of the most high-spirited pilots of 12 Group envied the 11 Group squadrons, who were constantly in the fight. Flying on the leash of strict ground control was particularly chafing for veterans of an era of open-cockpit flying. To be sent to guard the airfields of the pilots who were doing the fighting must have seemed the last straw to such men. Even the least critical members of this school of thought believed that ground Controllers should advise and ask rather than order. Squadron Leader Bader believed that very large formations of fighters should have enough latitude to engage the enemy at the time, the place, and in the fashion that the formation leader saw fit.

Had it not been for the times when German raids heavily bombed 11 Group's airfields entrusted to 12 Group's protection, the big-wing theories might have gone unremarked in spite of Bader's adjutant and those discussions with higher authority. But Park reacted sharply to having his fighter airfields left open to bombers. Leigh-Mallory's response was to criticize Park's entire strategy and to mention Bader's theories to his friends, among them Sholto-Douglas, by now Air Vice-Marshal and Deputy Chief of Air Staff.

The exaggerated combat claims by both sides were usually *in proportion to the number of aircraft in action.* (This was because several pilots would take a quick shot at an enemy plane, and then all report it as it went down.) Inevitably Leigh-Mallory's big wings benefited from this fundamental law of air fighting. On one occasion, the big wing claimed fifty-seven Germans downed, when post-war scrutiny of German records showed that only eight of the raiders failed to get home. Usually 12 Group's big wings met the Germans at the extreme limit of the Bf 109's range. This gave them a reputation for being able to turn the German raids back. And so it was that the big-wing theorists captured the imagination of the Air Ministry, and probably of Churchill too.

The attacks upon the sector airfields brought more people into the Battle. As electricity, telephones, teleprinters, sewage, and transport were destroyed, fighter aerodromes relied upon the ground staff, and civilians, to put the pieces back together. At Manston on Saturday 24 August, Post Office engineers sat down next to an unexploded bomb and sorted through hundreds of severed wires to reconnect the Operations Room and the fighters to Group Headquarters. Electricity workers, WAAFs, and fire brigade men were taking risks as great as the pilots, but it was not everyone's finest hour.

RAF Manston – built on a cliff-top alongside the sea –

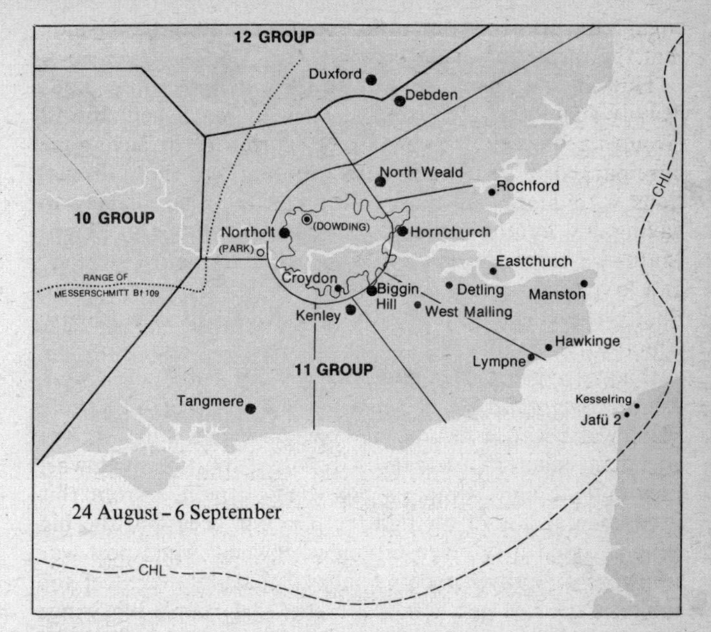

Figure 30

The time between 24 August and 6 September became known to Fighter Command as 'the critical period.' The attacks centred upon the sector airfields of 11 Group, which Park commanded. From these airfields (large solids) came orders of the Sector Controllers to fighters in the air. Other Fighter Command airfields (small solids) did not have such Operations Rooms.

During the critical period's first few days Messerschmitt Bf 109s were moved from the Cherbourg region to the command of *Jafü 2*, so that by the end of August a great concentration of single-seat fighters built up in the Pas de Calais. This changed the operational area (dotted line) slightly.

Note that Duxford airfield to the north is under the command of Leigh-Mallory of neighbouring 12 Group. Kesselring's advanced (underground) HQ is shown; his normal HQ was in Brussels. Note the way in which the short-range German fighters flying home from south-east England needed only a slight navigational error to miss the Pas de Calais.

The dotted line shows the extreme limit of the Bf 109's range (the westerly part of this was lost when the fighters were moved from the Cherbourg area). The range of the British radar for low-flying attacks (CHL) is also marked.

was suffering not only the scheduled bombing attacks, but also spontaneous ground-strafing from fighters which came in low over the sea and crossed the airfield at near ground level. Many airmen had been sitting in the air-raid shelters ever since the attack that Fink had delivered to the airfield at lunchtime on 12 August. (About one hundred raw recruits arrived just before the heaviest raids.) Now the terrified men would not budge, and the accountant officer could not even find enough airmen above ground to hold a pay parade. Squadron Leader J. A. Leathart, of 54 Squadron, had only just prevented another officer from going into the shelter to shoot the first man who refused to come out.

The chaplain disarmed an officer who was threatening to kill everyone in the Mess. While the RAF were in the shelters, local civilians took the opportunity to loot the damaged buildings for RAF tools and spares.

Manston was not the only airfield where men spent week after week petrified in the shelters. The provision that some far-sighted Air Ministry official had arranged to deal with bomb craters had now gone badly wrong. The civilians, who had been receiving wages for doing nothing until the action started, now decided that it was too dangerous to work while an air-raid alert was in force. So they, too, sat in the subterranean shelters, and the few men left to service the aircraft and keep the airfields and Operations Rooms running went out with the shovels and filled in the craters too. By this time most pilots had learned something of the job of refuelling and rearming the fighters.

But even the less glorious moments of the Battle retained their class-conscious nature. Europe's cataclysmic movements of nations and races and their social aftermath were still to come. This war in the air belonged to varsity men, with technical-school graduates as travelling reserves. Sharing the same middle-class values as their opponents, the Stuka crews – like those of Bomber Command – frequently carried their bombs back to base if they failed to identify their military targets. And at least one German flyer was reprimanded by Mölders for attacking such 'an unmilitary target' as a train. The survivors would live to wonder at such niceties.

Meanwhile they photographed each other patting pet dogs, playing cards, and relaxing in deck chairs on neatly trimmed grass. In 1940 there *was* honey still for tea, in this the world's last romantic battle.

25 August

To get to 11 Group's sector airfields – ringed round London – Kesselring often routed one raid direct and another along the great blind spot created by the Thames Estuary. In the small hours of Sunday 25 August a night raid used the Estuary route to the oil tanks at Thameshaven. The crew of one aircraft lost their way, continued too far westwards, and dropped their bombs. They hit the City of London. The raid caused more dismay among the British War Cabinet and the staff of Air Fleet 2 than among the Londoners. The outer suburbs had already been bombed and Londoners had been expecting raids. The bomb-load of just one errant bomber was a gentle introduction to total war.

Just as the Rotterdam bombing prompted the 15 May War Cabinet to send the RAF to bomb the Ruhr next day, so now did Churchill authorize an immediate reprisal raid upon Berlin. During this period RAF Bomber Command believed themselves to be 'reducing the scale of German air attack by bombing aircraft assembly plants.' Now eighty-one RAF bombers departed for Berlin on the night of Sunday 25 August. More civilians died. Here bombs were unexpected: the Nazi leaders had promised that Berlin was inviolable. They vowed to avenge the 'atrocities.' So began a chain of incidents that eventually ended not only the Battle of Britain, but – at Hiroshima – the war.

The German fighter formations had returned to the practice of flying well above the bombers. A Fighter Command Intelligence Summary of 30 August reported that fighters had been keeping to altitudes between 25,000 and 20,000 feet while the bombers were usually at 13,000 feet, with certain German units coming down to bomb at 4,000 feet.

For new pilots the high-altitude battles could be a frightening experience. It was very, very cold at 25,000 feet, and the Spitfires slipped and skidded through the thin air, as the propeller blades failed to bite. Invariably the Perspex misted over and reduced visibility. Only slowly did the aircraft add a few hundred feet, and for this reason the throttles remained wide open. It meant that if a pilot dropped back from his formation through lack of flying skill, he could never catch up with them again. And above them were the Bf 109s, watching and waiting for just such a straggler. This was the way that many young men died: alone and cold in the thin blue air, peering through the condensation into the glare of the sun, unable to see the men who killed them.

As a way of confusing the ground Observers, the Germans were now splitting the formations as they crossed the coast. This meant that Observer Corps reports were sometimes difficult to reconcile with the radar plots. Park ordered that his formation leaders should report the details of any enemy formation they saw, to help the Controllers form an accurate picture of what was happening.

But the uncertain weather of August brought more trouble to the Luftwaffe than to the British. If the raiders flew under the clouds they were visible to anyone who looked up. If they flew over them they were visible to fighters flying above. If they flew in the clouds it was dangerous, and they were unable to get the visual references they needed both for dead-reckoning navigation and for bombing the target.

And yet the defences could no longer be certain that the Luftwaffe depended upon dead-reckoning navigation. During the summer of 1940 there had been a second Battle of Britain in progress. It was fought by night fighters which each night sought, and usually failed to find, let alone shoot at, the lone night bombers that were ranging over southern England.

None of the senior British commanders – and certainly not Dowding – had any illusions about the chances of countering heavy forces of night bombers. In fact, there was a certain grim irony to their present predicament; they were engaged in a desperate race against time to find ways of countering the night bomber, and yet the more successful they were by day, the sooner would come the night attacks for which they were not yet ready.

It was June when the British first guessed at the sort of precision attacks that the Luftwaffe might be able to stage. A specially equipped RAF Avro Anson reconnaissance aircraft had found, in the night air above England, a mysterious beam that was only about 450 yards wide, and had all the characteristics of the Lorenz blind-landing system's beam.

It was this latter characteristic that was most worrying for the defences, for it implied – rightly – that any of the enemy bombers could be guided to their target by this system, without additional equipment. Examination of downed German bombers confirmed that the standard Lorenz equipment was suitable and sensitive enough for it, and by now intelligence officers, examining documents taken from German air crew, had come across references to such a device. It was code-named *Knickebein* (literally, dog-leg or bent-leg).

Investigating the beams drove the British to desperate measures. Listening Service men were sent to the tops of the tall radar towers. And a special RAF (No. 80) wing was created to counter *Knickebein*, which the British code-named 'Headache.'

Old Lorenz blind-landing sets were hunted up, and so was electro-diathermy equipment from hospitals. Both kinds of machinery were adapted into transmitters for jamming the German beams. By September jammers called 'Aspirins' were at work each night transmitting dashes that made it difficult for the German pilots to distinguish dots

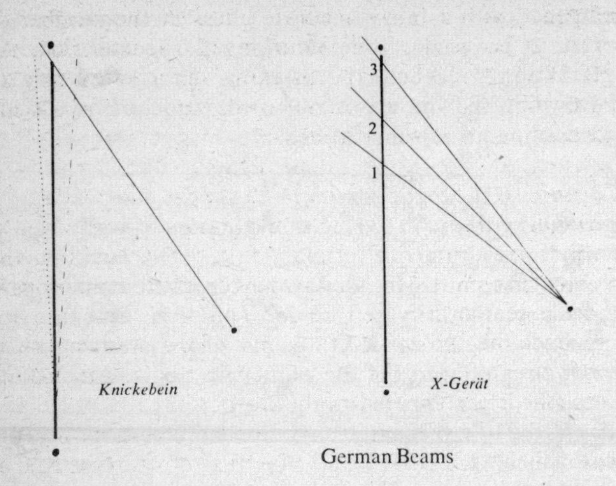

Figure 31 German Beams

LEFT The *Knickebein* (literally, bent-leg or dog-leg) system required no more equipment or experience than was needed to use the Lorenz blind-landing gear, fitted into most of the German bombers already. Just as in a landing, the pilot heard a continuous note if he was on a correct course to his target. If he wandered off course he heard in his earphones dots or dashes, according to which way he had wandered. At the target, a second beam intersected and told the bomb-aimer to release the bombs.

RIGHT The *X-Gerät* system was more complex and required trained crews with special equipment. The *Kampfgruppe 100* was the chosen unit and, as 1940 continued, the 'pathfinders' dropped only incendiary bombs to mark the target for the ordinary bombers.

The *X-Gerät* aircraft flew along a beam that took it to the target. It had receiving equipment for three other beams and also a simple clockwork device connected to the bomb-release gear.

The first beam alerted the crew to the nearness of the target. The second beam gave the signal to punch a time clock. The third beam told the operator to punch it a second time. This halted one hand of the clock. The second hand continued and released the bombs automatically.

The accuracy of this method (it was more accurate than *Knickebein*) depended upon the mathematical calculations that enabled the beams to be aimed, and also upon the way that the simple clockwork computer could compensate for the ground speed of the aircraft (between the operator's two signals) and thus adjust the time the bombs were released.

and dashes from their own transmitters (which worked on the basis of most blind-landing systems: dots mean too far left, dashes mean too far right, continuous note means you are on the correct course).

The difficulty with such counter-measures was measuring how successful they were. Bombers came wandering across darkened landscape (upon which towns, furnaces, and lighted factories could usually be seen if not recognized) and dropped bombs. How could anyone guess how near the enemy aviators had come to fulfilling their orders?

Most of these night raiders came from Hugo Sperrle's Air Fleet 3. With all his Bf 109s moved to the Pas de Calais, night raids had become largely his responsibility. He had been ordered to prepare a series of such attacks against Liverpool. After dark on 28 August the raids began and continued for four nights. Five Blenheim night-fighter squadrons – using their airborne radar sets – went on patrol but no enemy aircraft were shot down. Only one Blenheim crew – it was an aircraft from 600 Squadron – saw a German bomber but it was too slow to catch it.

The British counter-measures were certainly evident to Hugo Sperrle, whose crews were coming back baffled by the electronic jamming. German air crew talked about bombers which had gone in circles until the crew were dizzy. At least one Heinkel landed in England – on the beach near Bridport – believing that the jamming signal was their own guidance beam. The British did everything to spread the word about the effectiveness of the jamming. They succeeded only too well; even nowadays (nonsensical) stories are told about how the British bent the beams to cause the Luftwaffe to bomb Dublin, a neutral city.

Meanwhile 150 bombers delivered to Liverpool the heaviest attack so far suffered by any British target. Considerable damage was done to the docks and there were 470 casualties. Moreover, Sperrle's bombers did not have to depend solely upon the *Knickebein* apparatus.

Since 17 August a special unit – *Kampfgruppe* 100 – had been transferred from Kesselring's command to

Sperrle's. This Heinkel He 111 *Gruppe* was fitted with guidance equipment far beyond the limitation of the *Knickebein* beam. The *X-Gerät* (fitted only to these aircraft with specially trained crews) provided a beam down which to fly and a series of three cross-beams. The accuracy of *X-Gerät* was calculated as 120 yards, and as the highly skilled men of KGr 100 led long streams of bombers to Liverpool, there was no British counter-measure. For the time being, the British night sky belonged to the Germans.

Equally important was the use that could be made of *X-Gerät* in daylight, especially during the cloudy weather that Britain experienced at this time. For an example of the accuracy of the method, one had only to remember the lucky raid by four Heinkels, which scored a surprising number of hits on the Spitfire factory at Castle Bromwich, Birmingham, on the night of Eagle Day. The Heinkels were from KGr 100, and it wasn't luck.

26 August

The mixed weather gave enough cover for the Air Fleets to launch attacks on Fighter Command airfields in Kent and Essex. One wave came towards the English coast from the east and split for attacks on Debden, to the north-east of London, and Hornchurch, virtually in the capital's eastern suburbs.

Fearing an attack on London, Park put up seven squadrons to intercept the southern prong. The crews of the Dornier Do 17s had the terrifying experience of seeing their Bf 109 escorts turn for home just as the RAF fighters rose like a cloud of gnats. The long detour, which had let the raid approach the coast from an unexpected direction, made the Messerschmitts' fuel warning lights glow long before their targets were reached.

One of the fighter squadrons was from Croydon. It was about three o'clock that afternoon, as Peter Townsend led 85 Squadron's attack. Said Townsend, 'Thirty minutes later a dozen Dorniers came sailing majestically towards us – an impeccable phalanx in vics [vees] of three, stepped up in line-astern.' They were from KG 2 – Fink's crews – and some of them were later to recall it as a flight for which they carried no bombs. The bomber crews believed that their role was to provide a decoy to attract the RAF fighters. If that was true it was to prove a costly tactic, for now that the range of the Bf 109s forced them to withdraw, the Dorniers were to pay a heavy price. Some observers reported that the leading Dornier fired coloured signals, and the whole formation turned for home, knowing that they would be cut to pieces long before they reached their target.

Townsend said:

> I brought the squadron around steadily on a wide turn moving it into echelon as we levelled out about two miles ahead on a collision course. Ease the throttle to reduce the closing speed – which anyway allowed only a few seconds' fire. Get a bead on them right away, hold it, and never mind the streams of tracer darting overhead. Just keep on pressing on the button until you think you're going to collide – then stick hard forward. Under the shock of negative G your stomach jumps into your mouth, dust and muck fly up from the cockpit floor into your eyes, and your head cracks on the roof as you break away below.

Sammy Allard was flying with Townsend on that day. By now he had won the DFM and been promoted from Sergeant to Pilot Officer. He fired at one Dornier long enough to make both propeller blades stop, and then climbed and came round for another diving attack. He found a target and fired a three-second burst at it.

Two of the Dornier's crew jumped out. Its wounded pilot saw Rochford fighter airfield below, and decided to try to make a crash landing there.

Allard's victim lurched into the approach run for the airfield, watched with mixed feelings by those on the ground – who thought he was about to bomb – and by a Spitfire overhead. One of the people watching it from ground level was the Medical Officer from Hornchurch on a routine visit. The Dornier made a wheels-up landing, and with a scream of tearing metal slid on its belly all the way across the airfield, until it stopped almost where the MO stood. He ran to the wreck and with a struggle managed to get the injured pilot out of it and onto the grass:

> I then looked around to see if there were any other crew members and to my horror I found myself looking into the muzzle of a machine gun pointed at me from the top turret, with the machine gunner gazing unflinchingly down the sights. I confess I felt goose pimples breaking out all over me, and I deliberately turned away to give aid to the injured pilot as proof of my good intentions. When I looked up again the gun was still pointing at me, so I made a quick dash for the shelter of the aircraft's wing. From there I made my way along the side of the fuselage to the turret. One look was enough to tell me that the gunner had fired his last shot.

The horror of bloody wreckage, the smell of fuel and blood and vomit, the gloomy interior pierced by sunlight from a thousand bullet holes, an exterior gleaming with the silver discs that hot metal burned into paint work, the struggle to extricate dead and dying, and the cries of men who would never fly again, these were all well known to the men of the Luftwaffe's bombing units, across all the airfields of northern France. No wonder these flyers began to believe that they were being used as decoys.

29 August

The weather was beginning to stabilize as a high-pressure region centred on north-west Europe. England had sunshine and showers with enough cloud along the south coast to make interception uncertain.

The radar screens remained dark all morning but about 3 p.m. small formations of Heinkel He 111s and Dornier Do 17s headed for the English coast between Beachy Head and Hastings. Thirteen fighter squadrons went into the air that afternoon, for behind the Heinkels and Dorniers there were more green blips. But these waves were higher, and at closer quarters they were identified as fighters. There were more than 500 Bf 109s, with almost all the *Jagdgeschwader* represented: JG 3 (*Udet*), JG 26 (*Schlageter*), JG 51 (the unit that was later to be named after Mölders), JG 52, and JG 54 (*Grünherz*). And after them came a great wave of Bf 110s, from ZG 26 (*Horst Wessel*) and ZG 76.

As the trap closed upon the RAF fighter squadrons sent to intercept, the voices of the Controllers were heard calling their aircraft home again. It was Park's instruction that the German fighters must be left to fly unchallenged in the English skies, and for the most part that order was obeyed.

As the German crews were debriefed that evening, the Luftwaffe intelligence no longer had any doubt that the RAF tactics were working. The Spitfires and Hurricanes were being preserved, while the Germans were losing aircraft and gaining very little. Grieved by the losses among his young pilots, old Theo Osterkamp told Mölders and Galland that the Battle was going badly. He believed that the RAF were very far from the exhausted state that Göring described, and the Luftwaffe could not spare the high-quality air crews that were being sacrificed.

Some of 'Onkel Theo's' allegations were self-evidently true, but neither of the young aces could share the old man's pessimism about the outcome. Now Osterkamp decided that he should write a detailed report about the air battle. And yet by its very nature such a report must be critical of Göring. Osterkamp decided to send it to Milch.

Milch would not be difficult to contact. Since 20 August he had resumed his inspection trips. Piloting his own 'Storch' liaison aeroplane, he visited units large and small. For those without an airstrip he went by the sort of big black Mercedes that had become the status symbol of the top Nazis. Unceasingly Milch scribbled notes in a little green Collins diary that was four years out of date. Nothing was too trivial to get his attention: fuel supplies, replacement parts, tactics, morale, and the bombs. And Milch was quick to evaluate the men with whom he spoke; for them he carried supplies of Brazilian cigars and various grades of medals.

Milch was showing particular interest in any shortcomings of the Junkers Ju 88. This excellent machine had been one of Udet's pet projects, firmly supported by the young Luftwaffe Chief of Staff, *Generaloberst* Hans Jeschonnek. The devastating report that Milch was compiling about the bomber would strengthen his position in respect of both these rivals.

If Milch was looking for complaints, there was every reason to think that his inspection visit to KG 30, the *Adler-Geschwader*, at Gilze-Rijen and Eindhoven airfields in the Netherlands, delighted him.

Dowding's policy of seeking out the bombers and avoiding the fighters was eating into the confidence of the bomber crews. This Junkers Ju 88 unit had suffered terrible losses during the 15 August raid from Denmark across the North Sea. Now the men blamed the equipment, the tactics, the aircraft itself, and even their bombsights and

ILLUSTRATIONS

57 *The War Room, Whitehall* The history of warfare over the past couple of centuries can be thought in terms of soldiers lowering themselves closer and closer to the ground, and then deeper and deeper into it. During 1940, regular bombing raids, first by day and then by night, meant that more and more vital services and control centres went underground. These two photographs show the most important underground control room of the period – the War Room, Whitehall – from which Winston Churchill eventually controlled the whole war: (a) Churchill's desk and (b) his bed.

58 *A conversation I would like to have overheard (number one)* Göring and Udet at a pre-war flying display. Göring poses with his *Feldmarschall*'s baton; on his right breast pocket he wears the 'Blood Order' awarded only to old-time Nazis. At his neck (edge-on and difficult to see in this photograph) he has the *Pour le Mérite,* the highest German award for valour in the First World War, in which Göring had been an ace fighter pilot. Udet, another ace pilot of the First World War, is also wearing the *Pour le Mérite* at his neck. Below his left breast pocket he has (left to right) the First World War pilot badge, an Iron Cross first class and the 'double badge' that the Luftwaffe awarded to flyers who had qualified as aircraft captains (observers) and as pilots. Beyond Göring, Hitler can be seen, head thrown back and mouth wide open.

57a

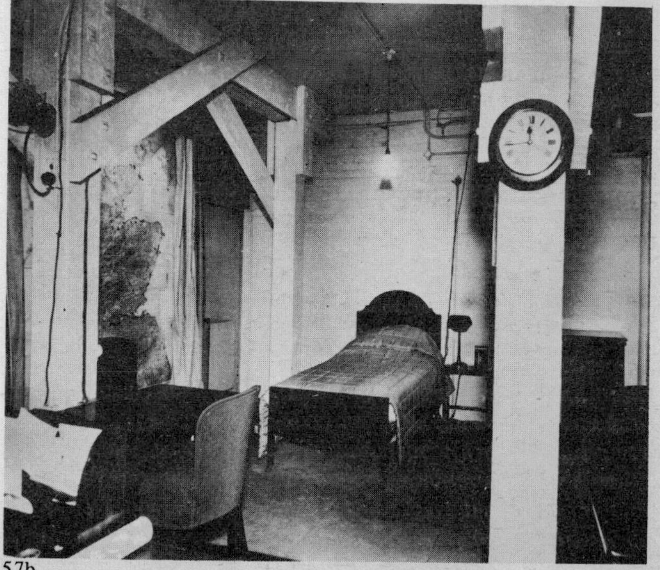

57b

58

59

defensive machine guns. *Oberleutnant* Werner Baumbach said, 'Milch seemed grateful for our frank statement and said he would immediately seek a remedy.

'He did produce a remedy,' added Baumbach. 'One *Gruppe* which had borne the heat and burden . . . was broken up "as punishment for mutiny and defeatism". The officers were transferred and reduced in rank.'

30 August

This Friday saw a change in tactics and the beginning of the battles that were to take the RAF fighters to the brink of defeat.

Sniffing the dawn air and the state of the defences, Kesselring's Dornier Do 17s went as far as the Thames Estuary to attack ships of a north-bound convoy. Their escorts were Bf 110s of III/ZG 76. By an outside chance, nine Hurricanes were already on an interception course,

59 A conversation I would like to have overheard (number two) A few weeks after the war was over, Dowding again put on the uniform of the RAF, from which he had been fired. He went to North Weald fighter airfield to see the preparations for the first peacetime Battle of Britain anniversary flypast. Leading it would be Douglas Bader, the legless ace recently liberated from a POW camp in which he had spent much of the war. Bader had evolved the big-wing theories that played an important part in Dowding's downfall. Here the two men exchange words before the take-off.

60 A conversation I would like to have overheard (number three) Long after 1940, Battle of Britain aces get together. Left to right: Al Deere, Peter Townsend and Denys 'Kill 'em' Gillam. On the far right is Johnnie Johnson.

61 A conversation I would like to have overheard (number four) At an International Radio Navigation conference in post-war Frankfurt is (centre) Robert Watson-Watt, creator of British radar and the system that went with it. On the right is the Luftwaffe Signals' chief *Generalmajor* Wolfgang Martini who failed to understand the part that radar played in the defence of the British coastline. On the left 'Smiling Albert' Kesselring, commander of Air Fleet 2, who suffered the consequences, lives up to his nickname.

62 A conversation I did not need to hear A German flyer is repatriated.

having been scrambled by a false alarm. The Hurricanes' 'Tally-Ho!' over the radio brought three Spitfires of 54 Squadron into the fight.

But the battle over the Estuary was designed to attract attention away from the main assaults of the day. A first wave of sixty Bf 109s crossed the south coast at 10:30 a.m. It was ignored by Park's Controller, who simply warned his squadrons to expect bombers as the second wave. Thirty minutes later he was proved exactly right when forty Heinkel He 111s and thirty Dornier Do 17s crossed the coast, escorted by nearly a hundred fighters. A cloud layer at about 7,000 feet made it impossible to see the raiders, and the Observer Corps posts could do no better than phone to report the sound of aircraft overhead.

By noon all of Park's fighter aircraft were in the air and most of them saw action. Park asked Leigh-Mallory – 12 Group Air Operations Commander – to send air cover south to protect Kenley and Biggin Hill airfields. But the 12 Group fighters sent to Biggin let a *Staffel* of Junkers Ju 88s, from a third wave of attacks, get through. The airfield and its neighbourhood suffered. This failure further inflamed the bad feeling between the two men.

A second German raid followed immediately. Again the attacks were directed upon fighter airfields: Kenley, Biggin Hill, Tangmere, and Shoreham. While the sounds of guns and aero-engines were heard from the cloudy sky, seven stations of the radar chain whimpered as the cathode-ray tubes went blank. The main electricity supply had been hit. Now there was no radar protection for the south-east coast.

A third attack was coming in waves over Dover before the second had withdrawn. Like the others, it was directed at the vital Fighter Command airfields. Ten raiders made a detour that brought them to the Thames Estuary and then south to Biggin Hill. It was a low-level attack pressed skilfully. It did considerable damage to hangars, armoury, workshops, stores, and WAAF quarters. It killed thirty-nine and injured twenty-six people and also severed water mains and gas, power, and telephone links.

In the middle of all this activity, a newsreel camera crew visiting Gravesend airfield asked for a squadron scramble. Obligingly the 501 Squadron pilots pretended to answer the phone at dispersal, and then raced out to the Hurricanes. The waiting ground crews helped their pilots into harness, fastened the straps, started the engines, and removed the chocks so that the fighters could lumber across the flattened grass and climb steeply into the air, tucking their wheels up the instant they were airborne – a favourite fighter pilot's conceit.

What the delighted camera crew didn't know was that the pilots had plugged in their helmet phones just in time to hear the Controller's voice giving them a genuine scramble, and vectoring them on the Thames Estuary.

The squadron met the raiders in a head-on attack. Keeping in formation, the whole squadron pressed their gun buttons together, as ordered by their commander. None of the enemy fell before the massed gunfire but the formation of Heinkels was broken.

By now RAF intelligence were giving great importance to the scattering of German formations. Intelligence Summary No. 166 noted that the Luftwaffe was flying higher, pattern-bombing from 20,000 feet. This tactic – all aircraft bomb when their leader bombs – was interpreted by the RAF as a sign of the Luftwaffe's shortage of trained personnel. The scattering of formations before they bombed was henceforward given high priority.

But 501 Squadron had no time to spare for self-congratulation. Sergeant pilot Lacey was one of the men who scattered the Heinkels, but no sooner had he come round for a second attack than he saw bullets hammering into his wings and engine. The cockpit cover went black as oil sprayed over it. He kicked his way into a steep turn but bullets continued to hit him: 'Whoever was doing the shooting was either very lucky or knew a lot about deflection, because it had been constantly changing.'

Unable to see what was happening, Lacey jettisoned his oily hood but was discouraged from the idea of bailing out by the grey water of the Thames Estuary that he saw beneath. He had considerable altitude and decided to glide as far as land. When he reached the Isle of Sheppey he decided to try to get all the way home in a shallow glide. As he neared Gravesend he pumped his undercarriage into the down position, and did the same for his flaps. With engine lifeless he made a perfect landing, and rolled to a stop almost exactly at the place from which he had taken off. The camera crew were delighted, and filmed the whole landing. There were eighty-seven holes in the Hurricane, not counting the exit ones.

Lacey was rather pleased with himself but the Engineering Officer wiped the smile off his face when he said, 'Why the hell didn't you bail out? . . . I'd have got a new aircraft tomorrow morning! Now I've got to set to work and mend it.'

Earlier that morning, over Maidstone, there had taken place one of the most sudden episodes of carnage of 1940, and in fact of the whole air war. Wing Commander Tom Gleave was one of the most senior officers flying in combat at this time. Born in Liverpool in 1908 he had founded a flying club while still in his teens and gone on to get a pilot's licence before joining the RAF in 1930. He started the war as Bomber Liaison Officer at Fighter Command HQ but talked his way into getting command of 253 Squadron in spite of being 32 years old. This was completely against Dowding's order that no Squadron Commander could remain in the job after becoming 26 years old. And in July Tom Gleave was promoted to Wing Commander, which meant he was both too old and too senior for the job. Desperate to continue flying his Hurricane, he asked the newly appointed Squadron Commander if he could remain in the squadron as 'an ordinary bloke,' but was generously invited to 'share the squadron' with the new Commanding Officer.

This day provided Wing Commander Tom Gleave with his first taste of combat. Detached from the rest of the squadron, his vee of three aircraft was vectored on to an enemy formation. Ahead of him and about 500 feet above Gleave saw line-astern formations of Bf 109s riding above the haze, well spaced out and stretching as far as the eye could see. It was the culmination of all Gleave's ambitions. Unhesitating, he flew right through the enemy fighters. He remembered the scene clearly, and described the smell of the cordite, the hiss of the pneumatics, and the way the Hurricane's nose dipped as the guns recoiled.

He gave the first Bf 109 a four-second burst and saw his bullets hitting the engine. He saw the Perspex of the hood shatter into fragments that sparkled in the sunlight. The Bf 109 rolled onto its back, slewed, and then dropped, nose down, to earth. Another enemy aircraft came into his sights. Gleave turned with him, firing bullets that brought black smoke from the wings before the Bf 109 dropped vertically, still smoking. Gleave narrowly missed colliding with his third victim, and then gave him a three-second burst as the Messerschmitt pulled ahead and turned into the gunfire. The cockpit seemed empty; the pilot slumped forward out of sight. The Messerschmitt fell. The German pilots were trying to maintain formation and by now there was so much gunfire curving through the air that Gleave had the impression of flying through a gigantic golden bird-cage. A fourth Messerschmitt passed slightly above Gleave, and he turned and climbed to fire into the underside of its fuselage. But after two or three seconds' firing Gleave heard the ominous clicking that told him he had used up all his bullets. But already the fourth victim was mortally hit, and rolled on its back before falling away.

In spite of his age and rank, Gleave possessed the one quality that distinguished the ace pilots on both sides. It was something more important than flying skill, more important than keen eyesight, even more important than quick reaction times and the ability to 'aim off' for the correct deflection. Such men as Gleave had the nerve to fly on collision courses (that forward-facing guns require) very, very close to the enemy. Gleave was 175 yards from his first victim (very close by 1940 standards) and 120 yards from the second one. But the third and fourth Messerschmitts were hit from only 60 and 75 yards respectively. Furthermore the RAF were discovering that the shortened, lightened version of the Oerlikon 20mm cannon that the Luftwaffe was using had severe limitations. The reduced muzzle velocity was causing the shells to explode before penetrating the RAF airframes, and the cannon shells were fragmenting into such small pieces that the monocoque structures were often being perforated but not always shattered. The extra armour plate that the fighters now carried, thanks to the efforts of No. 1 Squadron in France, enabled many pilots to escape from fighters suffering direct hit by cannon shells. Some pilots even brought such aircraft home.

The pre-war theories about the destructiveness of explosive cannon shells were eventually to prove right but in 1940 the short Oerlikon cannon that the Bf 109E used had such a low velocity and poor rate of fire that the armament of the opposing fighters was about equal. And the Messerschmitt wings were still imposing terrible limitations upon the Luftwaffe's fighter pilots. Even with bubbles on the lower surface of the wings, the cannon magazines could hold no more than sixty rounds. This gave the Bf 109 a mere nine seconds of gunfire compared with the RAF's machine guns which could deliver fourteen seconds of fire. And such gunfire could be equally destructive if the pilot flew very close.

And on this day of August, Tom Gleave had flown very close. It was an instructive insight into the ways of the Air Ministry assessment boards, and their indifference to the rules of evidence that, at a time when RAF claims were so far from reality, Gleave's claim to four Bf 109s shot down was allowed only as four 'probables.' It seemed to them unlikely that Gleave had shot down four aircraft in as many minutes and so they offered him a vague compromise. Dissatisfied, Gleave sought out the wrecks just south of Maidstone and proved his claims. They were all from JG 27.

As the day came to an end, Fighter Command could console itself with the news that thirty-six German aircraft had been destroyed for only twenty-five RAF fighters, and from these fifteen pilots were safe. But the Luftwaffe seemed to have discovered the way to hurt the defences. The attacks against the sector airfields had been delivered with resource and determination, and the relentless timing had scarcely been giving the RAF fighters enough time to rearm and refuel. Luckily none of the attacks had found the fighters on the ground but inevitably they would, and the results could prove as devastating as they had in France and Poland.

31 August

It was a day when the Luftwaffe did everything exactly right. Every available Bf 109 had been moved to airfields in the Pas de Calais under Kesselring and as close as possible to England. Today no less than 1,300 fighter sorties were flown, to protect 150 bombers.

The skills and experience of the German fighter pilots became evident early in the day. The newly operational Canadians of No. 1 Squadron RCAF were bounced by a *Staffel* of Bf 109s, and three Hurricanes were shot down before breakfast.

Following this wave of fighters came the first bombing raid. Again the attacks were directed against the sector airfields. The raids were delivered with skill and determination. No. 56 Squadron, out of the North Weald, went to intercept a raid heading for their base. They met the enemy over Colchester but the Bf 109 escorts knocked four Hurricanes out of the sky without suffering any casualties themselves or losing any bombers.

The raids continued with the same relentless energy as they had the previous day. Inevitably some RAF fighters were caught on the ground. At lunchtime the Kenley Controller phoned 85 Squadron at Croydon and scrambled them. As Squadron Leader Peter Townsend cleared the perimeter fence and reached for the undercarriage retraction gear, his engine stopped. It missed a few beats before roaring back into life again. 'Turning in the cockpit, I saw the rest of the squadron emerging from a vast eruption of smoke and debris.' The blast of the bombs had strangled his engine but the Hurricanes survived the bombing. Out of sight over the horizon were the vulnerable Dornier Do 17s discovering that their low-level diving runs gave their target no warning and gave themselves a chance of getting away.

As Townsend climbed steeply away at full boost, he saw in the distance black smoke from another attack, upon neighbouring Biggin Hill. Chasing after the raiders, 85 Squadron caught up with the Bf 110 fighter escort at 9,000 feet over Tunbridge Wells. But as they did so, Bf 109 high escorts dived into the fight. All Bf 110s were flown by selected crews but those attacked by Townsend were really *Experten.* They belonged to *ErprGr 210* (the precision light-bombing unit that had done such damage to the radar chain on 12 August). No. 85 Squadron shot down one of the Bf 110s and damaged two others, but as Townsend was aiming at a Bf 109 with thumb on the firing button, his Hurricane was rocked by a burst from a Bf 110. Townsend saw the winking light of the muzzle flashes before his windscreen went white, fuel poured over him, and the nose-cap of a cannon shell went into his foot, and stayed there. But his Hurricane was still in one piece, and Townsend climbed out and pulled the ripcord of his parachute. When still dangling in the air he remembers calling to two girls, 'I say, would you mind giving me a hand when I get down?' By 21 September, walking with the aid of a stick and minus one toe, Townsend was back with his squadron.

There were many such miraculous survivals and they were partly due to the low muzzle velocity of the shortened Oerlikons. On 9 August a Spitfire of 92 Squadron had been hit by cannon shells, one of which struck the control column, but the pilot had flown his fighter back to Kenley. On 24 August Pilot Officer Andy Mamedoff, an American flying with 609 Squadron, had an amazing escape when a cannon shell actually pierced his seat armour. The Spitfire was a total loss but Mamedoff had nothing worse than a bruised back. It was his first combat.

The smoke that Townsend had seen rising in a black cloud from Biggin Hill was the result of a formation of Heinkel He 111s bombing from about 12,000 feet. They turned away south-east and were intercepted by 253 Squadron. That morning Tom Gleave had inherited the squadron again when the new commander (with whom he was 'sharing') died after bailing out of his Hurricane. The squadron pilots were convinced that he had been deliberately shot up by the Germans while descending, but such incidents were rare simply because the combatants seldom had the time for such dangerous activities. As the brief combats ended, the fighters tried to re-form and/or gain height, rather than circle round parachutists expending valuable ammunition.

Now, with Tom Gleave in command, 253 Squadron found the homeward-bound Heinkels. Gleave's Hurricane took a direct hit from a Bf 109 that came up into the blind spot under his tail. Flames roared over him as he tried to tear himself loose of his radio and oxygen connections. He saw his skin bubble and crisp, and felt pain from his burning clothes as he undid the harness and slid back his hood. An explosion threw him out of the cockpit, and he managed to pull the ripcord of his parachute. By the time he landed in a farm, his burned flesh had swollen to close his eyes to thin slits. Put to bed in the farmhouse, Gleave politely objected because he would mark the clean linen.

The Heinkels that bombed Biggin Hill were part of a two-pronged attack of which the second half went for Hornchurch airfield. These Dorniers, hidden by a heat haze, bombed from 15,000 feet. Their bombs came down just as 54 Squadron were scrambled. Eight Spitfires escaped unhurt, but the final section of three was destroyed at the moment they became airborne. One was tilted far enough for a wing to touch the ground; it cartwheeled across two fields, and the pilot went into a river. The second was hammered back to earth minus a wing, and the leading Spitfire – flown by Flight Lieutenant Al Deere – was flipped onto its back and slid 100 yards across the airfield upside down. Deere remembered the violent impact 'and a terrifying period of ploughing along the airfield upside down, still firmly strapped in the cockpit. Stones and dirt were thrown into my face and my helmet was torn by the stony ground against which my head was firmly pressed.' The wrecked Spitfire – with engine and one wing missing – came to rest with Deere in complete darkness inside. Petrol fumes were almost overpowering him but, showing amazing agility, he crawled out through the tiny flap door. Incredibly, all three pilots were back flying again next day.

That afternoon, *ErprGr 210* returned to the task of bombing the radar stations. Beachy Head, Whitstable, Foreness, Rye, Dunkirk, and Pevensey were attacked, but as soon as the raiders disappeared the technicians started to repair the damage. By nightfall all the stations were working again.

At teatime the indefatigable *ErprGr 210* crossed the English coast yet again. This time they went to Hornchurch and Biggin Hill, escorting Junkers Ju 88s. Two Spitfires were destroyed on the ground but the squadrons were in the air. No doubt the raiders were heartened to see the chaos of wreckage that the previous raids had caused, but German intelligence were convinced that all RAF Operations Rooms were deep underground (they were not; they were on the surface and very vulnerable, as were the communication links that emerged from them). And in the summer months Spitfires and Hurricanes did not need runways – few fighter airfields had them – they could take off across any stretch of firm grass. But by now Biggin Hill was in bad shape. Two of its squadrons were withdrawn and its Operations Room was now a converted shop in the village.

Thirty-nine RAF fighters had been lost, with thirteen of the pilots killed. Luftwaffe losses were also thirty-nine aircraft. By any measure Kesselring's new tactics were paying off handsomely. But Dowding's greatest worry was not to be measured simply by the loss in numbers. The danger came from the lowering quality of his squadrons, as pilots were rushed through a few hours of operational training or converted from their duties with Bomber Command, Coastal Command, or the Fleet Air Arm. These men were diluting effectiveness of the defence. For instance, 616 Squadron had gone to Kenley in mid-August. In only fifteen days of fighting, four pilots were killed, five were wounded, and one became a POW. Additionally the commission of one officer was terminated and another was posted away from the squadron. There was no alternative but to withdraw it from the Battle.

It was not only newcomers who faced a terrible strain. The veterans were flying more sorties, and nursing inexperienced pilots too. At one squadron a Spitfire taxied to a standstill but no one got out. The ground staff climbed up on its wing expecting to find the pilot dead or wounded, but he was slumped over his controls, fast asleep. The pilots were tired, and so were the ground crews. Often men sat down to eat and fell asleep before even picking up a knife and fork.

The Germans had every reason to be more tired. They were not rotated as the RAF flyers were, and the need for fighter escorts – sometimes two relays for one raid – gave them little rest.

The fighting was hard and yet there was surprisingly little bitterness between the two sides. Erich Rudorffer, of the *Grünherz Geschwader*, JG 54 (who ended the war as one of the top German aces, with 222 victories), remembers the Battle of Britain as a time when no one fired upon men descending by parachute. He added:

> Once – I think it was 31 August 1940 – I was in a fight with four Hurricanes over Dover. I was back over the Channel when I saw another Hurricane coming from Calais, trailing white smoke, obviously in a bad way. I flew up alongside him and escorted him all the way to England and then waved

goodbye. A few weeks later the same thing happened to me. That would never have happened in Russia – never.

Oberleutnant Hans von Hahn, a Bf 109 pilot of I/JG 3 – the *Udet Geschwader* – remembered the ever-present obstacle of the Channel. He said, 'There were only a few of us who had not yet had to ditch in the Channel with a shot-up aircraft or a stationary propeller.'

Running out of fuel was a constant hazard for the Bf 109 pilots. It needed only a careless error to stretch the narrow Strait of Dover to the 70 miles of sea between the English coast and Abbeville. One Bf 109 pilot, his red fuel warning light glowing, watched seven of his *Gruppe* ditch in the ocean, and then saw another five make belly landings on the French beaches.

Forced landings and parachute descents had become commonplace. Of 85 Squadron's eighteen pilots at Croydon during this two-week period, fourteen were shot down, two of them twice. On 31 August its commander – Peter Townsend – added another Hurricane to the total. No. 56 Squadron had also suffered so badly that it was withdrawn from the Battle.

Brought to interceptions at a lower altitude than their enemies, the RAF fighters were at a serious disadvantage. Yet the Controllers had no option. The radar showed the German formations assembling over Calais, but the fighters' short endurance prevented them being scrambled until the raid was on its way. In the 20 minutes it took a Spitfire to climb to 25,000 feet, even the slower German bombers could travel 80 miles. Added to this was the imperfection of the radar, which was now suffering regular jamming. Few Controllers committed the bulk of their forces if the weather was good enough to wait for a confirmed visual report.

1 September

By Sunday 1 September, Dowding realized that he could no longer rotate his squadrons because he had no adequately rested and refitted ones to bring south into 11 Group. Forced to what he later admitted was 'a desperate expedient,' he classified the squadrons into three types, A, B, and C. The squadrons in 11 Group and Duxford and Middle Wallop were classified as A squadrons. The B squadrons (most of those in 10 and 12 Groups) were to be kept up to strength, so that they could be sent to relieve A squadrons. But the C squadrons, in the quieter parts of Britain, were now to be used like training units, preparing pilots for posting to A squadrons.

Even more tribute to Kesselring's tactics and the courageous determination of his crews was the price that Fighter Command was now paying for every victory in the air. The RAF were no longer destroying substantially more raiders than their losses in fighters. Sometimes losses were at parity. At least once, the Germans led. In the two weeks of the critical period, Fighter Command lost 200 more Spitfires and Hurricanes than they received.[1] Worse, of a total complement of about 1,000 RAF pilots, 231 had been killed, wounded, or were missing. Six out of seven sector airfields were badly damaged, and so were five forward airfields.

The Luftwaffe's morale was high. On 1 September a captured German pilot, under armed escort, looked out of the window when his train stopped at Chatham station. A waitress ran out of the buffet rattling a 'Mayor of Chatham's Spitfire Fund' collecting box. She shook it under the prisoner's nose. He asked the guard for his wallet, smiled, and put a five-mark note into the box before the train pulled out.

If what Göring wanted was air superiority over south-east England for the invasion, then by 1 September it was almost his.

Milch received Osterkamp's long, pessimistic report about the way the Battle was going and what would be the consequence of losing so many of the Luftwaffe's finest

[1]In the thirteen days from 24 August 466 fighters were destroyed and damaged. There were 269 new and repaired ones.

flyers. Milch reacted immediately. He ensured that 'Onkel Theo' was disciplined and reduced in rank. The old man was told that if in the future he expressed such defeatist views, either in writing or in conversation, he would be court-martialled.

However the tide of battle flowed, it wasn't all work and no play for Milch. He tasted some of the pleasures that were on offer to Generals of the victorious army in a conquered land. Accompanied by Hugo Sperrle and Udet's Chief of Staff, he visited the gambling casinos of Deauville, and enjoyed some winnings.

Soon he was to have his own train too. It was cobbled together by the French railways in the Gare St Lazare, Paris, and included Marshal Pétain's First World War dining car (complete with a bathroom and corduroy and green baize furnishings) and a dining car of President Lebrun, with two of his chefs in attendance, as well as ordinary coaches and locomotives.

2 September

Kesselring kept up his attacks against the airfields. Early that morning he sent a *Gruppe* of KG 3 Dorniers, escorted by Bf 109s from JG 51, to bomb the south-east airfields. By now 11 Group Controllers knew the dangers of leaving their airfields without some sort of air cover, and this meant a reluctance to send the fighters forward to meet the raiders. (Leigh-Mallory in 12 Group must bear much of the responsibility for these inadequate tactics.)

Significantly it was 603 Squadron Spitfires, out of Hornchurch, not threatened by the raid, which went forward to intercept. It was about 8 a.m. as they chased the Bf 109s over Kent and out to sea. Four of the Messerschmitts were shot down, the last two crashing in the Channel. One of these pilots was Heinz 'Pritzl' Bär, the NCO ace based at Wissant with the first *Staffel* of JG 51. He was nursing his damaged Messerschmitt over what the German pilots called '*der Bach*' (the stream) when a Spitfire gave him a last long burst. He hit the water, climbed out, and started swimming. It took him two hours before he found one of the brightly painted Channel rafts that the Luftwaffe had anchored for such emergencies. As it got dark, a German patrol boat found him there. Next day he was back on flying operations.

One of the four Messerschmitts downed in that breakfast-time action was claimed by Pilot Officer Richard Hillary, a skilful fighter pilot who had by now shot down three Bf 109s in five days. Hillary was later to become famous as the author of a book about the air fighting, *The Last Enemy*. In it he wrote:

> I wondered idly what he was like, this man I would kill. Was he young, was he fat, would he die with the Führer's name on his lips, or would he die alone, in that last moment conscious of himself as a man? I would never know. Then I was being strapped in, my mind automatically checking the controls, and we were off.

The next day, 3 September, at about the same time, Hillary himself was shot down into the sea near the North Foreland and rescued by the Margate lifeboat. But he was not as lucky as 'Pritzl' Bär. Richard Hillary's Spitfire burst into flames. He was hideously disfigured by burns.

Fire was the ever-present nightmare of many flyers. The RAF fighters had the fuel tank immediately in front of the pilot, and there was not always a fire-wall. The Bf 109's fuel was in a huge L-shaped container upon which the pilot sat. The rival merits and dangers of these designs were a favoured topic of discussion, and grim jokes, among fighter pilots on both sides of the Channel. Some pilots were so nervous about fire that they covered themselves with gloves, goggles, and scarf to be sure there was no exposed skin. Others preferred the precaution of flying always with the hood locked back, ready to bail out. It was freezing cold in the open cockpit but it reassured them. Tom Gleave was one of many who carried a loaded pistol, determined to shoot themselves at the first sign of flames. But Gleave, shot down in flames, had not used the pistol.

This was what was later called 'the critical period.' Since 24 August the Air Fleets had focused their assault upon 11 Group's airfields. The tactic had worked well. By now the defence depended upon the only two surviving sector airfields: Tangmere and Kenley.

Had the Luftwaffe commanders pursued these targets to the exclusion of everything else, they might well have gained command of the air over south-east England. But they did not do so. They added aircraft factories to the objectives, and so gave the sector stations a chance to patch up the damage. On 30 August, Fighter Command had flown 1,000 sorties for the first time. It was a great worry to Dowding and Park but the presence of so many Spitfires and Hurricanes must have been a blow to the morale of any German who still believed the figures about RAF losses that Luftwaffe intelligence were providing. Especially since the Luftwaffe's losses – 800 aircraft in two months – were now influencing the scale of the fighting. On 1 September, the Luftwaffe had flown only 640 sorties, and it failed to reach 1,000 sorties on any of the five days that followed. The Air Fleets' total fighter strength – now concentrated in the Pas de Calais – was less than 600 machines. This was reducing the effectiveness of the attacks, because Kesselring was insisting that the formations must be about 75 per cent fighters.

And yet this preponderance of fighters provided a grim prospect for the RAF squadrons that were sent to intercept the attacks. In recognition of this, whole squadrons deliberately disobeyed orders, if the orders were too dangerous. At Kenley, the Sector Controller repeatedly vectored 605 Squadron to fly due east, while watching the pip-squeak signals that showed them going west – away from the enemy. It was the same story with some of the Hornchurch squadrons, which refused to cross the Thames on an interception course unless they had climbed to at least 18,000 feet. Everywhere the pilots were learning that to intercept from below was suicidal. Sometimes this meant that the bombers got through unscathed. On 2 September, the commander of ZG 76 – the once so vulnerable Bf 110s – reported after returning from a mission, 'There's not much doing over there anymore.'

3 September

The Germans continued the attacks on Fighter Command airfields. This time the fighters and bombers were flying at the same level, and were mixed together to prevent the RAF getting to the bombers.

This seemed to work in the case of the thirty Do 17s that bombed North Weald, and in spite of the new instructions, these Dorniers had only Bf 110s escorting them. In the event, they sufficed. Hangars and the new Operations Block were hit and the airfield communications went out of action, including the high-frequency radio contact with its aircraft.

Göring chose this day to call his Air Fleet commanders to The Hague for a conference. They reached no agreement about results so far achieved. 'Smiling Albert' Kesselring was his usual optimistic self, and inclined to believe German intelligence reports that the RAF had very few fighter aircraft left. Hugo Sperrle's experiences had left him more sceptical. He preferred to believe that the RAF had anything up to 1,000 fighters left.

In spite of the sun at The Hague this day, there could be no arguing about the approach of winter weather. The three men agreed that the RAF fighter force must be brought into battle more quickly. London was surely a target that the British would defend with every fighter they possessed. Hitler had forbidden 'terror raids' against residential districts, but the Luftwaffe could send their bombers to the London docks, which were considered legitimate military targets.

For the RAF there was little comfort to come from the day's fighting. Sixteen RAF fighters were lost for sixteen of the enemy, the only consolation being that eight pilots were safe. In just two weeks of fighting Dowding had lost 25 per cent of his pilots. Neither did this mean that he could fight another six weeks with the remainder. Long before that, Fighter Command would cease to be a disciplined fighting force. Even at this moment, a quarter of his pilots were fresh from only a few flying hours at Operational Training Units, and with less than two weeks' squadron experience. He had only to keep September's skies too dangerous for a German invasion in order to force a postponement to 1941. But at this loss rate it seemed impossible.

4 September
In response to a Luftwaffe Operations Staff IA order dated 1 September, attacks were directed to thirty aircraft factories. On the first day of this new policy, the Vickers-Armstrong factory at Brooklands was bombed, causing 700 casualties.

Phase Four: 7 September Onwards, the Daylight Attacks Centre on London

7 September
Hitherto, Hitler had forbidden raids upon London but the RAF continued to bomb Berlin after the first attack on the night of 24–25 August, and Hitler became angry enough to relax his veto. He said terror raids on central London could begin.

After his capture, in 1945, Göring spoke of this period. He claimed that while he had wanted to continue the attacks on the airfields, Hitler had demanded retribution. However, no other evidence supports this claim. No Luftwaffe commander, no memoir, diary, or memo shows Göring reluctant about the new policy. In fact Göring recalled Milch to his Air Ministry desk and came west himself. And on the afternoon of Saturday 7 September, when Göring, Loerzer, and Kesselring stood on the cliffs at Cap Blanc Nez watching the German formations head for London, Göring had already announced over the radio, 'I

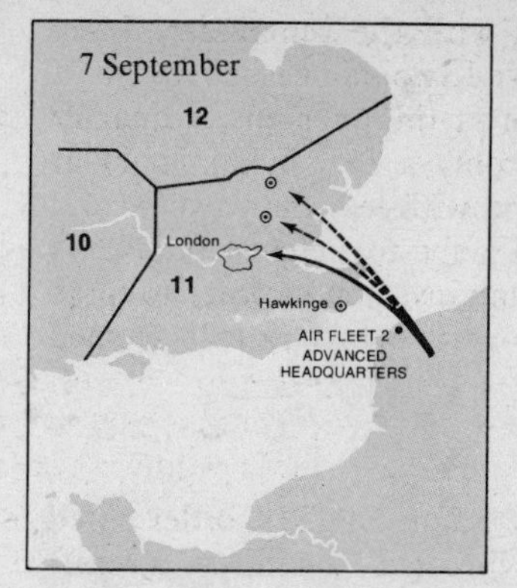

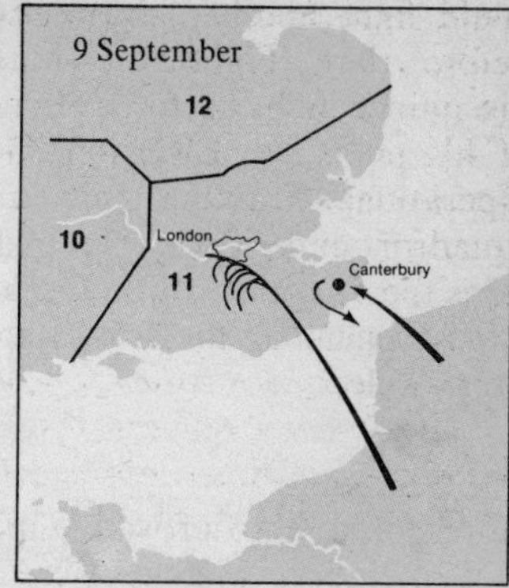

Figure 32

On 7 September, after morning attacks upon Hawkinge airfield, the Controller of 11 Group expected that the attacks against the sector airfields would continue.

Massed German formations passed over Air Fleet 2 advanced HQ, watched by Göring, who had brought his personal train to the Pas de Calais specially for this event.

The Controller plotted raiders as they came to the coast but thought that they were heading for fighter airfields north of London. Because 12 Group had failed to cover these airfields on previous occasions, he kept his fighters north of London.

For the first time the Luftwaffe deliberately bombed London, having got there almost unopposed.

On 9 September the Controller of 11 Group was prepared. Realizing that the Luftwaffe had changed its tactics to centre the attacks upon London, he sent great numbers of fighters to confront them. One attack was turned back at Canterbury, which was bombed. The other attack was deflected; the formations broke up and bombed targets to the south of London. Many RAF fighters were brought into action as the track of the Germans took them very close to many Fighter Command airfields.

myself have taken command of the Luftwaffe's battle for Britain.'

In order to supplement his forces, and replace so many bomber casualties, Kesselring had been given KG 26, the

Löwen-Geschwader, and KG 30, the *Adler-Geschwader*, from Air Fleet 5. It was a measure of the fighting that these two units, with a paper strength of 240 aircraft, could provide less than 40 serviceable ones.

Altogether the huge bombing formation that Göring watched numbered nearly 1,000 aircraft. About a third of these were bombers. The formation looked like a vast black storm cloud, for it was nearly two miles high, and covered about 800 square miles!

It has been suggested that the intercepted Enigma signals that British intelligence supplied to Dowding and Park (although not to the other commanders) warned them of German intentions, but on the English side of the Channel Park had no idea that London was to be the target for this daylight raid. On this Saturday he had gone to Fighter Command HQ, which shows that Dowding too had no warning of the huge air assault of this day.

Park had given his staff and all concerned a sharp rebuke about the practice of adding a little height to the estimation that came from the radar. By the time Group, and then the Sector Controller, and finally the squadron had all added to the estimated height of the 'bandits' (to avoid the risk of arriving under them), some of the lower German formations were getting in, and back, unintercepted. Park pointed out that on one occasion the previous day, only seven out of eighteen squadrons vectored on the enemy made contact.

Because of the way in which Leigh-Mallory had failed to protect Debden on 26 August, Park had now ordered his squadrons at North Weald, Debden, and Hornchurch not to fly south on interceptions until Leigh-Mallory's promised units had arrived over their bases.

The Observer Corps saw the Germans approaching the east coast of Kent, near Deal. From the course of the German raid Park's Controller guessed that their track would pass into an attack against those very sector stations that Leigh-Mallory was charged to defend. Therefore, instead of sending his squadrons well forward, as had become Park's routine for defending the sector stations south of London, the Controller played safe. He kept most of his squadrons north of the Thames.

Once again the 50-year-old Fink was leading KG 2 in the van of the attack. Already he had seen his fighter escort turn back as their fuel ran short. Unescorted, he turned to attack targets in East London. Behind him came other waves of bombers to hit docks and factories on London's river. Only after the main force had bombed did the RAF Controllers fully realize that London was the German target, and bring the full strength of Fighter Command into action.

In the subsequent fighting, the RAF suffered a marginal defeat. The German fighter escorts had evolved a series of counter-moves for each type of attack. For instance, an attack from the starboard side to draw the fighter escort away did not do so, because the top-cover moved down to cover the starboard flank while the port escort moved up to top-cover position. These tactics frustrated Park's system of sending a Hurricane and a Spitfire squadron into action in unison, the latter to attack the fighters, the former to attack the bombers. To add to Fighter Command's difficulties, the German formations were flying much higher than usual – 16,000 to 20,000 feet – at the very day when all concerned were meticulous about not adding a few thousand feet extra for safety's sake. This higher-altitude fighting left the blue sky woven with hundreds of condensation trails that made the Battle visible to watchers on the ground.

Bader was ordered to orbit 11 Group's sector airfield at North Weald, but according to his biographer, 'Bader disobeyed instructions again' and chased the Germans, climbing steeply to 15,000 feet so as to leave his big-wing formation 'trailing, unable to keep up.' He attacked the Germans, who were formed 'in a straggle from below with 109s on top. No chance to break them up. No time for tactics.'

Not surprisingly, Bader's big wing performed disappointingly enough for Leigh-Mallory to write excuses to Dowding, saying that they 'were at a disadvantage through the loss of any element of surprise, through having to climb up to get at the enemy, and through the enemy fighters coming down at them from the sun.'

One of the worst aspects of Leigh-Mallory's unilateral behaviour was the way in which it affected the co-operation between the Groups. At one time 12 Group Controllers had – like those of 10 Group on the right flank – been keen to help in concert with any tactics decided upon by 11 Group. By September, the feud between the two commanders had resulted in a complete loss of contact between their respective Controllers. So much so that 11 Group sometimes watched the Germans evade the big wings with no way of helping the interception except by sending messages through Fighter Command HQ.

To add to the confusion caused by the bombing of London, where the Luftwaffe had tried out its new 3,600-lb high-explosive bomb, the Joint Intelligence Committee decided that a German invasion was imminent; 'a significant item of intelligence' contributing to this notion was that four Germans had been found landing by rowing boat, and had confessed that they were going to report troop movements.

The Combined Intelligence Committee, and the Joint Intelligence Committee to which they reported, had a high opinion of the speed and efficiency of the men in the rowing boat, for they chose not to use Invasion Alert No. 3 (an attack is probable within three days) or No. 2 (an attack is probable within two days). They stampeded the Chiefs of Staff into issuing Invasion Alert No. 1 – attack is imminent.

Red-faced, the authorities later blamed the troops under their command for taking the warning too seriously. Special scorn was reserved for Home Guard commanders who ordered the church bells to be rung, for this was a signal that enemy parachutists were descending in the neighbourhood.

Churchill and the official historian wrote that the

invasion warning was justified on the strength of the information available. But, apart from the continued build-up of barges in the Channel ports, two understrength *Geschwader* transferred from Air Fleet 5, and the wretched men in the rowing boat, they provided none. It became expedient to say that the No. 1 Alert was the only invasion alert available, and that what the Chiefs of Staff wanted to do was to warn the troops in south-east England that there was a good chance of an attack by seaborne German forces in the next few days. Why this announcement could not have been sent by phone, teleprinter, messengers, by means of a conference, or even broadcast over the BBC was never explained.

However, impeded only slightly by the Chiefs of Staff, London continued to attend to the damage done by its first real bombing raid. The afternoon raids continued and more bombers came that night. In London's Surrey Docks the bombs set fire to 250 acres of timber. Warehouses of paint and rum blazed. Pepper caught fire and tormented the eyes of the Civil Defence workers. 'Send all the pumps you've got,' said one Fire Officer, 'the whole bloody world's on fire.'

Circling the burning city in his personal Hurricane, code-lettered OK1, Air Vice-Marshal Park prayed that it meant a respite for his vital sector airfields.

9 September

But bombing by daylight provided an accuracy that night bombing never could. Park was determined that the Germans should not repeat their daylight success on London. For the next big raid, he placed his squadrons well forward, to intercept a two-pronged attack that came towards London from Dover and Beachy Head. The former was intercepted skilfully enough for the Germans to bomb Canterbury instead. The southern raid was deflected from the docks – the prime German target – and in bitter fighting over south-west London, bombs were scattered in city and countryside.

But again Leigh-Mallory failed to protect Park's airfields north of London. Instead his squadrons came south, to join in the air battles south-west of London.

Leigh-Mallory's determination to send his squadrons down south into 11 Group is made more puzzling by the 'territorial' attitude he took about his own Group. There was an incident in which a lone raider flew along the Group boundary being chased by fighters of both 11 Group and 12 Group. One of Park's fighters shot it down, but it fell just inside 12 Group area. Within minutes a signal from Leigh-Mallory arrived at the desk of the 11 Group Controller: 'Full explanation required why 11 Group fighters have shot down enemy aircraft into 12 Group area.' From some commanders such a signal might have contained a measure of wry humour but Leigh-Mallory did not joke about such things.

Park's handling of the fighting of 9 September was as brilliant as any in the war. Virtually none of the German bombers achieved hits on its primary target.

By now the summer had gone and the weather deteriorated rapidly. Several times the daylight raids stole in unseen over the weather. Unintercepted, the German crews went home trying to believe their Intelligence Officers, who kept repeating that RAF Fighter Command had virtually ceased to exist. When, on the next raid, they saw huge formations rising to meet them, they were disillusioned again. 'Here they come,' said one German flyer bitterly, 'the last fifty Spitfires.'

It was the week ending 13 September that saw the RAF storage units down to the lowest point in the battle. Only eighty Hurricanes and forty-seven Spitfires were available. Although it would be unwise to place much emphasis upon this timing, it is certainly an indication of the skill with which Park and Dowding had fed aircraft into the battle.

15 September

Both sides had learned a great deal. At last German Signals had realized that the south-coast radar stations, difficult to destroy by bombing, could be nullified by radio interference. Some experts said the Germans would save their intensive jamming to coincide with the invasion.

Today came the climax of the daylight battles. Warning had come when the monitoring service heard intense radio activity from aircraft being tested and prepared for operations. And there was warning too from other sorts of radio activity by the Luftwaffe Air Fleets. From these various sources, collectively known as the Y service, it became evident that today's attack would come in two waves. Park knew that he would have to get his squadrons refuelled and replenished in record time, to engage the follow-up attack. The ground crews did not let him down.

The Luftwaffe was still experimenting with changes in formations. Today these were more complex and flew higher, having discovered that high-flying formations sometimes escaped without interception. (The radar was ineffective above 20,000 feet but the Germans did not know this for certain.) Both the height and the complexity of the forming-up gave Park a little extra time to position his defences. He had his squadrons well forward and fought the raids all the way to London, and all the way back again. The extra time gave him a chance to use his squadrons in pairs (usually from the same airfield), which he had always preferred but seldom had time to do.

Leigh-Mallory, on the other hand, persisted in using bigger and bigger big wings. Ignoring his orders, and failing to play a part in Dowding's whole strategy, Leigh-Mallory let his flyers fly south as far as London, and even beyond, leaving London completely undefended from the north.

And yet this day's fighting provided a vivid example of how impractical the big-wing operations were. Johnny Kent was flying with 303 (Polish) Squadron behind 229 Squadron. Over Croydon he sighted a large enemy formation approaching from the south. His aircraft had no common radio band with the other squadron, which was by now on a heading away from the enemy. Kent tried to call the ground Controller so that he could tell 229 about the 'bandits' but the high-frequency radios in use at this time were very poor, seldom ranging more than 40 miles. Kent's speech broke up and the Controller could not understand.

So as the other squadron moved away, Kent sent nine of his Hurricanes to attack the bombers while he led the remaining two in an attack on the fifty fighters. By that time, 303 Squadron had lost its initial advantage and the Germans were already bombing.

Kent was never an advocate of the big-wing theories but he shared some of the proponents' criticisms of the Controllers. On another occasion, vectored towards a dangerous-looking thundercloud, Kent, an ex-test pilot and one of the most capable aviators flying in the Battle, asked for another course. The Controller became angry, but not as angry as Kent did when he found himself in the middle of the London balloon barrage, having lost radio contact with the Controller. When eventually Kent regained radio contact he was told, 'Bandit ten miles ahead of you.'

'Good, he can stay there,' said Kent. 'I am at angels one half.'

'Apany Red Leader, increase Angels at once,' said the Controller.

'Apany Red Leader to Garta – to hell with that. I'm nearly out of fuel and you've already nearly had me into the balloons in this filthy weather, so I'm coming home.'

On landing, Kent was called to the phone and given 'a terrific tirade from the Controller – a certain Squadron Leader who never flew on operations – principally because I had compromised the secret of our weather conditions to the enemy. He would not listen to any explanation so I hung up – I would very much have liked to go along to the Operations Room and clouted him. . . '

Although the RAF were near to victory, there was no feeling of elation among the exhausted pilots. By now Fighter Command was badly mauled, and morale was at an all-time low. Sent to take over 92 Squadron, Johnny Kent sat down with his pilots at the meal table without identifying himself. His first impressions were not favourable: 'Their general attitude and lack of manners indicated a lack of control and discipline.' He had, he said, been sent to take over 'a disorganized, undisciplined, and demoralized collection of first-class material.'

That squadron had suffered losses about double those of 303 Squadron, from which their new commander came. They had lost four Commanding Officers in short succession, three of them in the previous month. One had only lasted two days.

This demoralization was reflected by the squadron's fighting. On patrol the Hurricanes were subjected to diving passes by some small formations of Bf 109s. Their new commander, Kent, turned his formation to meet the attackers head-on. Each time the Germans turned away. But after this had happened several times Kent noticed that a number of his Hurricanes turned round and headed for home. 'One-oh-nine-itis,' he called it. 'These pilots had lost all confidence in their ability to cope with the German fighters.

'When we returned to our airfield,' said Kent, 'I had all the pilots in and gave them a really good talking to and announced that if I had any more people breaking away – and by so doing exposing not only themselves to attack but the rest of the squadron – I would not wait for the Germans to shoot down the offender but would do it myself.'

The great battles of 15 September – celebrated as Battle of Britain day – gave Londoners the spectacle of nearly 200 Spitfires and Hurricanes over the capital. Twice that same day, 300 RAF fighters were in the air over the southern counties.

Kesselring sent 400 fighters to protect not much more than 100 bombers. And the fighters were put in as a high-altitude sweep ahead of the bombers too. What is never mentioned about the air activity of this day is the element of bluff that was part of the Luftwaffe's plan. It was a double bluff. Says then *Oberleutnant* Johannes 'Macky' Steinhoff, who eventually commanded the post-war West

German air force, 'For demonstration purposes everything that we had in the way of bombers and fighters was thrown into the air.'

However controversial Leigh-Mallory's behaviour, the resulting high concentration of fighters in the London area countered this great bluff. It convinced the Luftwaffe that Fighter Command was far from the depleted force that German intelligence described.

Bader's big wing found the enemy, and the sight of a larger RAF fighter formation than they had ever seen before did much to shatter German hopes. The fact that the RAF claimed 185 victories instead of the 60 credited after the war, or the 50 that recent German researchers record, was less important. Churchill's message to Dowding that evening was intended for German consumption: 'Aided by Czech and Polish squadrons and *using only a small proportion of their total strength*, the Royal Air Force cut to rags and tatters separate waves of murderous assault upon the civil population of their native land.'

RAF Fighter Command did not gain command of the sky. In darkness and by daylight the German Air Fleets continued to raid Britain for a long time to come. The air above the Channel and southern England was still disputed, but nothing short of German command of the air could provide security for a seaborne invasion.

Just by remaining intact, Fighter Command had won the Battle of Britain. On 16 September the weather was too poor for large-scale air fighting and on 17 September turbulent winds were predicted. On this same day, British intelligence intercepted a secret radio message that authorized the dismantling of air-transport facilities in Holland. In the absence of the 'flat calm' that the navy wanted for an invasion, it was officially decided to postpone Sea-lion until further notice. It was just as well: the Luftwaffe was also exhausted by the summer battles. The bomber units were depleted and their morale low. Many spares were in short supply, and the High Command was growing uncomfortably aware of its lack of reserves. The Luftwaffe turned its attentions to the techniques of night bombing and Hitler turned to maps of Russia.

PART FIVE

The Results

'The Reichsmarschall *never forgave us for not having conquered England.'*
Oberst Karl Koller, Staff Officer and later Göring's Chief of Staff

The great battles of 7 September had begun late in the autumn afternoon. Not until teatime did the first raid develop but the waves of bombers kept coming. They came back that evening, and then kept coming through the night until daybreak.

There was no need for radio aids or target markers, the East End of London was a vast lake of flames that guided the airmen from miles away.

The next night the bombers returned. They returned every night for 76 consecutive nights (except for 2 November when the weather was too bad). Douhet's theories got a fair trial.[1]

It was inevitable that the Luftwaffe should succumb to the temptation of London: Europe's largest city, a great port, centre of communications, seat of government, residence of the King. The radar stations, the fighter airfields, the sector stations, these must all have seemed indecisive targets to men across the Channel dazzled by this huge and ancient city. They rationalized its destruction by telling each other that it was the only target that Fighter Command would give everything to defend, but Britain's senior commanders breathed a sigh of relief when the Luftwaffe began to dump their high explosive into the lucky-dip of Greater London. As Churchill wrote in his memoirs, 'London was like some huge prehistoric animal, capable of enduring terrible injuries, mangled and bleeding from many wounds, and yet preserving its life and move-

[1]See p. 41.

ment.' Some said that the bombing of London was the very reaction that Churchill had hoped to provoke when he sent the RAF to Berlin on Sunday 25 August. If that was his intention – and Churchill was a master of strategy – he never admitted it was so.

To have contrived that London was bombed, even as a war-winning master-stroke, would still have damaged his reputation.

The night bombing of London had little effect upon the progress of the war. The raids did not cause enough damage to commerce, industry, or morale to bring Britain nearer to surrender. The residents of London adapted to a new style of life that often included sleeping every night in an air-raid shelter underground. The cold and damp of such places brought a 10 per cent increase in tuberculosis – statistically it was a worse danger than the Luftwaffe.

And as the long winter nights continued, British electronic experts struggled with the problem of jamming the *X-Gerät*. Even as early as 23 August, *Kampfgruppe 100* had used the frightening new technique of giving its electronic 'pathfinder' aircraft incendiary bombs to set the target alight. This enabled other units to dump high explosive into the flames, which were visible for many miles.

It was an act of faith to send the jamming signals into the ether, not knowing how effective were these countermeasures. And yet on the night of 14–15 November there came a horrifying indication of what was being achieved; it was one that the experts would readily have forgone. An error in the adjustment of the modulation made it relatively easy to distinguish the sound of the signal from the sound of the jamming.[1] KGr 100 put over 1,000 incendiaries precisely onto Coventry to lead three separate streams of bombers there with high explosive.

But that was the high-water mark of *X-Gerät*. And the

[1]In spite of recent nonsense written about Churchill and the Enigma machine, this technical error was the sole reason that the German attack was so successful.

effectiveness of the marking technique was reduced by the way in which decoy fires were lighted in the open country-side, while town fire-services did all they could to extinguish the German incendiary attack.

As Christmas approached, the German Embassy in Washington made secret contact with their British counter-parts to say that they would observe a bombing truce from Christmas Eve until 27 December if the RAF would do the same. They did.

As the air assault against England dwindled into harass-ing daylight attacks and a night offensive, the RAF High Command acted more vindictively against the two men who had succeeded than did Göring against the men who had failed.

Dowding and Park had committed an unforgivable sin in the eyes of the Air Ministry and their other critics: they had proved their theories right. In a manner more appro-priate to the already obvious failure of Bomber Command than to the remarkable achievements of Fighter Command, the Air Ministry called a meeting to discuss the Battle.

Not knowing what to expect, Park and Dowding went along to find a gathering of what Beaverbrook always referred to as 'the bloody Air Marshals.' It must have been an astonishing experience for these two weary victors. The room was arranged so that they faced a mighty array of top brass. Conspicuous among it there was only one low-ranking officer. It was Douglas Bader.

Although Sholto-Douglas was only an Air Vice-Marshal, he now held the office of Deputy Chief of Air Staff, which gave him authority over Dowding. He chaired this Alice-in-Wonderland meeting, and was, in Park's words, 'the public prosecutor,' while, 'sitting in an honoured place at the table, was Air Vice-Marshal Leigh-Mallory, supported by Squadron Leader Douglas Bader.'

Bader had been a civilian after his flying accident in 1931. Still young, the legless ace had now completed eight months' RAF service. It was perhaps awesome for him to face Dowding, by now the most senior officer – by rank and experience – of anyone still serving. Dowding had been an Air Chief Marshal since 1937.

Leigh-Mallory explained to the meeting the way in which, according to him, the big-wing tactics had proved superior to the methods of Park. Not content with this, he then called upon the young Douglas Bader to elaborate upon Park's shortcomings.

Although Leigh-Mallory had no practical experience of the special problems of commanding the vital south-east region, he was an eloquent critic of his colleague. He contended that he could get the five squadrons of the Duxford wing into the air in 6 minutes. In another 25 minutes they could be as far as Hornchurch. But as the ace fighter pilot and historian Johnnie Johnson later pointed out, 'the Duxford wing had recently taken 17 minutes to leave the ground and a further 20 minutes before it set course from base.' And Johnson also remarked on the way in which such a concentration of aircraft left many important Midlands targets without air protection.

Young Bader went much further than his boss. He, according to his biographer, told the meeting 'that the chap in the air, not the Controller, should decide when, where and how to meet the enemy.' It was a complete rejection of the whole interception system, and radar too.

Park had no doubt that the whole humiliating charade was contrived as a pretext for sacking Dowding and himself. He remembered the way that the Deputy Chief of Air Staff seemed pleased at the way the meeting was conducted.

Dowding did not fight them; it was not his style. By now his career should have taken him into the back-stabbing world where the military met the politicos, but Dowding had spent four wearying years preparing Fighter Command for the battle he had only just won. And the years before that had been entirely concerned with the technicalities of fighter aircraft design, equipment, organization, research, and radar. Like many technicians he was a political innocent.

It is sad comment on Dowding's lonely life that General Sir Frederick Pile, the AA gun commander, perhaps the only associate to whom Dowding spoke freely, described him as voluble, not realizing that he was Dowding's only friend. That Dowding made so many enemies isn't surprising, but that the Air Ministry and RAF should subject him to petty humiliations and harassments, even during the Battle, is one of the most extraordinary episodes of the war. That Churchill permitted it is a reflection upon that great man's judgment.[1]

Many years later Park said, 'To my dying day I shall feel bitter at the base intrigue which was used to remove Dowding and myself as soon as we had won the Battle of Britain.'

Dowding had a curt phone call telling him to vacate his office in twenty-four hours. The Air Council 'have no further work to offer you,' said the official letter. He was not even permitted to stay in the RAF. Park was relegated to Training Command and Leigh-Mallory took over his Group.

The German High Command

Hitler had taken close interest in the plans for the attack on Poland, and made improvements in it. For the assault on Denmark and Norway, he had used his office of OKW (command of the combined armed forces) to keep a large degree of personal control. Planning the invasion of France, Belgium, and the Netherlands he had encouraged the idea of putting the weight of the thrust upon Sedan, which in

[1] It is sometimes said that Churchill knew nothing of the sacking of Dowding and Park, and that he had no authority to prevent it. But Churchill had day-to-day control of the war and wrote detailed memos on everything from providing sugar rations for bee keepers to allowing women in the army (ATS) to leave the service when they married. And he was Minister of Defence, and was not only kept informed of such decisions but had the authority to instruct the Chiefs of Staff without reference to other Ministers.

the event proved the key to the victory. In the air assault against Britain, Hitler took no interest at all.

Hitler was one of the most successful opportunists of the twentieth century. (As the historian A. J. P. Taylor has shown in detail, there was no Nazi *plan* of war and expansion.) His interest in Sea-lion was a long-shot wager on the hope of Britain's intimidation and collapse. It failed; Hitler shrugged and fingered maps of Russia.

Although the British considered themselves fully engaged in a desperate and dangerous war, Hitler saw the situation differently. The western front was secure – no danger there of any British invasion of the mainland – and there was time enough for a 'quick war' against Russia.[1]

In any case, it had long been a fundamental belief of the German military thinkers that victory over Britain could only be gained by severing its sea routes. Although virtually all nations prepare contingency plans for war against their neighbours (including their closest allies), Germany did not draft any plans for a war against Britain until June 1937. And the Luftwaffe did not draw up memoranda about air attacks on Britain until February 1938. It is worth looking at these evaluations.

The German Predictions

The Luftwaffe's evaluation and study[2] were not optimistic. Accepting the opinion that Britain could only be conquered by a drastic curtailment of its sea traffic, the Luftwaffe

[1]Hitler's decision to invade the USSR has been interpreted as a contradiction of his previous statements. In November 1939, he said, 'We can oppose Russia only when we are at peace in the west.' In June 1940 while still fighting against the French, he said he would move against Russia 'when the military position makes it at all possible.' The end of the Battle of Britain did bring peace in the west by Hitler's standards – the attacks by Bomber Command were no more than pin-pricks – and considering the speed of the blitzkrieg he envisaged, the military position did make the attack on the USSR possible.

[2]Luftwaffe Operations Staff evaluation of August 1938, and the Luftwaffe General Staff (Operations Branch I) study of May 1939.

pointed out that the most important western and south-western ports were beyond bombing range.

The study continued with a pronouncement that Britain's fighter defences would make German attacks too costly to continue, and that terror bombing against the towns and cities – including London – would not bring a decision. The study said that the most effective targets would be the British aero industry, oil storage, ports, and harbours. War industry and supply centres, as secondary ones, were almost as important.

It was not an encouraging view and of course it could not take into account the losses the Luftwaffe suffered before the Battle of Britain. In the three months April, May, and June, the Luftwaffe lost 2,784 aircraft, including 579 single-engine fighters. In the light of these losses, it is surprising that the Luftwaffe virtually ignored what their own study had chosen as the prime target – Britain's aero industry. Even better would have been Britain's fighter aircraft factories. But such targets were essentially strategic ones, not really suitable for a programme that called for invasion before the end of summer. Obviously the destruction of radar stations – a tactical target – would have put Britain's eyes out, and made the rest of the plan easier.

What plan? Was the Luftwaffe trying to:

1 Reduce Great Britain by bombing alone, as Douhet said was possible but had no historical precedent?
2 Deprive the RAF of air superiority so that a landing could not be harassed by attacks from the air? In effect this would have meant destroying Fighter Command and Bomber Command.
3 Establish its own air superiority so that it could attack the British army and navy? This would have meant the destruction of Fighter Command and it would have enabled the German fighter force to withdraw and defend Germany.
4 Prepare the way for a seaborne invasion? This would

mean neutralizing Bomber Command, and Royal Navy units, while preserving British ports and Harbours so that the German invaders could use them. Mine-laying from the air would have little or no place in such a plan.

The answer is yes to all four questions. At one time or another these were each stated to be the Luftwaffe's objectives. But it was Göring's ambition to achieve the first of these objectives that doomed the campaign from the very start. Probably Göring realized that Hitler had no intention of launching the invasion except against a passive shore.

For the pinpoint destruction of tactical and strategic targets the Luftwaffe possessed magnificent equipment. The *Knickebein* could put a bomb into any chosen target with an accuracy of 300 yards, which was good enough for any average *Gruppe* to wipe out a factory. And *Knickebein* equipment was already fitted to all the German bombers. For smaller targets KGr 100 had *X-Gerät,* which was even more accurate.

German experiments and training flights warned the British about both types of beam. Working feverishly, they found it possible to jam the *Knickebein* by the time that heavy night attacks began on 28 August. But the jammers had only been ready for one week! And the jamming of the *X-Gerät* was not completely effective until 1941. There is no need to elaborate upon what the Luftwaffe could have achieved during May and June had the night-bombing units been given even the muddled list of targets that Luftwaffe intelligence had prepared.

But the Germans decided to fight the Battle in daylight, and most historians agree that Dowding and Park showed masterly generalship in husbanding their fighter aircraft. There had been no precedent for such ideas as letting the German fighters range across southern England without engaging them, and constantly ordering fighters to attack only bombers. These responses are now universally regarded as the right ones.

Many Germans object to the way in which the results of the fighting are presented to the British and American reader. The RAF Bomber Command squadrons flying over Germany by night during the summer of 1940 suffered considerable losses. If German bomber losses in the daylight raids are to be included in the British totals, why, ask the Germans, aren't these RAF bomber losses included as German victories? In fact, few British historians include in their figures even the RAF aircraft destroyed on the ground by bombs or gunfire.

There is also a dispute about the number of Hurricanes and Spitfires that were written off because of German action. The official British figure for Hurricanes and Spitfires lost is 1,960, yet only 934 were entered as lost by German action. This has yet to be satisfactorily explained.

Many German historians also feel that the British have deliberately inflated the German losses. The German High Command diary records figures well below the ones that British sources still use. Four days of the Battle can be used to illustrate the discrepancy (see Table 3, p. 295).

Of course, the figures issued by the propaganda men at the end of each day's fighting bear no relationship to the truth. As Figure 33 shows, the Germans simply divided their losses in half, while the RAF multiplied their victories by two (the RAF provided accurate figures of their own losses). As a basis for these inflated claims the RAF used the reports that their fighter pilots submitted after combat.

It would have been simple for the British government to get more accurate figures. Most of the air fighting took place over land, and aircraft crashed in an overcrowded island, networked with constantly manned Observer Corps posts. The fully alerted civil police, and the ambulance services, were promptly on hand to arrest German air crew and succour the wounded. The RAF recorded each crash too, immediately providing round-the-clock armed sentries to prevent souvenir hunters removing vital parts from wrecks both British and German.

To collate these reports would have been an easier task

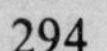

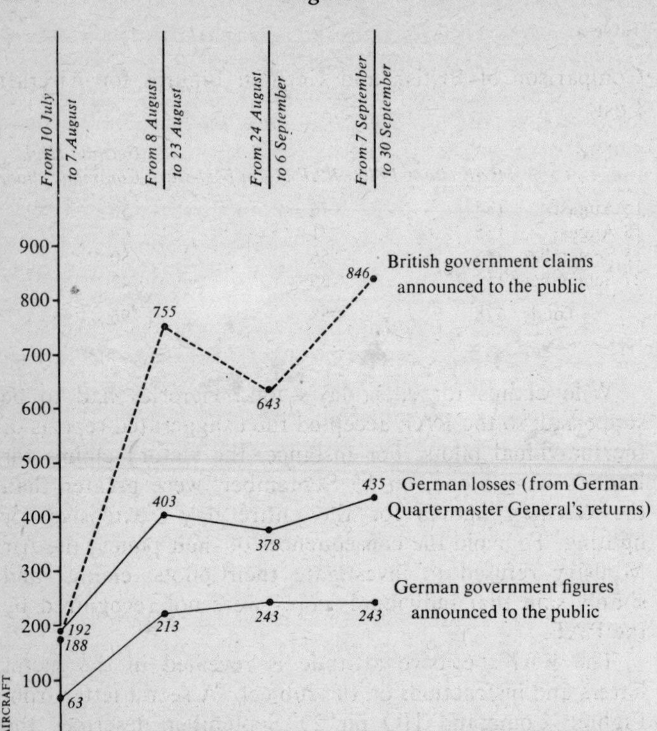

Figure 33 German Aircraft Losses

than sifting and sorting the claims and contradictions of excited and exhausted fighter pilots, with overlapping claims that were sometimes shared with squadrons based miles away.

It is interesting to note that the figure for the period in July, when 60 per cent of all fatal air battles took place over the sea and inflated figures might be expected, is the most accurate. The worst distortions come at the time when the RAF most needed its propaganda victories.

Table 3

Comparison of British and German Figures for Aircraft Lost

	RAF claim 1940	*RAF claim post-war*	*German High Command diary*
15 August	185	76	55
18 August	155	71	49
15 September	185	56	50
27 September	153	55	42
Totals	678	258	196

Wild claims for each day's total victories had to be supported, so the RAF accepted the exaggerated reports of the individual pilots. For instance, the victory claims for Bader's wing alone, on 15 September, were greater than the German figures for the entire day's extensive air fighting. To avoid the consequences of their policy, the Air Ministry refused to investigate their pilots' claims, and simply said that individual scores were not recognized by the RAF.

The RAF's evasive attitude is revealed in the secret letters and instructions on the subject.[1] A secret letter from Fighter Command HQ on 23 September describes the inflated RAF claims as disquieting. An accompanying analysis of the five weeks from 8 August to 11 September showed that the RAF announced that 1,631 enemy aircraft were destroyed and 584 aircraft were 'probably destroyed.' If one assumes that half of the probables were downed, this makes a claim of well over 1,900 aircraft for the five weeks under review. Yet during this period a mere 316 enemy aircraft wrecks were counted. Even allowing for the fact that the pilot of a crippled German plane will head for

[1]For instance, Air Ministry letter to RAF Commands 30 March 1940, Air Ministry letters dated 7 May 1940 and 28 May 1940, 12 Group HQ to Fighter Command 7 October 1940, and Fighter Command letter to 74 Squadron dated 21 September 1941.

home (and so possibly fall into the sea), this is obviously highly inaccurate.

The Luftwaffe formed an *Abschusskommission* to investigate the individual claims of its pilots. Sometimes it took a year to reach a decision, and there was a firm rule that *without a witness no claim would be even considered.* Its regulations were stringent and its results conservative. Although the RAF usually awarded a half-share to all the pilots who contributed to the destruction of a downed enemy aircraft, the Germans simply credited the unit with one victory but did not allow any individuals to share it. For this reason, German unit scores do not tally with the sum of their individual pilots' victories. But German unit scores for this period come remarkably close to known RAF losses. (The average *Jagdgruppe* shot down fifty-five aircraft.[1])

Anyone reading about 'official RAF scores' should remember that there are no such things. But in the light of recent research, the scores generally accepted as the largest are seventeen aircraft shot down by Sergeant Frantisek, a Czech flying with 303 (Polish) Squadron, and sixteen destroyed by Flight Lieutenant McKellar of 605 (County of Warwick) Squadron.

The tactics of the air war – as they emerged – were not very much different from the lessons that had been learned from 1914 to 1918. Height was still the trump card, with attacks out of the sun the most reliable tactic. Heavier fighters, that accelerated more quickly into the dive, were often forgiven other faults. Acceleration in level flight is a quality not listed in any aircraft specification, but for a pilot coming under fire, it often meant the difference between life and death. The twin-engined Bf 110 and the Hurricane were sluggish in this respect.

The most common type of attack was a dive out of the sun, pulling out behind, and under the tail of, the enemy,

[1]And by reason of continued combat, the Luftwaffe ended the war with 35 aces who had shot down 150 or more enemy aircraft. There is no reason to believe that such scores are less than authentic.

and firing while in this blind spot. A cliché of the fiction inspired by the First World War, this tactic continued in use right until the end of the war in 1945.

The head-on formation attacks that were invented by the pilots of 111 Squadron were abandoned during the Battle, because of the number of collisions suffered. However, this tactic was reintroduced by German fighter pilots and used against the big USAAF daylight formations later in the war. It became a standard tactic because it minimized the ability of the bombers to return fire during the head-on approach, while the heavy cannon of the fighters gave them a good chance of inflicting fatal damage.

The fighter pilots themselves had the same physical advantages that marked the First World War's aces: above average eyesight and the ability to see distant aircraft (not quite the same thing), coupled with very quick reactions. For this reason, many of the younger pilots were more successful than their more experienced elders, although experience improved a pilot's chance to survive.

No less vital than eyesight was the ability – and the willingness – to fly very close to the enemy. The aces would not open fire until they were 100 yards away, while the average pilot was breaking off attacks at that distance. The design of the reflector gun-sights – used by both sides – did nothing to help. When the German gun-sight ring was completely filled by the wings of a Spitfire, the two aircraft were still 335 yards apart, too far away for effective shooting.

Scrutiny of Air Ministry secret records (only now released) shows the cloud-cuckoo land that the RAF High Command enjoyed at this time. Fictitious German fighter aircraft are reported in great detail, and the writers of Intelligence Summaries are obsessed with highly unlikely secret devices, such as tin boxes thrown by bomber crews at RAF fighters, and repeatedly report that the Germans are using captured RAF aircraft in all kinds of bizarre colour schemes.

About 3,000 RAF men flew in the Battle of Britain,

although this number is marginally reduced if only single-seat fighters are included. Over 80 per cent of these flyers were from the United Kingdom; the remainder included one hundred and forty-seven Poles, eighty-seven Czechs, twenty-nine Belgians, fourteen Frenchmen, seven Americans, ten Irishmen, a Palestinian, and many men from the Commonwealth nations, including ninety-four Canadians and one hundred and one New Zealanders.

But these figures do not reflect the skill, daring, and determination of this 'remainder.' Poles and Czechs were not permitted to participate in the air fighting until they had mastered the rudiments of the English language and flying procedures. When they did start operations these homeless men, motivated often by a hatred bordering upon despair, fought with a terrible and merciless dedication.

The Australians, New Zealanders, Rhodesians, and Canadians were often men who had paid their own fare to England in order to join the peacetime RAF. Perhaps this sort of determination explains why their contribution was of an exceptional kind. The Commonwealth provided some of the best and bravest flyers[1] and suffered disproportionate casualties. For instance, of twenty-two Australians, fourteen were killed. South Africa also contributed twenty-two flyers, and of these nine were killed during a period in which the average air-crew fatalities in Fighter Command were 17 per cent.

And the skills of this 'remainder' can be recognized among the aces of the Battle. Of the top ten fighter pilots (scoring fourteen or more victories), one was Czech, one was Polish, two were New Zealanders, and one Australian. Only five were from the UK. From such tiny samplings it would be reckless to draw any conclusions, but it is interesting to note that in this list of aces the Hurricane

[1]A study of air combat in the Second World War, *The Fighter Pilots*, by E. H. Sims (London: Cassell, 1967), listed the eight top RAF aces. Of these only two, Johnson and Duke, were English. The others were Canadian, Australian, Irish, French, and two South Africans.

and Spitfire are distributed evenly down the list from top to bottom, with one pilot flying both types of aircraft.

German fighter pilots came to the end of 1940 with considerable reservations about the Bf 109E. When the new Bf 109F arrived, some liked it even less. The difficulties with the Messerschmitt wings had now persuaded the design team to omit any kind of wing guns. A vastly improved cannon, firing through the airscrew boss, had been made to function, but this was now the sole armament, apart from two machine guns mounted on the cowling. Galland, who thought machine guns ineffective for air fighting, said that such armament was quite inadequate for the average fighter pilot. *Major* Walter Oesau, a Battle of Britain ace, preferred his old E model and kept it going until lack of replacement parts forced him to fly the Bf 109F. Mölders, on the other hand, thought one centrally mounted cannon was worth two in the wings. Armament experts pointed out that any kind of wing gun suffered a high rate of jamming. A compromise was reached by sending a kit of parts to the front-line units, so that an extra cannon (20-mm MG 151) could be bolted under each wing. It up-gunned the Messerschmitt but it impoverished its performance and made it unwieldy in combat.

Men who had been watching the intense rivalry between Galland and Mölders throughout that summer were perhaps amused to see both of these legendary air fighters' totals (fifty-two and fifty-four respectively) passed by *Major* Helmut Wick, whose string of fifty-six successes had made him *Kommodore* of JG 2 (*Richthofen*), which he took over from Harry von Bülow-Bothkamp, the First World War ace. At forty victories Wick was, like his rivals, awarded the oak leaves to the Knight's Cross.

The 25-year-old Wick was highly regarded by the lower ranks in the fighter force for his readiness to answer back to the top brass. When Wick's unit was paraded for a visit by *Feldmarschall* Sperrle, Wick was gently told that his ground crews were unmilitary in appearance. Wick asked his Air Fleet commander innocently if he didn't think that refuelling, rearming, and servicing the fighters, to maximize the operational status, wasn't more important than getting a haircut.

As the Battle came to an end, the most successful fighter pilot the RAF had put into the air – Sergeant pilot Josef Frantisek – died. The Czech, who declined to fly with the Czech Squadron, preferring to remain 'a guest' of the Poles with whom he got on so well, failed to get home. Soon after this, Wick also was killed in action. He parachuted down into the wintry waters of the Channel while his men circled, unable to save him. 'It was as if a curtain went down, and the play ended,' remembered one of Wick's flyers.

As already described, the importance of the German fighter squadrons became more and more evident as the battle progressed. In the later stages, the bomber fleets were greatly outnumbered by the necessary fighter escort, and the bombers' use was limited by the availability of fighters. And so it seems incomprehensible that the Luftwaffe did not provide their single-seat fighters with an external fuel tank, until the E-7 version came along too late for the battle.

The first thing that must be said is that the range and endurance of the Spitfire and Hurricane were no better than those of the Bf 109E that fought in the Battle.[1] And certainly the Spitfire and Hurricane had no long-range tanks at this time. But this comparison does not take into account the role of the Luftwaffe as an offence arm, used with the army, to penetrate enemy air space. The RAF Fighter Command was designed entirely to defend Britain from foreign attackers.

Luftwaffe planners saw no need for long-range fighters because of the extraordinary fleet of Junkers Ju 52/3m, three-engined transport aircraft available to them to move

[1]Exact comparisons are difficult because of the varying endurance at different speeds and different heights for all three aircraft. Certainly all fuel-injection systems are theoretically more economical on fuel than carburettor engines.

their support units forward to captured airfields. By this means German squadrons could leap-frog ahead, always operating from fields near to the front line.

Milch said that he had recommended the use of drop tanks for the Bf 109 fighters 'many months before,' but this had been followed up too late. He says that at the Karinhall conference with Göring and the Air Fleet commanders on 15 August, this subject was raised, because 'the fighters were refusing to use the drop tanks unless they were armour plated.' This is probably a reference to the curious old moulded plywood tanks which split if subjected to rain.

But Milch's allegation is nonsense. The Messerschmitt Bf 109E was not equipped with the belly shackles and the fuel lines for fitting the external fuel tank until the E-7 model. And the first example of this did not arrive until the end of August 1940. The shackles for the bomb-racks were available and in use from mid-July. These might have been adapted to hold the fuel tank but the fuel connection was more complicated. Perhaps such adaptations were made unofficially but there is no record of it, and so far no Luftwaffe orders and instructions have been discovered to support Milch's face-saving allegations.

Galland says:

> With additional tanks which could be released and discarded after use, a device employed later by both sides and one which we had already tried successfully in Spain, our range could have been extended by 125 to 200 miles. At that time this would have been just the decisive extension of our penetration.

In Spain Galland had flown Heinkel He 51s with jettisonable tanks. The He 51B was the first to have fuel leads and shackles for this purpose and was in production in late 1935.

So it seems that the lack of external tanks for the Bf 109E-3 was yet another example of Luftwaffe staff bungling and mismanagement. The RAF must remain grateful, for the 300-litre tanks that equipped the E-7 dramatically changed the potential of this fighter. With such a machine the necessary escort could have been provided for attacks against any British targets, for example, the two Rolls-Royce factories (at Derby and Crewe) then making the Merlin engines for Hurricanes and Spitfires. And the extra fuel meant extra duration, so that the fighter sweeps could have proved a far more serious threat to trains and road transport. Or the fighters could have remained over targets, to provide an air umbrella, or over fighter airfields to attack RAF fighters that were taking off or landing (when aircraft are very vulnerable).

In 1940 the Bf 109 averaged about 90 minutes' flying time. But climbing and getting into formation, as well as finding airfields on the return, meant that the German fighters never had more than about 30 minutes over English soil.

External fuel tanks would have eliminated the relay escorts that forced fighter pilots to fly four or five sorties a day, and consequently would have changed the tactical map. Luftwaffe fighter units could have been situated in Holland, beyond British radar coverage, and raids could have been flown by indirect routes over the water. Many pilots lost at sea in 1940 would have had enough fuel to get home safely and have flown again.

But instead of extra fuel, the rack under the new Bf 109E-7 usually held a bomb. This made these aircraft suitable only as nuisance raiders. Most pilots were anxious to release their bomb as soon as possible rather than risk combat while carrying it. Relegating the Bf 109E-7 to such a role demonstrated a profound misunderstanding of the importance of the single-seat fighter.

It is impossible to be sure how important was the part the British anti-aircraft guns played in the battle. Anti-aircraft devices (searchlights, balloon-supported cables, etc.) are usually deterrent rather than combative, although by 1939 the German anti-aircraft units were changing that. By German standards, the British AA of 1940 was very poor. The Kerrison predictor and the Bofors guns, Britain's most efficient AA weapons (according to General Pile, the G.O.C. in C.), were in a very short supply. The GL (gun-laying) radar was still not working properly, and the proximity fuse (which was later to make the guns a deadly accurate destroyer of flying bombs) was not yet invented. More than one fighter pilot having a claim disallowed was told that it was being credited to the guns 'because they must be encouraged.'

Only the really big guns could do much damage to any formation above 20,000 feet (which many raids were), and these really big guns were usually cemented into permanent emplacements. Some of these gun-sites saw little or no action.

As the Battle progressed, it was the airfields that got the lion's share of the AA defences. The few available Bofors guns, the precious big mobile guns, ancient Lewis machine guns, and 20-mm cannon manufactured for aircraft were all provided for airfield protection. Eventually low-level attacks by German aircraft became very hazardous. So – only too often – did low-level flight by friendly aircraft.

Both sides learned from each other. The loose formations that were, according to Galland, evolved by Mölders became standard for both air forces. Armour plate, which the RAF had adopted in spite of Air Ministry objections, was put into the Bf 109 fighters. It became vital to the pilot's safety as cannon fire was used more and more. Self-sealing fuel tanks (in 1940 only in bombers) were also used by both sides. German night-bombing techniques were later copied by the RAF, and British counter-measures – such as jamming and decoy fires – were borrowed by the Germans.

The Battle of Britain saw the end of the Luftwaffe's reputation as an invincible force. The 'yellow-nosed Abbeville boys,' a unit of Bf 109 fighters with yellow-painted cowlings that had achieved an awesome reputation during the summer of 1940, proved no more than a reflection of Fighter Command's state of mind. There were no 'Abbeville boys': many Bf 109 units had painted their cowling with a yellow patch so that friend and foe could be easily distinguished in battle.

For the RAF, the quantity and quality of pilots had come nearest to bringing disaster. Bravery was no substitute for training, skill, and experience, and as the Battle progressed, Fighter Command put into combat squadrons of men who should not have been asked to meet the Germans on equal terms. There were fifty-eight naval pilots, an American parachutist with virtually no experience of military flying, and Polish pilots who had had only a brief experience of the British high-speed monoplanes and even less of the English language. As the fighting progressed, and the men leading the formations suffered unduly heavy casualties, too many of them were replaced by outside officers without combat experience. This extraordinary procedure had a doubly bad effect upon the other pilots, for it deprived them of promotion and sent them into battle with inadequate leaders. Worst of all was the way in which pilots 'went operational' before they had properly mastered their machines – ten hours on fighters was not unusual – and without any realistic operational training.

This desperate shortage of trained pilots becomes even more incomprehensible when read in conjunction with a memo from Winston Churchill to Archibald Sinclair (Britain's Air Minister, well remembered by the pilots of 64 Squadron for a brief visit he had paid to them in 11 Group during the Battle; he'd walked round their Spitfires while addressing them as Hurricane pilots, and kept referring to them as a part of 12 Group):

PRIME MINISTER TO SECRETARY OF STATE FOR AIR

3 June 1940

The Cabinet were distressed to hear from you that you were now running short of pilots for fighters, and that they had now become the limiting factor.

This is the first time that this particular admission of failure has been made by the Air Ministry. We know that immense masses of aircraft are devoted to the making of pilots, far beyond the proportion adopted by the Germans. We heard some months ago of many thousands of pilots for whom the Air Ministry declared they had no machines, and who consequently had to be 're-mustered': as many as seven thousand were mentioned, all of whom had done many more hours of flying than those done by German pilots now frequently captured. How then therefore is this new shortage to be explained?

Lord Beaverbrook has made a surprising improvement in the supply and repair of aeroplanes, and in clearing up the muddle and scandal of the aircraft production branch. I greatly hope that you will be able to do as much on the personnel side, for it will indeed be lamentable if we have machines standing idle for want of pilots to fly them.

But Churchill himself was not entirely blameless in respect to the quality of the fighter pilots. Professor Frederick Lindemann (later Lord Cherwell), the man Churchill had made his scientific adviser, in July pressed for the shortening of the operational training. It was a reckless expedient, for, in spite of Lindemann's contention that 'the final polish should be given in the squadrons,' it was the six months at OTU that made a pilot into a fighter pilot. At Lindemann's suggestion, the time had been reduced to a mere four weeks and the training was to become more and more perfunctory.

Lindemann exerted powerful influence upon Britain's progress in the war.[1] However controversial Lindemann's contribution to victory, the way the British were able to bring scientists, generals, and businessmen together, to help the war effort, was something the Germans failed to do and suffered because of it.

Already many great names of German science had fled the country, or gone into concentration camps. Surely by now few can doubt that a Nazi regime without anti-

[1]Millions of pounds were spent, in six years of experiments, in the absurd idea of sowing aerial minefields through which the enemy bombers would have to fly. Another Lindemann obsession was infrared. As late as 1939, Lindemann was still writing to Churchill telling him that radar would never fulfil its expectations.

Semitism would have produced long-distance rockets with nuclear war heads and won the war.

Instead of husbanding the remainder of their scientists, the German armed forces conscripted them into the army, along with manual labourers and clerks. The curious political system of Nazi Germany had manufacturers pursuing parallel research, in pursuit of the same contract, so too much scientific time and effort were spent in perfecting equipment that was already good enough.

British scientific weaponry was often hastily lashed together and imperfect but – unlike so much German equipment in beautiful cases – it could be modified with a can-opener and soldering iron – and was.

The German scientists enjoyed a higher status than their British counterparts, but they did not enjoy the right to roam through military establishments, from Sergeants' Messes to War Cabinet, as the British did. And it is hard to imagine scruffy German civilians, in ill-fitting suits, telling German staff officers where they were going wrong. This the British scientists did, and so were able to bring science from laboratory to battlefield at surprising speed.

All this was a result of the confidence that Britain's soldiers, businessmen, and politicians had in science. A large measure of this confidence was due to the part that radar played in the Battle of Britain.

Germany did little or nothing to revise the role of science in the war. In 1940 the German General Staff had decreed that no research or development should be pursued unless it promised military results within four months.[1] As a part of this ill-considered and Draconian measure, work on Messerschmitt's amazing Me 262 jet fighter was forbidden. Messerschmitt continued with some work, but in the spring of 1941 Milch went to Messerschmitt's home and

[1] I refer here to the conference on 7 February 1940 at which Göring presided and Keitel, Milch, and Economics Minister Funk discussed acceleration of the armaments programme. It was the report and recommendations of the Quartermaster General (Air) that led to the ban on new designs.

insisted that all work on the jet should end. Galland considers that the 1940 order delayed the Me 262 by about two years.

The failure to understand the importance of the Me 262 was only a part of the failure to understand the importance of the fighter plane. Even after the 1940 fighting, the Luftwaffe failed to give fighter production the priorities it needed. Not until late 1943 can fighters be said to have been produced in large quantities, and then only because the totals include later variants of the by then obsolescent Bf 109.

Many German failures were due to the way that the country's leaders clung to the hope of the 'quick war.' Even after the Battle of Britain's stalemate, Germany still made no long-term war plans. Hitler decided that Britain's reluctance to make peace was due to its belief that one day the USSR would fight Germany. To cut this Gordian knot, Hitler decided upon a 'quick war' against the USSR. After this, he said, Britain will make peace. As the air battles of 1940 continued, and the German army stood waiting, Hitler gradually confided to his generals his ideas for 'Barbarossa.'

Yet, if the British looked for salvation, most looked not to the east, but west to the USA.

'Wild Bill' Donovan's brief trip to Britain had convinced him that Britain would survive and should be supported in every way possible. This report ran counter to everything that Ambassador Kennedy had been telling Washington, and it did not please the ambassador. Early in September, Kennedy's car had been damaged by blast as he was driving through an air raid. He said he would endure a month of bombing, and did exactly that. In October he went home to resign, angry at the British for being bombed, at the Germans for dropping bombs, at Donovan for contradicting his reports, and at Roosevelt for allowing it all. The British were polite. The King and Queen gave him lunch at Buckingham Palace. The *Evening News* wrote, 'It is Mr Kennedy single-handed who has strengthened Anglo-

American friendship in London.' Even less restrained was the socialist *Daily Herald*: 'Goodbye, Joe! Heaven bless you!' He let everyone know that he was going to denounce the Roosevelt administration, and intended to time his statement for maximum effect on the 5 November elections. He took with him a British air-raid siren. Asked if it was a souvenir, he said he wanted it for his Cape Cod mansion to call the Kennedy children home from their boats. Once back in Boston, Kennedy told the *Globe*, 'Democracy is finished in England.'

When the election came, Kennedy gave Roosevelt all the support he needed to win. The mystery of his turn-round has never been satisfactorily explained. On the matter of Britain's imminent defeat, Kennedy also changed his mind, but now Britain no longer cared. Robert Vansittart – Halifax's Chief Diplomatic Adviser – wrote, 'Mr Kennedy is a very foul specimen of double-crosser and defeatist. He thinks of nothing but his own pocket. I hope that this war will at least see the elimination of this type.'

Already many Americans were realizing that the USA had little option but to enter the war. The German successes in Europe had weakened the colonial powers in the Pacific. Raw materials – not the least of which was oil in Dutch possessions – would alter the balance of power, and bring Japan into confrontation with the USA.

In 1940 Roosevelt asked for 50,000 warplanes. It makes the combats of 1940 seem puny by comparison. Asked for a time limit, Roosevelt blandly said that it was the number he wanted each year. Inevitably the war grew larger and larger. Before it ended, the Luftwaffe was to lose, in one day's combat, the same number of planes that it lost in the whole summer of 1940.

In 1940 the Royal Navy had brought its destroyers back to British ports to be ready for the German invasion. Deprived of such protection, Britain's Atlantic convoys suffered grievous losses, and the German U-boat crews were ever after to know this period as 'the happy time.'

RAF Bomber Command had devoted a great deal of

effort to bombing the barges in the Channel ports but with accuracy no better than in their attacks against other German targets. In the autumn of 1940, according to the official history, Bomber Command decided that hitting German civilians, hospitals, churches, and cultural monuments, hitherto a by-product of the intention to hit military targets, 'should become an end-product . . . the time had come to launch a direct attack upon the German people themselves.'

And now it was time to write history. The men at the Air Ministry issued the official account of 'The Battle of Britain.' A 32-page booklet recounted the story without once mentioning the name of either Park or Dowding.

In RAF Fighter Command, the men who had humiliated, judged, and sentenced Dowding and Park turned their attentions to a war game that was intended to vindicate their big-wing theories.

They used historical data to re-create one of the big air battles of September. Umpires were appointed to watch the way the battle went. Leigh-Mallory, now Commander of Park's old Group, reacted to the German threat with exactly the kind of large formations that he and Bader had argued were best.

The exercise was a fiasco. The Umpires decreed that the vital Fighter Command airfields of Biggin Hill and Kenley were bombed before the big wings were even airborne. This did not affect Leigh-Mallory's career. He stayed in Park's job and then took over Dowding's.

Göring's influence declined. Even by the beginning of October the 'Iron Man' had lost interest in his Air Fleets and their struggle. When Galland went to see the *Reichsmarschall* after getting the oak leaves (a new award for flyers with forty aerial victories), he met Mölders coming out of the hunting estate. Mölders said, 'Fatty promised he would detain you at least as long as he did me,' and hurried off to get more victories.

Galland described the 'log cabin made of huge tree trunks, with a thatched roof jutting far over the eaves.

Göring came out of the house to meet me, wearing a green suede hunting jacket over a silk blouse with long, puffed sleeves, high hunting boots, and in his belt a hunting knife in the shape of an old Germanic sword. . . That night no mention was made either of the war in general or the Battle of Britain in particular.'

'I myself have taken command of the Luftwaffe's battle for Britain,' Göring had told a radio audience in September. In spite of this, the Luftwaffe commanders now denied that there had ever been any such battle. Kesselring blandly argued that the Air Fleets had changed their tactics many times during the summer of 1940. In September the tactic of night bombing was employed. That did not mean, he insisted, that the Luftwaffe was defeated any more than had the previous changes.

But the men who had flown over England knew differently. The Luftwaffe's failure generated a mood of discontent. Complaints about the equipment – some of them generated by Milch but many of them genuine – reflected upon the inadequacies of Udet, Director of Air Armament. Called to account before Göring, Udet usually managed to turn the conversation round to old times, and nothing was done.

Well aware of the campaign against him, Udet was never sure who was behind it. During the final stages of the Battle of Britain it was the urbane Milch who had taken Udet on a shopping spree in Paris, ending in Cartier's. And when Milch went back to Berlin, he resumed his dinner parties at Horcher's restaurant and included Udet as a regular guest. And yet Udet was depressed and the outcome of the Battle of Britain made him worse. He was drinking too much; he also chain-smoked and used the pep pills that were available to front-line units for men under stress. Abuse of these pills made Udet moody and irritable. Finally Udet was persuaded to get medical attention. Milch sent him to his own personal physician.

Udet's Chief of Staff might have helped him sort out the chaos of the department and salvage his career, but he was also in trouble. During the summer he had visited Deauville with Milch and Sperrle and spent all his money gambling with them. Now he owed far more than he could repay, and was under considerable pressure from both his creditors.

And Göring, too, realized that the Luftwaffe had suffered a set-back, and was reminded of it when Hitler showed him the reaction of the foreign press. Soon Göring gave Milch the sort of power that would be needed for the onslaught against the USSR in the following summer. Milch immediately started an ambitious programme to expand the Luftwaffe to four times its strength. Delighted with his new power, the wily Milch named his plan 'The Göring Programme.' One of his most important decisions was to keep the Bf 109 in full production no matter how superior the Focke-Wulf FW 190 proved to be. As always the Luftwaffe went for quantity at the expense of quality. In the same cause, Milch forbade Messerschmitt to do any work on his jet fighter and told him to get on with his Bf 109 production.

On Göring's advice, Udet took some sick leave. During the time he was in hospital Milch had Udet's unfortunate Chief of Staff – a close friend of Udet – banished to the eastern front. And he replaced Udet's chief engineer with a man of his own choice. When Udet came out of hospital he was upset. He clashed with Milch on the subject of fighter production (Bf 109 versus FW 190). Milch won the fight but diplomatically suggested that Udet go with him to Paris for a few days' vacation, 'to straighten things out again.' Udet agreed that they would meet at Tempelhof airport at Monday noon, and then went to spend the weekend with his mistress and with his one-time Chief of Staff, who still owed gambling debts and was now on leave before departing to the Russian front.

On Monday morning, Udet was found dead with two empty cognac bottles and a revolver. On the wall he had scrawled a message accusing Göring of selling out to 'the Jew' Milch: 'Iron Man, you deserted me!' he'd written.

Göring dictated a press notice that said that Udet had died from injuries suffered while testing a new weapon. In his diary Milch blamed everything on Udet's one-time Chief of Staff, adding as a contributory cause a rumour that Udet's mistress had threatened to leave him.

Hitler was present at the state funeral. Werner Mölders was summoned to be a pall-bearer for Udet (who after von Richthofen was the most successful fighter pilot of the First World War). His aircraft hit a factory chimney. Mölders died.

Milch took over Udet's department, in addition to his own.

Acknowledgments

It was A. J. P. Taylor who suggested initially that I should write a history book. My first thanks, therefore, must go to him for his sustaining encouragement throughout the six years it has taken to produce *Fighter*. I also thank Albert Speer for our talks and for reading the manuscript.

Some years ago, Derek Coyte arranged for me to fly as one of the crew delivering a Heinkel He 111 to a museum in Germany. It was the first aircraft to fly over Germany in Luftwaffe colours since the end of the war. Adolf Galland, the fighter ace, was waiting to greet us when we landed, and from that moment many doors were opened to me for my enquiries. So to all the many RAF and Luftwaffe flyers, too numerous to mention by name, who recollected for me their experiences and adventures, and discussed with me details of the battle, go my grateful thanks. In particular, I am indebted to those who brought me long-forgotten diaries and documents, finished and unfinished memoirs, and other valuable material, and to those war-gamers who tested out ideas and drew my attention to new ways of looking at the course of events.

I would also like to thank the staff at the Imperial War Museum and Group Captain E. B. Haslam, F.R. Hist. Soc., and Denis Bateman of the Ministry of Defence (Historical Branch), all of whom gave me every possible assistance with research.

For permission to reproduce the photographs in this book, some of which have never been published before, I acknowledge Associated Press, Flight International, Imperial War Museum, Keystone Press Agency, Orbis Publishing Ltd, Popperfoto, Radio Times Picture Library, Rairpix, Robert Hunt Library, Syndication International, and U.S. Information Agency.

I thank Group Captain John A. Kent and his publishers, William Kimber, for permission to quote from *One of the Few* on pages . I also acknowledge my debt to Robert Wright and his publishers, Macdonald, whose book *Dowding and the Battle of Britain* was a most valued research source.

Finally, I thank Derek Jewell and Peter Giddy for help and encouragement, Ellenor Handley, who for many years has helped to transform my scribbling into proper text, Ray Hawkey, Anton Felton and everyone at Jonathan Cape who worked on the book. Some additions and changes I made to the text when the book was later published in America have also been embodied in this paperback edition.

Bibliography

Books

Anon., *Psychological Disorders in Flying Personnel of the RAF, 1939–1945,* HMSO, 1946

Anon., *The Origins and Development of Operational Research in the RAF,* HMSO, 1963

Anon., *Radar: A Report on Science at War,* Government Printing Office, Washington, n.d.

Anon., *The Rise and Fall of the German Air Force,* Ministry of Defence (restricted access), n.d.

Bekker, C. *The Luftwaffe War Diaries,* translated from the German by F. Ziegler, Macdonald, 1967

Churchill, Winston S., *The Second World War,* six volumes, Cassell, 1960

Collier, Basil, *Leader of the Few,* the authorized biography of Air Chief Marshal the Lord Dowding, Jarrolds, 1957

The Battle of Britain, Batsford, 1962

Collier, Richard, *Eagle Day,* Pan, 1968

Cross, Roy, and Scarborough, Gerald, *Classic Aircraft, Their History and How to Model Them,* four series, P. Stephens, 1971–4

Crowther, J. G., and Whiddington, R., *Science at War,* HMSO, 1947

Deere, Alan C., *Nine Lives,* Hodder and Stoughton, 1969

Douhet, Giulio, *The Command of the Air,* translated from the Italian by Dino Ferrari, Faber and Faber, 1943

Fest, Joachim, *Hitler,* translated from the German by R. and C. Winston, Weidenfeld and Nicolson, 1974

Galland, Adolf, *The First and the Last: German Fighter Force in World War II,* translated from the German by M. Savill, Eyre Methuen, 1973

Green, William, *War Planes of the Third Reich,* Macdonald, 1970
Hillary, Richard, *The Last Enemy*, Macmillan, 1942
Irving, David, *Destruction of Dresden,* Elmfield Press, 1974
The Rise and Fall of the Luftwaffe, Weidenfeld and Nicolson, 1974
Kent, John, *One of the Few,* Kimber, 1971
Lewis, Peter, *The British Fighter Since 1912,* Putnam and Co., 1974
Mason, Francis K., *Battle Over Britain,* McWhirter, 1969
Olmsted, Merle, *Aircraft Armament,* Modern Aircraft Series, Sports Car Press, 1970
Postan, M. M., *Design and Development of Weapons: Studies in Government and Industry Organization,* HMSO, 1964
Price, Alfred W., *Instruments of Darkness,* Kimber, 1967
Speer, Albert, *Inside the Third Reich*, translated from the German by R. and C. Winston, Weidenfeld and Nicolson, 1970
Spandau: Secret Diaries, translated from the German by R. and C. Winston, Collins, 1976
Taylor, A. J. P., *The Origins of the Second World War,* Hamish Hamilton, 1963
English History 1914–1945, O.U.P., 1965
Beaverbrook, Hamish Hamilton, 1972
The Second World War, Hamish Hamilton, 1975
Essays in English History, Hamish Hamilton, 1976
Taylor, J. W. R., *Combat Aircraft of the World,* Ebury Press and Michael Joseph, 1969
(ed.) *The Lore of Flight,* Nelson, 1975
Taylor, Telford, *The March of Conquest: The German Victories in Western Europe, 1940,* Edward Hulton, 1959
The Breaking Wave: The German Defeat in the Summer of 1940, Weidenfeld and Nicolson, 1967
Townsend, Peter, *Duel of Eagles,* Weidenfeld and Nicolson, 1970
Wallace, G. F., *Guns of the RAF,* Kimber, 1972

Watson-Watt, Sir Robert, *Three Steps to Victory*, a personal account by radar's greatest pioneer, Odhams, 1957

Webster, Sir Charles, *The Strategic Air Offensive Against Germany, 1939–45*, four volumes, HMSO, 1961

Wood, Derek, and Dempster, D., *The Narrow Margin,* Arrow Books, 1969

Wright, Robert, *Dowding and the Battle of Britain*, Macdonald, 1969

Ziegler, Frank H., *Under the White Rose: The Story of 609 Squadron,* Macdonald, 1971

Journals and Documents

Adler

Aeroplane

Aircraft Profiles

Fighter Command Intelligence Summaries, Public Record Office

Flight

Icare

Signal

Die Wehrmacht

Note: This is a selected bibliography of English publications. For a more exhaustive list of reading matter I strongly recommend the bibliography in Richard Collier's *Eagle Day*, listed above.

Index